DOES ETHICS
HAVE A CHANCE
IN A WORLD OF
CONSUMERS?

Institute for Human Sciences
Vienna Lecture Series

The Institute for Human Sciences
(Institut für die Wissenschaften vom Menschen, or IWM),
founded in 1982, is an independent international institute for
advanced study based in Vienna, Austria.
The IWM publishes books in cooperation with
Harvard University Press, Suhrkamp Verlag (Frankfurt),
and Znak (Kraków).

DOES ETHICS HAVE A CHANCE IN A WORLD OF CONSUMERS?

·

Zygmunt Bauman

·

HARVARD UNIVERSITY PRESS

Cambridge, Massachusetts · London, England

174.
BAU

Printed in the United States of America

A Caravan book. For more information, visit www.caravanbooks.org.

First Harvard University Press paperback edition, 2009.

Library of Congress Cataloging-in-Publication Data

Bauman, Zygmunt, 1925–
Does ethics have a chance in a world of consumers? / Zygmunt Bauman.
p. cm.—(Institute for Human Sciences Vienna Lecture Series)
Includes bibliographical references and index.
ISBN 978-0-674-02780-0 (cloth : alk. paper)
ISBN 978-0-674-03351-1 (pbk.)
1. Consumption (Economics)—Moral and ethical aspects.
2. Globalization—Moral and ethical aspects. I. Title.
HC79.C6B353 2008
174—dc22   2007052153

Contents

◆

DOES ETHICS HAVE A CHANCE IN A WORLD OF CONSUMERS?

•

Introduction

Threats or Chances?

•

THIS BOOK is a report from a battlefield—the battlefield on which we wage our struggle to find the new and adequate ways of thinking *of, about,* and *for* the world we live in, and our lives within it.

The ongoing effort to understand the world—this world, here and now, apparently familiar yet sparing us no surprises, denying today what it yesterday suggested was true, while giving little assurance that what we hold true at sunset today won't be refuted tomorrow at dawn—is indeed a struggle. One would say an uphill struggle—and surely a daunting and unending task—always unfinished. Final victory in the struggle remains obstinately beyond the horizon. And vexingly, the hope of coming to some understanding of the world seems even more unattainable now than it did in the not-so-distant past—as older people remember but the young find difficult to imagine.

Life appears to be moving too fast for most of us to follow its twists and turns, let alone anticipate them. Planning a course of action and sticking to the plan is an endeavor fraught with

risks, whereas long-term planning seems downright dangerous. Life trajectories feel as if they are sliced into episodes; any
connections between the episodes, not to mention the causal,
determining connections, are discernible (if at all) only in ret-
rospect. Worry and apprehension about the sense and destination of the journey are as abundant as the pleasures promised
by this world full of surprises, this life punctuated by "new beginnings."

Our plight, once cast into such a setting and obliged to act in
it, is not made any easier by the "conceptual nets" we have inherited or learned to use to grasp the elusive realities, or by the
vocabularies we commonly deploy to report our findings. So
many concepts and words intended to convey our meaning to
ourselves and others now prove unfit for the purpose. We desperately need a new framework, one that can accommodate
and organize our experience in a fashion that allows us to perceive its logic and read its message, heretofore hidden, illegible, or susceptible to misreading.

In this book I offer a preliminary and tentative attempt to
assemble such a framework. I cannot pretend that it is anything more than a "career report": no more than an attempt to
catch the shape of a world on the move, a world that, infuriatingly, keeps changing faster than we—our ways of thinking and
talking about it—can adapt. Rather than suggesting solutions to
our quandaries, I ask how our quandaries tend to be shaped
(by what sort of experience), where their roots lie, and what
questions need to be asked if we are to uncover them.

My ambition is merely to help myself and my readers shar-
pen our common cognitive *tools;* perfecting the cognitive *products* must remain a do-it-yourself enterprise. It is undoubtedly
true that, whether big or small, improvements in our thinking about the lived world will not suffice to ensure fulfillment
of the hope to improve the world and our lives in it, yet it is

no less true that without such improvements, that hope will not survive.

Just to clarify what the proposed reshaping of our cognitive framework would involve, and what obstacles it is likely to face along the way, let us look at the intellectual adventure of a group of researchers from the Zoological Society of London who went to Panama to investigate the social life of local wasps. The group was equipped with cutting-edge technology, which it used over the course of 6,000 hours to track and monitor the movements of 422 wasps from 33 nests.[1] What the researchers found out has overturned centuries-old stereotypes of the social insects' habits.

Indeed, ever since the term "social insects" (a category embracing bees, termites, ants, and wasps) was coined and popularized, learned zoologists and the lay public have shared a firm belief, hardly ever questioned: that the "sociability" of insects is confined to the nest to which they belong—in which they were hatched and to which they bring the spoils of their regular foraging ventures, shared with the rest of the hive's inhabitants. The possibility that some working bees or wasps would cross the boundaries between nests, abandon the hive of *birth* and join another one, a hive of *choice,* was seen (if it was ever contemplated) as incongruous. It was axiomatic, rather, that the "natives," the indigenous and therefore "legitimate" members of the nest, would promptly chase the maverick newcomers away and destroy them if they refused to flee.

Like all axioms, that assumption had never theretofore been questioned or tested. True, technically it could not have been: electronic equipment for tagging individual wasps had only quite recently been invented. More important, however, the thought that tracing the traffic between nests or hives might be called for did not occur in the first place—either to ordinary folks or to the learned experts. For the scholars, the assumption that the instinct to socialize is limited to "kith and kin," in other words to the "community of birth and *therefore* of belonging," stood to reason. For the ordinary folks, it made sense. Instead, a lot of research energy and funds were dedicated to the question of how social insects spot a stranger in their midst: Do they distinguish it by sight? By sound? By smell? By minute nuances of conduct? The intriguing question was how the insects manage what we humans, with all our smart and sophisticated tools and weapons, only half succeed in achieving—that is, how they keep the borders of "community" watertight and maintain the separation between "natives" and "aliens," between "us" and "them."

What passes for reason (in its role as the supreme authority when it comes to making judgments and recognizing them as beyond dispute), like what is taken to make "good sense" (in its role as *doxa* or paradigm), tends, however, to change over time.[2] It changes together with the human condition and the challenges it presents.

All or most currently held views of reason and good sense tend to be *praxeomorphic*. They take shape in response to the realities "out there" as seen through the prism of human practices—what humans currently do, know how to do, are trained, groomed, and inclined to do. Scholarly agendas are derivatives of mundane human practices, whereas it is the *sociocultural* agenda, dictated by problems of daily human cohabitation, that sets the topical relevance of issues and suggests the hypotheses that research projects seek subsequently to confirm or disprove.

We are therefore entitled to surmise that if no effort has been made to test received popular wisdom, it is not so much for lack of research tools as from the absence of suspicion that such a test was needed because the credibility of such common wisdom was at issue. Consequently, we may also suppose that if for most of modern history nothing in the commonsense view (no belief formed and reinforced daily by common experience) had cast doubt on the "naturalness" and universality of the "inborn" limitations on sociality, the research escapade of the Zoological Society team hints that this may not be the case any longer.

Contrary to everything known (or believed to be known) for centuries, the London team found in Panama that an impressive majority, 56 percent, of "working wasps" change their nests in their lifetime, and they move to other nests not just as temporary, unwelcome visitors, discriminated against and marginalized, always suspected and resented, but as full and rightful (one is almost tempted to say "card-carrying") members of the adoptive community, collecting food and feeding and grooming the native brood just as the native workers do. The inevitable conclusion was that the nests the Londoners researched were *as a rule* "mixed populations," inside which the native-born and the immigrant wasps lived and worked cheek by jowl and shoulder to shoulder—becoming indistinguishable from one another, at least for the human outsiders, except through the help of electronic tags.

What the news from Panama points up above all is the astonishing reversal of perspective: beliefs that not so long ago were imagined to be reflections of the "state of nature" have been revealed now, retrospectively, to have been but a projection onto the insects' habits of the scholars' own human, all-too-human, preoccupations and practices (though practices of a kind now dwindling and receding into the past). Once these scholars of a somewhat younger generation brought to the forest of Panama their own experience (and ours) of the life practices acquired and absorbed in their newly multicultural home of interlocking diasporas, they duly "discovered" the fluidity of membership and perpetual mixing of populations to be the *norm* also among social insects: and a norm apparently implemented in "natural" ways, with no help from royal commissions, hastily introduced bills of law, high courts, or asylum seekers' camps. In this case, as in so many others, the praxeomorphic nature of human perception of the world prompted the scholars to find, out there in the world, what they have learned to do and are doing here at home, and what we all carry in our heads or in our subconscious as an image of how things truly are. In confrontation with the unexpected evidence from social insects, something clicked: the intuitive, half-conscious, or unconscious premonitions were articulated (or perhaps articulated themselves); and then the intuitions were recycled into an alternative synthesis of that different reality corresponding to the novelty of the researchers' own reality. But for this recycling to take place, there already had to be an accumulation of raw material waiting to be recycled.

"How could that be?!" asked the Londoners on their research trip to Panama, at first hardly believing their findings, which were so different from what their professors had told them to expect. Feverishly, they sought a convincing explanation of the Panamanian wasps' bizarre ways and, as might be expected, found it in the warehouse of tested and familiar methods for recycling anomalous evidence to conform to the image of an orderly world. The scientists declared that the newcomers who had been allowed to settle in the hives "were not truly aliens"—strangers no doubt, but not as strange as the other, *genuine* strangers. Perhaps they joined the nests of closely related wasps—cousins, maybe. Indeed, such an explanation might have sounded foolproof to the human researchers: it seemed incontrovertible, precisely thanks to being pleonastic. The right of close relatives to visit and to settle in the family home had been for them, since time immemorial, a birthright; as we all know, this is exactly what sets close relatives apart from all other visitors. But how do we know that the alien wasps were close relatives of the natives? Well, they must have been, mustn't they? Otherwise, the insiders would have forced them to leave or killed them on the spot—Q.E.D. Circular reasoning is infallible even if not exactly logical, and this is why so many of us so often resort to it—not so much to resolve baffling problems, but to be absolved of the obligation to worry about them.

What the London researchers clearly forgot or failed, for the sake of convenience, to mention is that it took a century or more of hard work, sometimes sword brandishing and other times brainwashing, to convince the Prussians, the Bavarians, the Badenians, the Württembergers or Saxons (just as it takes now to convince the "Ossis" and "Wessis," until recently East and West Germans) that they were all close relatives, cousins or even brothers, descendants of the same ancient German stock animated by the same German spirit, and that for this reason they should behave the way close relatives do: be hospitable to each other and cooperate in protecting and increasing the common welfare. Or similarly, that on the way to the modern centralized nation-state and the identification of nationhood with citizenship, revolutionary France had to include the slogan of *fraternité* in the call it addressed to "locals" of all sorts—now appointed *les citoyens*—to people who had theretofore seldom cast a glance, let alone traveled, beyond the frontiers of Languedoc, Poitou, Limousin, Burgundy, Brittany, or Franche-Comté; *fraternité*, brotherhood: all Frenchmen are brothers, so please behave as brothers do, love each other, help each other, and make the whole of France your common home, and the land of France your shared homeland. Or for that matter, that since the time of the French Revolution all movements bent on proselytizing, recruiting, expanding, and integrating the populations of previously separate and mutually suspicious kingdoms and duchies have been in the habit of addressing their current and prospective converts as "brothers and sisters." Or that, as any anthropologist will tell you, *all* known cultures habitually link individual rights and the duties and norms of mutuality to the areas outlined on mental maps of kinship, even though the substance of those rights and duties varies considerably from one culture to another, such variation being one of the principal reasons to consider them *different* cultures.

But to cut a long story short: the difference between the cognitive maps the older generations of entomologists carried in their heads and those acquired or adopted by the youngest reflects the passage from the nation-building stage in the history of modern states to the multicultural phase in their history—more generally, from "solid" modernity, bent on entrenching and fortifying the principle of territorial, exclusive, and indivisible sovereignty, and on circumscribing the sovereign territories with impermeable borders—to "liquid" modernity, with its fuzzy and eminently permeable borderlines, the unstoppable (even if bemoaned, resented, and resisted) devaluation of spatial distances and the defensive capability of territories, and the intense flow of human traffic across all and any frontiers.

Human traffic goes both ways; frontiers are crossed from both sides. Britain, for instance, is today a country of *immigration* (even if the successive home secretaries go out of their way to be seen as trying hard to erect new barriers and stem the influx of foreigners); but also, according to the latest calculations, almost a million and a half native Britons are currently settled in Australia, almost a million in Spain, several hundred thousand in Nigeria, even a dozen in the North Korea. The same applies to France, Germany, Poland, Ireland, Italy, Spain; in one measure or another, it applies to any bordered-off territory on the planet, except a few remaining totalitarian enclaves that still deploy the anachronistic panopticon-style techniques designed more to hold the inmates (state subjects) *inside* the walls (state borders) than to keep the aliens *out*.

The population of every country is nowadays a collection of diasporas. Every sizable city is now an aggregate of ethnic, religious, and lifestyle enclaves in which the line dividing insiders from outsiders is a hotly contested issue, while the right to draw that line, to keep it intact and make it unassailable, is the prime stake in the skirmishes over influence and battles for recognition that follow. Most of the *states* and left their nation-building stage behind—and so are no longer interested in assimilating the incoming strangers (that is, forcing them to shake off and forfeit their separate identities and to dissolve into the uniform mass of autochthons); and so the settings of contemporary lives are likely to remain protean and kaleidoscopic, and the yarn of which the life experience is woven is likely to remain variegated, for a long time to come. For all that it matters and for all we know, they may well keep changing forever.

We are all now, or are fast becoming, like the wasps of Panama. But more precisely, it fell to the lot of the wasps of Panama to make history, as the first social entity to which the emergent, precocious cognitive framework (still waiting to be recognized and endorsed) was applied—a framework derived from our novel experience of an increasingly and probably permanently variegated setting of human cohabitation, the fuzziness of the line separating inside from outside, and the daily practice of mixing with and rubbing elbows with difference. Immanuel Kant predicted more than two centuries ago that designing, elaborating, and putting into operation rules of mutual hospitality must at some point become a necessity for the human species, for we all inhabit the surface of a *spherical* planet, and that prediction has now been realized. Or rather the necessity has become the seminal challenge of our time, the one that calls for the most urgent and most thoroughly considered response.

No place on the planet is spared a point-blank confrontation with that challenge. If any is seemingly exempt from the universal rule, it is for the time being only. The challenge faces every direction at once, and from the point of view of any place it simultaneously prompts inward and outward tensions and urgencies. However self-confident it might currently be or pretend to be, and however resourceful, each ostensibly sovereign territorial enclave on the planet is bound to be weighed down by the sheer magnitude of the global challenge and sooner or later lose its defensive battle (if it wages that battle, as it most often will, alone, resorting solely to the internally available resources and internally feasible measures). At the same time, a fully authoritative planetary center that could set the rules for a universal alliance for a proper response to the challenge, and that could make those rules universally binding, is today conspicuous by its absence.

The composition of the more than two hundred "sovereign units" on the political map of the planet is increasingly reminiscent of that of the thirty-three wasps' nests investigated by the research expedition of the London Zoological Society. When trying to make sense of the present state of human cohabitation, we could do worse than borrow the models and the categories that the researchers in Panama were obliged to deploy in order to make sense of their findings. Indeed, none of the nests they explored had the means to keep its borders watertight, and each had to accept the perpetual exchange of its population. At the same time, each seemed to manage quite well under the circumstances: to absorb newcomers without friction and suffer no malfunction because of the departure of some residents. Furthermore, there was nothing in sight remotely reminiscent of an "insect center" able to regulate the insect traffic—or, for that matter, anything else amenable to regulating. Each nest had to cope with the tasks of life more or less on its own, though the high rate of "personnel turnover" probably ensured that the know-how gained by any one nest could and did travel freely, and contributed to the survival success of all other nests.

Moreover, the researchers seem, first, not to have found much evidence of internest wars. Second, they found that the internest flow of "cadres" appeared to compensate for the locally produced excesses or deficits of nest populations. Third, they realized that the coordination and indirect cooperation among social insects of Panama were, it seems, sustained without either coercion or propaganda; without commanding officers and headquarters in sight; indeed, without a *center*. And whether we admit it or not, whether we relish it or fear it—we, the humans scattered among more than two hundred sovereign units known as the states, have also managed for some time now to live without a center—even though the absence of a clear, unquestionably authoritative, and uncontested global power at the center creates a constant temptation for the mighty and the arrogant to try to fill that void themselves.

The centrality of the center has been decomposed, and links between intimately connected spheres of authority have been broken, perhaps irreparably. Local condensations of economic, military, intellectual, or artistic power and influence no longer coincide (if they ever did). Maps of the world on which we painted political entities in various colors to mark their relative share and importance in, respectively, global industry, trade, investment, military power, scientific achievements, or artistic creation would not overlap. And the paints we use would need to wash off easily, since the rank of any land in the pecking order of influence and impact is by no means assured to last.

As we try desperately to grasp the dynamics of planetary affairs today, our old and hard-dying habit of organizing the balance of power with the help of such conceptual tools as center and periphery, hierarchy, and superiority and inferiority serves more as a handicap than, as before, an asset; more as blinders than as searchlights. The tools developed and applied in the research on Panama wasps may well prove much more suitable for this task.

The absence of a clear-cut and stable division between planetary center and periphery, coupled with the new multidimensionality of superior-inferior relations, does not augur the planetwide "leveling" of human conditions; most certainly they do not mean the advent, or even gradual advance, of equality. In the present constellation of global conditions necessary for a decent and agreeable life (and so also of the global prospects of living such a life), the star of *parity* shines ever brighter, where once the star of equality shone. As I will argue in Chapter 3 of this book, parity is, most emphatically, *not* equality; or rather it is an equality stripped down to the equal or at least equitable *entitlement to recognition,* to the "right to be" and to the right (if needed) to be left alone. Being left alone means, first and foremost, the right to self-definition and self-assertion, and having a realistic chance to act effectively on that right. It is that so-called self-governance (attained and enjoyed, postulated or putative), rather than the material boundaries, that holds together the totalities striving to achieve or retain parity. The totalities of our time are more reminiscent of hard-pitted avocados than hard-shelled coconuts.

The ever more frequent substitution of the metaphor of "network" for the terms most commonly used in narrating social interactions of the past (terms like *systems, structures, societies,* or *communities*) reflects the gathering realization that social totalities are hazy at the fringes, remain in a state of constant flux, are always *becoming* rather than *being,* and are seldom meant to last for the duration. It suggests, in other words, that the totalities struggling today for recognition are more fluid than they used to be or were believed to be when the terms we now yearn to replace were designed and adopted.

In Chapter 3 I argue that the most consequential feature of a network is the formidable flexibility of its contents—the extraordinary facility with which its composition may be, and tends to be, modified. If structures are all about comprising and enclosing, holding, keeping, restraining, containing, a network, in contrast, refers to the perpetual interplay of connecting and *dis*connecting. The process of "identity formation" becomes primarily an ongoing renegotiation of networks.

I also suggest that identities exist today solely in the process of continuous renegotiation. Identity formation, or more correctly their re-formation, turns into a lifelong task, never complete; at no moment of life is the identity "final." There always remains an outstanding task of readjustment, since neither conditions of life nor the sets of opportunities and threats ever stop changing. That built-in "nonfinality," the incurable inconclusiveness of the task of self-identification, causes a lot of tension and anxiety. And for that anxiety there is no easy remedy.

There is no radical cure, at any rate, because the efforts of identity formation veer uneasily, as they must, between the two equally central human values of freedom and security. These values, indispensable for decent human life, are difficult to reconcile, and the perfect balance between them remains still to be found. Freedom, after all, tends to come in a package with insecurity, while security tends to be packed together with constraints on freedom. And as we resent both insecurity and "un-freedom," we would hardly be satisfied with any feasible combination of freedom with security. Hence, instead of following a path of linear progress toward more freedom and more security, we can observe a pendulumlike movement: first overwhelmingly and staunchly toward one of the two values, and then a swing away from it and toward the other. Currently, it seems, in perhaps most places on the planet, the resentment of insecurity prevails over the fear of not being free (though no one can tell how long this tendency will last). In Britain, for instance, a vast majority of people declare that they would be willing to give up quite a few civil liberties in order to reduce the threats against them. Most are ready, in the name of more personal safety, to accept identity cards, until now stubbornly rejected in Britain in the name of individual freedom and privacy, and most want the state authorities, again for the sake of security, to have the right to tap private telephone lines and open private mail. It is in the realm of security, and under the banner of "more security," that the link between the political authorities of the day and the individuals, their subjects, is forged and mutual understanding and coordinated actions are sought.

The dismembering and disabling of the orthodox, supra-individual, tightly structured, and powerfully structuring centers seem to run parallel with the emergent centrality of the orphaned self. In the void left behind by the retreat of fading political authorities, it is now the self that strives to assume, or is forced to assume, the function of the center of the *Lebenswelt* (that privatized, individualized, subjectivized rendition of the universe). It is the self that recasts the rest of the world as its own periphery, while assigning, defining, and attributing differentiated relevance to its parts, according to its own needs. The task of holding society together (whatever "society" may mean under the liquid-modern conditions) is being "subsidiarized," "contracted out," or simply falling to the realm of individual life-politics. Increasingly it is being left to the enterprise of the "networking" and "networked" selves and to their connecting-disconnecting initiatives and operations.

All that does not mean that the normal, weekday conduct of the individual has become random and uncoordinated. It means only that the nonrandomness, regularity, and coordination of individually undertaken actions can be attained by means other than the solid-modern stratagems of enforcement, policing, and following the chain of command—those means preferred and deployed by the totalities of the past in their bids to be greater than the sum of their parts and to force/train/drill their human "units" into repetitive, routine, and regulated conduct.

Having pondered all that, we can note another striking similarity between the way the wasps of Panama live and the way we live. In a liquid-modern society, *swarms* tend to replace *groups,* with their leaders, hierarchies, and pecking orders. A swarm can do without all those paraphernalia without which a group could not exist. Swarms need not be burdened by the group's tools of survival: they assemble, disperse, and come together again from one occasion to another, each time guided by different, invariably shifting relevancies, and attracted by changing and moving targets. The seductive pull of shifting targets is as a rule sufficient to coordinate the swarm's movements—and so commands or other means of enforcement "from the top" are redundant (in fact the "top" itself—the center—is redundant). A swarm has no top, no center; it is solely the direction of its current flight that casts some of the self-propelled swarm units into the position of "leaders" to be followed for the duration of a particular flight or a part of it, though hardly longer.

Swarms are not teams; they know not of the division of labor. They are (unlike bona fide groups) no more than sums of their parts, or rather aggregates of self-propelled units, linked only by the mechanical solidarity manifested in similar patterns of conduct and movement in a similar direction. A swarm can be visualized best as being like Warhol's endlessly copied images without an original, or with an original that was discarded and impossible to trace and retrieve. Each unit of the swarm reenacts the moves made by the others, while performing the whole job, from beginning to end and in all its parts, alone (in the case of consuming swarms, that job is the job of consuming).

In a swarm, there is not much division of labor. There are no specialists—no holders of separate (and scarce) skills and resources whose task is to enable or assist other units to complete their jobs. Each unit is expected to be a jack-of-all-trades, in possession of the complete set of tools and skills necessary for the jobs to be done. In a swarm, there is no complementarity and little or no exchange of services—just physical proximity and roughly coordinated movement. In the case of humans, feeling, thinking units, the comfort of swarming comes from the security of *numbers*—the belief that the direction of action must have been properly chosen, since an impressively large number of people are following it: the supposition that so many feeling, thinking, freely choosing humans couldn't all be fooled at once. As for imparting self-assurance and a feeling of security, the coordinated movements of a swarm are the next best thing to, and no less effective than, to the authority of group leaders.

Jorge Luis Borges famously suggested in one of his short stories that, given the randomness of good or bad luck that befalls human individuals, and the all-too-frequent lack of causal connections between a person's fortune and his deeds, merits, and vices, one could hypothesize that the fate of individuals is decided by drawing numbers in some clandestine lottery office. Judging from individual experience, one could not either prove or disprove the existence of such a lottery. I wonder whether a similarly insoluble mystery haunts the issue of center and periphery in the liquid-modern setting.

Indeed, when watching a swarm in pursuit of a target, we might well guess that it was following a command—though we would be hard put to locate the headquarters from which the command was issued. Watching any *individual* "unit" in the swarm, we might suggest that it was moved by its own desires and intentions, though we would find it daunting to explain the twists and turns it followed, and even more daunting to grasp the secret behind the amazing similarity and synchronicity of moves made by the great number of individual units. I suspect that if we want to comprehend the world as it currently presents itself to us, and to acquire the skills needed to operate in such a world, we need to learn to live with this dilemma.

Everywhere, interhuman bonds, whether inherited or tied to the course of current interactions, are losing their former institutional protections, which are increasingly viewed as irritating and unbearable constraints on individual freedom of choice and self-assertion. Liberated from their institutional frame (now censured and resented as a "cage" or "prison"), human bonds have become tenuous and frail, easily breakable and more often than not short-lived.

Our lives, whether we know it or not and whether we relish the fact or bewail it, are works of art. To live our lives as the art of living demands, we must—just as artists must—set ourselves challenges that are difficult to confront up close, targets that are well beyond our reach, and standards of excellence that seem far above our ability to match. We need to attempt the impossible. And we can only hope, without benefit of a trustworthy prognosis, let alone of certainty, that with long, grinding, and often exhausting effort we may still manage to meet those standards and reach those targets and so rise to the challenge. Uncertainty is the natural habitat of human life—although it is the hope of escaping uncertainty that is the engine of human pursuits.

In a remarkable synthesis of the life experiences most common in our individualized society, François de Singly lists the dilemmas that tend to cast individual practitioners of the art of life into a state of acute and incurable uncertainty and perpetual hesitation.[3] Life pursuits continually oscillate between mutually incompatible, even starkly opposite goals—such as joining and opting out, imitation and invention, routine and spontaneity—all oppositions that are but derivatives or exemplifications of the meta-opposition, the supreme opposition in which individual life is inscribed and from which it is unable to free itself: the opposition between security and freedom—both ardently coveted in equal measure but also excruciatingly difficult to reconcile and virtually impossible to satisfy at the same time.

The product of self-creation, the process operated by the art of life, is supposed to be the "identity" of the creator. Given the oppositions that self-creation struggles in vain to reconcile, and the interplay between the constantly changing world and similarly unstable self-definitions of the individuals trying hard to catch up with the changing conditions, identity can't be internally consistent, nor can it at any point exude an air of finality, leaving no room (and no urge) for further improvement. Identity is perpetually *in statu nascendi,* each of the forms it assumes suffering from more or less acute inner contradiction, each to a greater or lesser extent failing to satisfy and yearning for reform, each lacking in the self-confidence that could be offered solely by comfortingly long life expectancy. As Claude Dubar suggests, "Identity is nothing else but a result simultaneously stable and provisional, individual and collective, subjective and objective, biographical and structured, of diverse processes of socialization which at the same time construct the individuals and define the institutions."[4] We may observe that "socialization" itself, contrary to once universally held and still frequently expressed opinion, is not a one-directional process but a complex and unstable product of the ongoing interplay between yearning for individual freedom of self-creation and the equally strong desire for security that only the stamp of social approval, countersigned by a community (or communities) of reference, can offer. The tension between the two seldom subsides for long, and hardly ever vanishes altogether. De Singly rightly suggests that in theorizing about present identities, the metaphors of "roots" and "uprooting" (or, let me add, the related trope of "disembedding"), all implying the one-off nature of the individual's emancipation from the community of birth as well as the finality and irrevocability of the act, are better abandoned and replaced by the tropes of dropping and weighing anchor.[5]

Unlike "uprooting" and "disembedding," there is nothing irrevocable, let alone ultimate, in weighing anchor. While roots torn out of the soil in which they were growing are likely to desiccate and die, anchors are drawn up only to be dropped again elsewhere, and they can be dropped with similar ease at many different and distant ports of call. Also, roots are part of the plant's design and predetermined shape—there is no possibility that any other type of plant will grow from them—but anchors are only tools that facilitate the ship's temporary attachment to or detachment from a place, and by themselves they do not define the ship's qualities and capabilities. The times between when an anchor is dropped and when it is drawn up again are but phases in the ship's trajectory. The choice of haven in which the anchor will be dropped next is most probably determined by the kind of load the ship is carrying; a harbor good for one kind of cargo may be entirely inappropriate for another.

All in all, the anchor metaphor captures what the metaphor of "uprooting" misses or keeps silent about: the intertwining of continuity and discontinuity in the history of all or at least a growing number of contemporary identities. Just like ships anchoring successively or intermittently in various ports of call, so the selves in the communities of reference to which they seek admission during their lifelong search for recognition and confirmation have their credentials checked and approved at every successive stop; each community of reference sets its own requirements for the kind of papers to be submitted. The ship's record and the captain's log are more often than not among the documents on which approval depends, and with every next stop, the past (constantly swelled by the records of preceding stops) is reexamined and revalued.

There are of course ports, as there are communities, that are not at all particular about checking credentials and that care little about the past, present, or future destination of their visitors; they would allow virtually any ship to drop anchor (or any "identity"), including such ships (or identities) as would probably be turned away at the entrance to any other port (or at the gates of any other community). But then visiting such ports (and such communities) is not wise and would be better avoided, since given the haphazardness of the company there, the offloading of precious cargo there might be an imprudent (risky) decision. Also, visiting such ports (or communities) could be an unreasonable step to take, or at best a sheer waste of time, since those visits would carry little weight when it comes to gaining recognition and confirmation of self-created identities, the principal objective of the voyage.

Paradoxically, emancipation of the self and its effective self-assertion need strong and demanding communities. Self-creation is a must, but self-affirmation feels like a figment of the imagination (and tends to be widely decried for that reason as a symptom of autism or a case of self-delusion). And what difference to the individual's standing, confidence, and capacity to act would all that effort invested in self-creation make, were the confirmation, its finishing act and purpose, not to follow? But confirmation capable of completing the labor of self-creation can be offered only by an authority: a community whose admission *counts* because it has, and uses, power to refuse admission.

"Belonging," as Jean-Claude Kaufmann suggests, is today "used primarily as a resource of the ego."[6] He warns against thinking of "collectivities of belonging" as necessarily "integrating communities." They are better conceived of, he suggests, as a necessary accompaniment to the progress of individualization, or, we may say, as a series of stations or road inns marking the trajectory of the self-forming and self-reforming ego.

The idea of an integrating community is a notion inherited from the now bygone panoptical era: it refers to the organized effort to fortify the borderline separating the "inside" from the "outside," to keep the inmates inside while barring the outsiders from entry and the insiders from deviating, breaching norms, and scheming to escape the grip of the routine. It refers to the enforcement of a uniform, monotonous, space- and time-ascribed code of conduct. That notion is associated with restrictions imposed on movement and change: an integrating community is essentially a conservative (conserving, stabilizing, routine-imposing, and preserving) force. It is at home in a strictly administered and tightly supervised and policed setting—which hardly describes the liquid-modern world, with its cult of speed and acceleration, novelty, and change for the sake of changing.

Today, panoptical instruments in their traditional form inherited from the solid-modern past are deployed mostly at the social periphery in order to bar the excluded from reentering the mainstream—that preserve of bona fide members of the society of consumers—and to keep the outcasts out of mischief. Elsewhere, what is deceptively similar in form to the orthodox panoptical tools, and is often mistaken for an updated version of Big Brother, that prison warden supreme, has been redeployed in the service of *exclusion* instead of *confinement*, or "keeping in" and "keeping in line." It monitors the movement of unwelcome and undesirable outsiders to keep them out—so that the insiders can be relied upon to stay in line, without having to resort to the tools of surveillance, policing, and enforcement.

The supraindividual "totalities" to which the mainstream individuals offer their allegiance at some stage of their life (only to withdraw it at the next stop or a stop after the next), are anything but integrating communities: they do not monitor the human traffic at their fringes, they do not register those who cross borders in either direction, and are hardly aware of the individual decisions to "join" or "leave"—and they do not run the offices that could seriously engage in all that monitoring, registration, and recording. Rather than integrating those currently "belonging," these entities are being "integrated" (though in an admittedly loose and easily arrested and reversed manner) by individual offers of allegiance—from the moment the offers begin to flow in, that is, and until the start of a massive desertion.

There is another seminal difference between the references to contemporary-style "belonging" and the orthodox "integrating communities." To quote Kaufmann once more—"a large part of the identification process feeds on rejection of the Other."[7] There is no access to a group, and there can't be, without the simultaneous opting out or retirement from another group. The act of selecting a group as one's site of belonging in fact constitutes some other groups as alien and, potentially, hostile territory: "I am P" always means (at least implicitly, but often explicitly) that "most certainly, I am *not* Q, R, S, and so on." "Belonging" is one side of the coin, and the other side is separation and opposition—which all too often evolve into resentment, antagonism, and open conflict. Identification of an adversary is an indispensable element of identification with an "entity of belonging"—and, through the latter, also a crucial element of self-identification. Identification of an enemy construed as an incarnation of the evil against which the community "integrates," gives clarity to life purposes and to the world in which life is lived.

What has been said thus far applies to all instances of "belonging," access, and offers of allegiance. But in the course of the modern era, with the passage from "identity building" to the ongoing, lifelong, and for all practical purposes infinite process of identification, this universal feature undergoes significant modifications.

Perhaps the most important modification is the fading of the monopolistic ambitions of the "entity of belonging." As signaled before, the referents of belonging, unlike the orthodox integrative communities, have no tools to monitor the strength of the members' dedication; nor are they interested in demanding and promoting the members' unswerving loyalty and undivided allegiance. And they are not jealous in the manner of monotheistic deities. In its contemporary liquid-modern rendition, belonging to one entity may be shared and practiced simultaneously with belonging to other entities in almost any combination, without necessarily provoking condemnation or repressive measures of any kind. Accordingly, attachments have lost much of their past intensity. Much of their vehemence and vigor, just like the partisan pugnacity of those attached, are as a rule tempered by the parallel allegiances. Hardly any belonging engages the "whole self," as each person is involved, not just in the course of her or his life but at any moment of life, in multiple belongings, so to speak. Being loyal only in part, or loyal "à la carte," is no longer viewed as necessarily tantamount to disloyalty, let alone betrayal.

Hence the present recasting of the phenomenon of (cultural) "hybridity" (combining traits derived from different and separate species) as a virtue and a sign of distinction, rather than, as it was viewed until quite recently, as a vice and a symptom of either cultural inferiority or condemnable declassment. In the emergent scales of cultural superiority and social prestige, hybrids tend to occupy top ranks and the manifestation of one's own "hybridity" becomes the prime vehicle for upward sociocultural mobility. Being condemned in perpetuity to one self-enclosed and invariable set of values and behavioral patterns is, at the same time, increasingly viewed as a sign of sociocultural inferiority or deprivation. The old-style jealous and monopoly-seeking integrative communities are now to be found mostly, perhaps even exclusively, on the lower rungs of the sociocultural ladder.

For the art of life, this new setting opens unprecedented vistas. Freedom of self-creation has never before achieved a similarly breathtaking scope—simultaneously exciting and frightening. Never before was the need for orientation points and guidance as strong and as painfully felt. Yet never before were firm and reliable orientation points and trustworthy guides in such short supply (at least in relation to the volume and intensity of need). Let me be clear: there is a vexing shortage of *firm and reliable* orientation points, *trustworthy* guides. That shortage (paradoxically, yet not at all accidentally) coincides with a proliferation of tempting suggestions and seductive offers of orientation and with a rising wave of guidebooks amid swelling throngs of counselors. This circumstance, however, makes yet more confusing the task of navigating through the misleading or deceitful propositions in order to find an orientation likely to deliver on its promise.

To sum up the seminal departures discussed thus far: The presently emergent human condition augurs an unprecedented degree of emancipation from constraints—from a necessity experienced as coercion and therefore resented and rebelled against. This sort of emancipation tends to be experienced as the reconciliation of Sigmund Freud's "pleasure principle" with the "reality principle," and therefore as the end of the epoch-long conflict that in Freud's view made civilization a hotbed of discontent.

All that does not mean, however, that the changed human condition has been cleansed of the hardships endemic to its previous form. It means only that the hardships are of a different kind, that they are experienced in a different way, and that they escape the cognitive frames created to serve the old hardships and therefore need to be articulated anew. The purpose of the new articulation ought to be, first, consideration of the ways in which the current human condition could be improved and rendered more inviting and hospitable to a "good" (or "better") life; and, second, the designation of the range of options that contemporary men and women must confront if they contemplate the achievement of such a condition and such a life. Those two intimately connected tasks were in the past the mission and vocation of the intellectuals. The big question, therefore, is whether that mission is likely to be taken up once more by the "knowledge classes" of our time.

The immediate or foreseeable future prospects for this, one is inclined to admit, are not encouraging. The "historical pact" between intellectuals and the people looks today like an episode related to the first, solid phase of modernity—the era of intense nation building and the modern state's authority-building effort. That era also saw the territorial enclosure of the knowledge classes and the working classes in the same space, confined by the territorial sovereignty of the emergent nation-state—a time when both classes remained, for all practical intents and purposes, *glebae adscripti*. But these conditions bind no longer. "Knowledge classes" (including the intellectuals) increasingly inhabit the extraterritorial cyberspace, emancipating themselves to a steadily growing extent from local dependencies and local populations. A new encounter and reunion, this time on the planetary scale, seems for the moment still some way ahead—and a new reunion must and can be arranged on the planetary, global level.

Indeed, globalization looks now inescapable and irreversible. The point of no return has been reached—and passed. There is no way back. Our interconnections and interdependence are already global. Whatever happens in one place influences the lives and life chances of people in all other places. Calculation of steps to be taken in any one place must reckon with the responses of people everywhere else. No sovereign territory, however large, populous, and resourceful, can single-handedly protect its living conditions, its security, long-term prosperity, preferred form of life, or the safety of its inhabitants. Our mutual dependency is planetwide and so we are already, and will remain indefinitely, *objectively* responsible for one another. There are, however, few if any signs that we who share the planet are willing to take up in earnest the *subjective* responsibility for that objective responsibility of ours.

At the moment, the knowledge classes (and most intellectuals in their number) seem to settle in the planetary "space of flows" (to borrow a concept from Manuel Castells) and thereby to keep their distance from "the people," who are left behind in the "space of places." But what about a somewhat more distant future? In the long term, so to speak?

To Marx, as Theodor Adorno suggested, the world seemed ready to turn into a paradise then and there. The world appeared to be prepared for an instantaneous U-turn, as "the possibility of changing the world 'from top to bottom' was immediately present." However, noted Adorno, this is no longer the case—if it ever was ("only stubbornness can still maintain the thesis as Marx formulated it").[8] The possibility of finding a shortcut to a world better fit for human habitation has been lost. Instead, one would say that between this world, here and now, and that other world, hospitable to humanity and "user friendly," there are no visible bridges left, whether genuine or putative. Neither are there crowds that would be eager to stampede across the length of the bridge if such a bridge were designed, nor vehicles able to take the willing to the other side and deliver them safely. No one is sure how a usable bridge could be designed and where the bridgehead could be located along the shore to facilitate smooth and expedient crossings. Such possibilities, one would conclude, are *not* immediately present.

Drawing the maps of utopia (represented as the model for "good society") that accompanied the birth of the modern era came to the intellectuals, their draftsmen, easily; the draftsmen just filled in the blank spots or repainted the ugly parts in the public space whose presence was, and with good reason, taken for granted and seen as unproblematic. The pursuit of happiness was understood as a search for a good society. Images of a good life were matter-of-factly public and social, since the meanings of "social" and "public" were not in doubt—they were not yet the essentially contested issue they became in our day, in the aftermath of the Reagan-Thatcher neoliberal coup d'état. Who would implement the blueprint and preside over the transformation was not a problem: it could be a despot or a republic, a king or the people; whoever it was, the seat of "public authority" was never empty. One or the other authority was firmly in place, waiting, apparently, only for enlightenment and the signal to act. No wonder that it was this *public* or *social* utopia that fell as the first casualty of the dramatic change in the public sphere.

Like everything else once securely located in that sphere, models of a good life have now become the game and prey of lone rangers, hunters, and trappers—and have become some of the many spoils of deregulation, privatization, individualization, of the conquest and annexation of the public by the private. The grand social vision has been split into a multitude of individual and personal, strikingly similar but decidedly not complementary portmanteaus. Each one is made to the measure of consumers' bliss—meant, like all consumer joys, for utterly individual, lonely enjoyment even when relished in company.

Can public space be made once more a place of lasting engagement rather than casual and fleeting encounters? A space of dialogue, discussion, confrontation, and agreement? Yes and no. If what is meant by public space is the public sphere, wrapped around and serviced by the representative institutions of the nation-state (as it was through most of modern history), the answer is, probably, no. That particular variety of the public stage has been stripped of most of the assets that enabled it to sustain the dramas staged on it in the past. Those public stages, originally constructed for the nation-state's political purposes, remain stubbornly local, whereas contemporary drama is a humanity-wide production, and so is obstreperously and emphatically global. An answer of yes, to be credible, would require a new *global* public space: genuinely planetary (as distinct from international) politics and a suitable planetary stage. Also a truly planetary responsibility: acknowledgment of the fact that all of us who share the planet depend on one another for our present and our future, that nothing we do or fail to do is indifferent to the fate of anybody else, and that no longer can any of us seek and find private shelter from storms that originate in any part of the globe.

The logic of planetary responsibility is aimed, at least in principle, at confronting the globally generated problems point-blank—at their own level. It stems from the assumption that lasting and truly effective solutions to planetwide problems can be found and made to work only through the renegotiation and reforming of the web of global interdependencies and interactions. Instead of aiming to control local damage and local benefits derived from the capricious and haphazard drifts of global economic forces, it would pursue results in a new kind of global setting, one in which economic initiatives enacted anywhere on the planet are no longer whimsical and guided by momentary gains alone, with no attention paid to the side effects and "collateral casualties" and no importance attached to the social dimensions of the cost-and-effect balances. In short, that logic is aimed, to quote Habermas, at the development of "politics that can catch up with global markets."[9] We feel, guess, suspect what needs to be done, but we cannot know in which shape and form it eventually will be done. We can be pretty sure, though, that the shape will not be familiar. It will be different from all we've gotten used to.

Not that long ago I took part in the celebration held in Prague of the seventieth birthday of Václav Havel, one of the most active and effective intellectuals of the past century. How come Havel left such a powerful trace on the shape of the world we inhabit? Havel is on record as having stated that "hope is not a prognostication." Indeed, hope pays little if any respect to statistics, to pedantically calculated trends and fickle majority opinions. Hope, as a rule, looks and stretches it-self beyond today and tomorrow (and, to the amazement of most practicing politicians, even well beyond the next elec-tions!)—and this is why most seasoned politicians wouldn't touch it with a barge pole. Havel, who almost single-handedly managed to topple one of the most sinister barracks in the Soviet-communist camp, had no bombers, aircraft carriers, smart missiles, or marines—all those weapons that (as we are repeatedly told) decide the course of history. He had only three weapons: hope, courage, and stubbornness. These are primitive weapons, nothing high-tech about them. And they are the most mundane, common weapons: humans all have them, and have since at least Paleolithic times. Only we use them much too seldom.

And this is why I believe that the obituaries of the intellectu-als are grossly exaggerated. This is also why I believe that the rupture between their concerns and those of the rest of the people will be healed, their dialogue with human experience will continue, and the changing human condition will be taken hold of again, with all the threats and chances it presents to our shared humanity.

CHAPTER ONE

What Chance of Ethics
in the Globalized World of Consumers?

THE CALL TO love thy neighbor as thyself, says Sigmund Freud, is one of the fundamental precepts of civilized life (and, according to some, one of its fundamental ethical demands).[1] But it is also most contrary to the kind of reason that such civilization promotes: the reason of self-interest, of pursuit of happiness. Is civilization therefore based on an irresolvable contradiction? So it seems; if one followed Freud's suggestions, one would come to the conclusion that the founding precept of civilization might be embraced only if one adopted Tertullian's famed admonition to *credere quia absurdum* (believe because it is absurd).

Indeed, it is enough to ask "Why should I do it?" "What good will it do me?" to realize the absurdity of the demand to love one's neighbor "as thyself"—any neighbor, just because he or she happens to be within sight and reach. If I love someone, he or she must deserve it in some way. He deserves it if he is so much like me in so many important ways that I can love *myself* in him; she deserves it yet more if she is so much more perfect than I am that I can love in her the *ideal* of my own self. "But if he is a stranger to me and if he cannot attract me by any worth of his own or any significance that he may already have acquired for my emotional life, it will be hard for me to love him."[2] The demand feels even more inane and, above all, irksome because all too often I cannot find much evidence that the stranger whom I am supposed to love *loves me,* or even shows me "the slightest consideration. When it suits him, he would not hesitate to injure me, jeer at me, slander me and show me his superior power." And so, Freud asks, "What is the point of a precept enunciated with so much solemnity if its fulfilment cannot be recommended as reasonable?" One is tempted to conclude, he says, against good sense, that "love your neighbour" is "a commandment which is really justified by the fact that nothing else runs as strongly counter to the original nature of man."

The less likely a norm is to be obeyed, the more likely it is to be stated with resolve and obstinacy. And the injunction to love one's neighbor is perhaps less likely to be obeyed than any other norm. When the Talmudic sage Rabbi Hillel was challenged by a prospective convert to explain God's teaching while the challenger stood on one foot, he offered "love thy neighbor as thyself" as the only—and yet complete—answer, encapsulating the totality of God's injunctions. But the Talmudic story does not tell whether the challenger's conversion followed that answer. Indeed, accepting Rabbi Hillel's command would be a leap of faith; a decisive but awfully difficult leap, through which man breaks out of the carapace of "natural" drives, urges, and predilections and sets himself against nature, turning into the "unnatural" being that humans are, unlike the beasts (and indeed the angels, as Aristotle pointed out).

Accepting the precept of loving one's neighbor is the birth-act of humanity. All other routines of human cohabitation, as well as the predesigned or retrospectively discovered norms and rules, are but a never-complete list of footnotes to that precept. We can go a step further and say that, since this precept is the preliminary condition of humanity, civilization, and civilized humanity, if this precept were to be ignored or thrown away, there would be no one extant to recompose that list or ponder its completeness.

But let me add right away that although loving your neighbor may not be a staple product of the survival instinct, neither is self-love, which is designated the model of neighborly love. Self-love—what does that mean? What do I love "in myself"? What do I love when I love myself?

It is true that self-love prompts us to "stick to life," to try hard to stay alive for better or worse, to resist and fight back against whatever may threaten life's premature termination and to protect, or better yet increase, that fitness and vigor that we hope will make the resistance (and so the protection) effective. In this, however, our near or distant animal cousins are masters no less accomplished and seasoned than the most dedicated and artful fitness addicts and health fiends among us. Our animal cousins (except the domesticated ones, whom we have managed to strip of their natural endowments so that they can better serve our survival, rather than their own) need no experts to tell them how to stay alive and be fit. Nor do they need self-love to instruct them that staying alive and fit is the right thing to do.

Survival (the animal survival, the physical, bodily survival) can do *without* self-love. As a matter of fact, it may do better without it than with it. The survival instinct and self-love may be parallel roads, but they may also run in opposite directions. Self-love may rebel *against* the continuation of life if we find that life hateful rather than lovable. Self-love can prod us to *re-*

ject survival if our life is not up to love's standards and therefore not worth living.

What we love when we "love ourselves" is a self *fit to be loved*. What we love is the state, or the hope, of *being loved*—of being an object worthy of love, being recognized as such, and being given proof of that recognition.

In short: in order to have self-love, we need to be loved or to have hope of being loved. Refusal of love—a snub, a rejection, denial of the status of a love-worthy object—breeds self-hatred. *Self-love is built of the love offered to us by others.* Others must love us first, so that we can begin to love ourselves.

And how do we know that we have not been snubbed or dumped as a hopeless, unworthy case? How do we know that love is, may be, will be forthcoming, that we *are* worthy of it? We know it, we believe that we know it, and we are reassured that our belief is not mistaken when we are talked to and listened to; when we are *listened to attentively,* with an interest that signals the listener's readiness to respond. We gather then that we are respected. It is from the state of being respected by others that we derive the conclusion that what we think, do, or intend to do *counts.* That we matter. That our staying alive makes a difference. That we are worthy of being cared for.

If others respect me, then, obviously, there must be "in me" something that only I can offer to others; and obviously there are such others who would be glad to be offered it and grateful if they were. I am important, and what I think and say and do is important as well. I am not a cipher, easily replaced and disposed of. I "make a difference," and not just to myself. What I say and what I am and do matters—and this is not just my own flight of fancy. Whatever there is in the world around me, that world would be poorer, less interesting, and less promising if I were suddenly to cease to exist.

If this is what makes us right and proper objects of self-love, then the call to love our neighbors as ourselves (that is, to expect our neighbors to wish to be loved for the same reasons that prompt our self-love) invokes the neighbors' desire to have the dignity of *their* unique, irreplaceable, and undisposable value similarly recognized and confirmed. That call prods us to assume that the neighbors do indeed represent such value—at least until proven otherwise. Loving our neighbors as we love ourselves would mean, then, *respecting each other's uniqueness*—valuing each other for our differences, which enrich the world we jointly inhabit and make it a more fascinating and enjoyable place.

This is, however, one side of the story—the brighter side. To be in the presence of an Other also has its dark side. The Other may be a promise, but it is also a threat. He or she may arouse contempt as much as respect, fear as much as awe. The big question is, which of the two is more likely to happen?

Philosophers have been divided in their answers to this question. Hobbes, for instance, famously suggested that if people were not coerced to behave nicely, they would be at each other's throats. Rousseau, however, equally famously supposed that it is because of coercion that people become cruel and harm each other. Some others still, for example, Nietzsche and Scheler, suggested that either possibility may come out on top, depending on what kinds of people engage (or are cast) in the mutual relationship, and under what circumstances.

Both Nietzsche and Scheler point to *ressentiment* as a major obstacle to loving the Other as thyself. (While they wrote in German, they used the French term *ressentiment,* the complex meaning of which is less than perfectly conveyed by the more straightforward English term "resentment." To fully grasp what the two philosophers had in mind, when writing and thinking in English it would be better to deploy such terms as rancor, repugnance, acrimony, grudge, umbrage, spite, malignancy—or better still, a combination of all of them.) Though they use the same term, however, Nietzsche and Scheler refer to somewhat different types of enmity.

For Nietzsche, *ressentiment* is what the downcast, the deprived, the discriminated against, and the humiliated feel toward their "betters" (the self-proclaimed betters and self-established betters): the wealthy, the powerful, the free to self-assert and capable of self-asserting, those who claim the right to be respected together with the right to deny (or refute) their inferiors' right to dignity. For those "inferiors" (the "lesser people," the "lower classes," the masses, plebeians, hoi polloi), acknowledging the rights of their "betters" would be tantamount to accepting their own inferiority and lesser, or nonexistent, dignity. *Ressentiment* is for that reason a curious, inherently ambiguous mixture of genuflection and acrimony, but also of envy and spite. We might say that the deepest cause of *ressentiment* is precisely the agony of that irresolvable ambivalence, or as Leon Festinger would say, that "cognitive dissonance": approving of the qualities one does not possess necessarily involves disapprobation, and respect for the "betters" entails for the "lesser people" the surrendering of self-esteem. One would therefore expect in the case of *ressentiment,* as in all cases of acute cognitive dissonance, the emergence of an overwhelming desire to deny that double bind: to recover one's own self-esteem (that is, the right to dignity) through denying the superiority of superiors—in other words, through postulating an equality of rank, at least, and the right to deference. For Nietzsche, this was the source of all religions, and of Christianity above all, with its postulate of the equality of all men before God and the same commandments, the same ethical code, binding all. In Nietzsche's rendition, *ressentiment* leads not to more freedom but to mitigating the pain of one's own un-freedom by denying freedom to all, and to alleviating the pain of one's own indignity by pulling others down from the heights they managed to make their exclusive property to one's own level of lowliness or mediocrity, slavery or semi-slavery.

For Max Scheler *ressentiment* is, however, a feeling most likely to appear among equals—felt by the members of the middle classes toward each other and prompting them to compete feverishly for similar stakes, to promote themselves while demoting the others "like them." Scheler's concept of *ressentiment* and of the role it plays in society is essentially opposite to Nietzsche's. For Nietzsche, *ressentiment* results in a fight against inequality and a pressure to level down the extant social hierarchies. For Scheler, it is quite the opposite: starting from an equal social standing and a similar predicament, members of the middle classes—as self-asserting and self-defining free agents—strive to lift themselves up and push the others down. Freedom comes as part of a package deal with inequality: my freedom manifests itself in, and is measured by, the degree to which I manage to limit the liberty of others who claim to be my equals. *Ressentiment* results in competition, in an ongoing struggle for the redistribution of power and prestige, social reverence and socially recognized dignity. "Ostentatious consumption," famously described by Thorstein Veblen—that shameless display of one's own opulence and wealth to humiliate others who don't have the resources to respond in kind—is a vivid example of the kind of behavior that Scheler's variety of *ressentiment* tends to generate.

We may add a third instance of *ressentiment,* a timeless kind, but in our times probably the most indomitable obstacle to "loving thy neighbor." Seemingly unstoppable, it rises in importance with the growing "fluidity" of social settings, the dissipation of comfortable routines, the increasing frailty of human bonds, and the atmosphere of uncertainty, insecurity, and diffuse, underdefined, free-floating, and unanchored fear in which we live. This is the *ressentiment* toward strangers—people who, precisely because they are unfamiliar and thus unpredictable and suspect, are vivid and tangible embodiments of the resented and feared fluidity of the world. They serve as natural, handy effigies in which the specter of the world falling apart may be burned; as natural props in exorcism rituals against the evil spirits threatening the orderly lives of the pious.

Among the resented strangers, pride of place is accorded today to the refugees, asylum seekers, and simply impoverished exiles from impoverished parts of the planet. They are, as Bertolt Brecht once put it, "the harbingers of ill tidings." They remind us, on whose doors they knock, just how insecure our security is, how feeble and vulnerable our comfort, how poorly safeguarded our peace and quiet.

Tribal wars and massacres, the proliferation of guerrilla armies (often little more than bandit gangs in thin disguise) busy decimating each other's ranks while absorbing and annihilating the "population surplus" (mostly the unemployable and prospectless youth)—these are some of the most spectacular and horrifying outcomes of the "negative globalization" that threatens conditions of life for everyone but affects most directly the so-called latecomers to modernity. Hundreds of thousands of people are chased from their homes, murdered or forced to run for their lives beyond the borders of their own country. It seems the sole thriving industry in the lands of the latecomers to modernity (deviously and deceitfully dubbed "developing countries") is the mass production of refugees.

Refugees are stateless, but stateless in a new sense: their statelessness is raised to an entirely new level by the nonexistence of the state to which their statehood could be referred. They are, as Michel Agier put it in his most insightful study of the refugees in the era of globalization, *hors du nomos*—outside law; not this or that law of this or that country, but law as such.[3] They are outcasts and outlaws of a novel kind, the products of globalization and the epitome and incarnation of its frontier spirit. To quote Agier again, they have been cast into a condition of "liminal drift," which may be transitory or permanent; even if stationary for a time, they are in a state of movement that will never be complete because their destination (arrival or return) remains unclear, and a place they could call "final," inaccessible. They are never to free themselves from the gnawing sense of transience, the indefiniteness and provisional nature of any settlement. They represent every premonition and fear that haunts our sleepless nights, even when we stifle and repress them with the busyness of our working days.

The human waste of the global frontier, the refugees, are the outsiders incarnate, the absolute outsiders, outsiders resented and greeted everywhere with rancor and spite. They are out of place everywhere except in places that are themselves out of place—the "nowhere places" that appear on no maps that ordinary tourists use on their travels. And once outside, indefinitely outside: a secure fence with watchtowers is all that is needed to make the "indefiniteness" of the out-of-place hold forever.

Emmanuel Levinas, acclaimed by many as the greatest ethical philosopher of the last century, was a disciple of Edmund Husserl. His own first studies and publications, starting with his prize-winning essay of 1930 on the role assigned to intuition in Husserl's work, were dedicated to the exegesis and interpretation of the teachings of the founder of modern phenomenology; they remain explicit testimonies to that intellectual debt. And this starting point determined to a great extent the trajectory of Levinas's own oeuvre—though his mode of reasoning and his methods, rather than his cognitive targets or his findings and substantive propositions, were in quite a few crucial respects the opposite of Husserl's.

What Levinas owed to Husserl in the first place was the daring feat of phenomenological reduction—in Levinas's own words, that "act of violence that man does to himself . . . in order to find himself again as pure thought"—and the stimulus, encouragement, and authoritative endorsement for the even greater boldness to allow the intuition of a philosophy to precede (and pre-form) the philosophy of intuition.[4] It was on the authority of phenomenological reduction—the procedure conceived, practiced, and legitimized by Husserl—that the concept of putting ethics before ontology, the founding act of Levinas's own philosophical system, was arrived at and endorsed.

Following the itinerary sketched and tested by Husserl's phenomenological reduction, and deploying the tools of "bracketing away" and epochē (detachment, elimination, suspension), Levinas embarked on cracking the mystery of Kant's "moral law inside me." He began an exploration of "pure ethics"—absolute, pristine, extemporal, and exterritorial, unsoiled by the products of societal recycling and unadulterated by illegitimate, heterogeneous, accidental, and dispensable admixtures—and of the ethic's pure meaning (intentional, as for Husserl all pure meanings must be), which makes all other ascribed and imputed meanings conceivable while also calling them into question and to account.

That voyage of exploration led Levinas, in stark opposition to Husserl, not to transcendental *subjectivity* but to the indomitable and impenetrable transcendental *otherness* of the Other. The ultimate station of the phenomenological reduction in Levinas's style is *alterity,* that irreducible otherness of the Other that awakes the self to its own unique responsibilities and thereby assists, even if obliquely, at the birth of subjectivity. At the far end of Levinas's reductive labors towers the encounter with the Other, the shock of that encounter and the silent challenge of the Other's Face—and not the always-already-there, introverted, solitary, lonely, and unperturbed subjectivity that weaves meanings, spider-style, out of its own abdomen. In Harvie Ferguson's masterly interpretation of Levinas's findings, "The other is not a differentiated fragment, or projection, of what is first internal to consciousness, nor can it be assimilated to consciousness in any way; it is and remains 'outside the subject' . . . What emerges with the reduction of the actively constituted object-world of everyday life is neither the transcendental ego, nor the pure transition of temporality, but the mysterious, brute fact of exteriority."[5]

It is not (as Husserl would aver) that the object-world is daily secreted by the transcendental ego and so could be returned to it, to its roots and original primeval purity, through the determinate effort of phenomenological reduction. The ego—the self and its self-awareness—is brought into being in the confrontation with, simultaneously, the limits to its creative potency and the limits-transcending challenge to its intentions and intuitions: by the absolute alterity of the Other as an ensconced and sealed, forever-external entity that stubbornly refuses to be absorbed and assimilated, and thereby simultaneously triggers and refutes the ego's unstoppable effort to cross the abyss that separates them. In stark opposition to his philosophy teacher, Levinas uses the teacher's methodology to reassert autonomy of the world as against the subject: emphatically *not* the world's God-like designer and creator, the subject is called into being through assuming responsibility for the world's indomitable and uncompromising alterity. If for Heidegger *Sein* (Being) was *"ursprünglich" Mitsein*—"from the beginning" being with—for Levinas it is (similarly *ursprünglich*) *Fürsein,* or being for. The self is born in the act of recognition of its being *for the Other* and thereby in the revelation of the insufficiency of a mere *Mitsein*.

The world in which the ego is immersed, the socially construed world, interferes in the confrontation of the thinking, feeling self with the Face of the Other. It does so by reducing the modality of "being for," by its nature boundless and forever underdefined, to the finite set of commandments and prohibitions. Following Husserl, Levinas embarked on an exploratory voyage in search of the *Sachen selbst* (things themselves), in his case the essence of ethics, and found it at the far end of the phenomenological reduction, once he had "bracketed away" everything accidental, contingent, derivative, and supernumerary superimposed on ethics in the course of the human's being-in-the-world. And like Husserl, he brought back from his voyage of discovery rich trophies hardly accessible in any other, less tortuous way: the inventory of the invariants of moral existence and ethical relationships—features of the pristine condition from which all moral existence starts and to which it returns in every moral act.

"The Other" and "the Face" are generic names, but in every moral encounter found in the heart of the "moral law inside me" mystery, each name stands for just one being—one only, never more than one: *one* Other, *one* Face. Neither name may appear in the plural at the far end of phenomenological reduction. The otherness of the Other is tantamount to its uniqueness; each Face is one and only, and its uniqueness defies the endemic impersonality of the rule.

It is their uncompromising singularity that renders redundant and irrelevant most or perhaps all of the things that fill the daily life of every flesh-and-blood human: the pursuit of survival, self-esteem, or self-aggrandizement, the rational juxtaposition of ends and means, the calculation of gains and losses, the search for pleasure, desire for peace or power. Entering Levinas's moral space requires taking time off from the daily business of living and leaving aside its mundane norms and conventions. At the "moral party of two," both I and the Other arrive disrobed, without our social trappings, stripped of status, social distinctions, and socially concocted or socially imposed identities, positions, or roles. We are neither rich nor poor, high nor lowly, mighty nor disempowered—neither "deserving" nor "undeserving." None of those qualifiers applies, let alone matters, for the partners in the moral twosome. Whatever we might yet become will emerge only in and from our twosome-ness.

Within such a space, and only there, the moral self cannot but feel uncomfortable—confused, lost—the moment the moral party of two is broken into by a Third. And it is not just the moral self that feels uncomfortable but also Levinas, its explorer and spokesman. No better proof of his discomfort is needed than the obsessive, almost compulsive urgency with which he returns in his late writings and interviews to the "problem of the Third": that is, to the possibility of salvaging the ethical relationship, born, raised, and groomed in the greenhouse of the twosome, in the setting of ordinary, mundane life, where interventions, intrusions, and "break-ins" of the uncountable "Thirds" are the daily norm.

As Georg Simmel pointed out in his groundbreaking comparison between dyadic and triadic relationships, "The decisive characteristic of the dyad is that each of the two (partners) must actually accomplish something, and that in case of failure only the other remains—not a supra-individual force, as prevails in a group even of three."[6] This, Simmel insists, "makes for a close and highly specific coloration of the dyadic relationship," "as the dyadic element is much more frequently confronted with All or Nothing than is the member of the larger group."

One can see why the dyadic relationship tends to turn almost naturally into (or even be identical with) the "moral party of two," and why it tends to be a natural habitat (or even a nursery) for that unconditionality of responsibility that would be unlikely to emerge and take root otherwise; and why it would be well-nigh inconceivable for such *un*conditional responsibility to emerge spontaneously in the midst of larger groups, in which mediated relations prevail upon the unmediated face-to-face ones, providing a matrix for many alternative alliances and divisions. One can also see why a thinking, feeling entity brought up in the secure confinement of the dyad is unprepared and feels out of its element when drawn into a threesome setting. One can see why the tools and habits developed inside a dyadic relationship need to be overhauled and complemented to make a triad viable.

There is a remarkable similarity between the late Levinas's keen yet ultimately inconclusive and frustrating effort to bring the pristine moral self he discovered at the end of phenomenological reduction back into the selfsame world from whose deforming traces he struggled all his life to free it, and the ageing Husserl's exorbitant, indeed Herculean, yet similarly frustrated and frustrating effort to return to intersubjectivity from the "transcendental subjectivity" he spent his life cleansing of all "inter"-bound adulterations. The question is: can moral capacity and aptitude, made to the measure of responsibility for the Other as the Face, be capacious and potent enough, as well as sufficiently determined and vigorous, to carry an entirely different burden of responsibility for the "Other as such," an indefinite and anonymous Other, a faceless (because dissolved in the multitude of "other others") Other? Is the ethics born and cultivated inside the moral party of two fit to be transplanted into the imagined community of human society and, further, into the imagined global community of humanity?

To put it bluntly: does the moral initiation, upbringing, and education we receive inside the moral party of two prepare us for life in the world?

Before the world stubbornly and vexingly inhospitable to ethics had become his major preoccupation, Levinas visited it on relatively few occasions, and only briefly and gingerly—and seldom on his own initiative, unprompted by inquisitive interviewers. In "Morality Begins at Home; or the Rocky Road to Justice" I traced those visits, from *Le moi et la totalité* of 1954 up to *De l'unicité,* published in 1986.[7] As time went by, however, the space and attention devoted by Levinas to the chances that the moral impulse would match on the broad societal stage "the kindness which gave it birth and keeps it alive" grew visibly; although gradual, it was unstoppable.[8] The major message hammered home by Levinas toward the end of his life was that the moral impulse, though sovereign and self-sufficient within the moral party of two, is a poor guide once it ventures beyond that party's limits. The stultifying infinity and unconditionality of moral responsibility (or, as the great Danish ethical philosopher Knud Løgstrup would say, the noxious silence of the ethical demand that insists that something needs to be done but stubbornly refuses to specify what) simply can't be sustained when the "Other" appears in a plural, as he or she does in human society. In the densely populated world of human daily life, moral impulses need codes, laws, jurisdiction, and institutions that install and monitor them all: on the way to being thrown onto the large screen of society, *moral* sense reincarnates as, or is reprocessed into, *social justice.*

In the presence of the Third, says Levinas in conversation with François Poirié, "We leave what I call the order of ethics, or the order of saintliness or the order of mercy, or the order of love, or the order of charity—where the other human concerns me regardless of the place he occupies in the multitude of humans, and even regardless of our shared quality of individuals of the human species; he concerns me as one close to me, as the first to come. He is unique."[9] Simmel would certainly add that "the essential point is that within a dyad, there can be no majority which could outvote the individual. This majority, however, is made possible by the mere addition of a third member. But relations which permit the individual to be over-ruled by a majority devalue individuality."[10] And they thereby devalue uniqueness, and privileged closeness, and uncontested priorities, and unconditional responsibilities—all those foundation stones of a moral relationship.

The oft-repeated assurance "This is a free country" (meaning it is up to you what sort of life you wish to live, how you decide to live it, and what kind of choices you make to see the decision through; blame yourself and no one but yourself in case all that does not result in the bliss you hoped for) suggests the joy of emancipation closely intertwined with the horror of defeat. "A free man," Joseph Brodsky would say, "when he fails, blames nobody" (nobody else, that is, except himself).[11] However crowded that world out there, it contains no one onto whom the blame for my failure may be shifted. And as Levinas would repeat after Dostoyevsky, "We are all guilty of all and for all men before all, and I more than the others," and comment, "Responsibility is *my* affair. Reciprocity is *his* affair. The I always has one responsibility *more* than all the others."[12]

The arrival of freedom is viewed as an exhilarating emancipation—be it from harrowing obligations and irritating prohibitions or monotonous and stultifying routines. Soon after freedom settles in, however, and becomes our daily bread, a new kind of horror, the horror of *responsibility*, not a bit less frightening than the terrors chased away through the advent of freedom, makes the memories of past sufferings pale. Nights that follow days of obligatory routine are filled with dreams of *freedom from constraints.* Nights that follow days of obligatory choices are filled with dreams of *freedom from responsibility.*

It is therefore remarkable but hardly surprising that the two most powerful and persuasive cases for the necessity of society (that is, of a comprehensive, solidly grounded, and efficiently protected system of constraints and rules), advanced by philosophers from the start of the world's modern transformation, were prompted by the recognition of physical threats and spiritual burdens endemic to the condition of *freedom.*

The first case, articulated by Hobbes, elaborated at great length by Durkheim and Freud, and toward the middle of the twentieth century turned into the *doxa* of social philosophers and scientists, presented societal coercion and the constraints imposed on individual freedom by normative regulations as necessary, inevitable, and in the end salutary and beneficial means of protecting human togetherness against a "war of all against all," and as guarding human individuals against a "life that is nasty, brutish and short." The advocates of this case argued that the cessation of social coercion, if such cessation were at all feasible or even conceivable, would not liberate the individuals; on the contrary, it would only make them unable to resist the morbid pressures of their own essentially antisocial instincts. It would render them victims of a slavery more horrifying than that which all the pressures of tough social realities could possibly produce. Freud would present social coercion and the resulting limitation of individual freedom as the very essence of civilization: since the "pleasure principle" (the drive to seek immediate sexual gratification, for instance, or the inborn inclination to laziness) would guide, or rather misguide, individual conduct toward the wasteland of asociality or sociopathy unless it were constrained, trimmed, and counterbalanced by the power-aided, authority-operated "reality principle," civilization without coercion is unthinkable.

The second case for the necessity, indeed the unavoidability, of socially operated normative regulations, and therefore also for the social coercion that constrains individual freedom, has been founded on the opposite premise, that of the ethical challenge to which humans are exposed by the very presence of others, by the "silent appeal of the Face"—a challenge that precedes all socially created and socially run ontological settings, which if anything try to neutralize, trim, and limit the otherwise boundless challenge to make it endurable. In this version, most fully elaborated by Emmanuel Levinas and Knud Løgstrup, society is primarily a contraption for reducing the essentially unconditional and unlimited responsibility-for-the-Other, or the infinity of "ethical demand," to a set of prescriptions and proscriptions more on a par with human abilities to cope and manage. The principal function of normative regulation, and also the paramount source of its inevitability, is to make the exercise of responsibility (Levinas) or obeying the ethical demand (Løgstrup) a realistic task for "ordinary people," who tend to stop short of the standards for saintliness—and must stop short of them—for society to be conceivable. As Levinas himself put it, "It is extremely important to know if society in the current sense of the term is the result of limitation of the principle that men are predators of one another, or if to the contrary it results from the limitation of the principle that men are *for* each other. Does the social, with its institutions, universal forms and laws, result from limiting the consequences of the war between men, or from limiting the infinity which opens in the ethical relationship of man to man?"[13]

To put it in a nutshell: is "society" the product of bridling the selfish, aggressive inclinations of its members with the duty of solidarity, or is it, on the contrary, an outcome of tempering their endemic and boundless altruism with the "order of egoism"?

Using the vocabulary of Emmanuel Levinas, we may say that the principal function of society, "with its institutions, universal forms and laws," is to make the essentially *unconditional* and *unlimited* responsibility for the Other both *conditional* (in selected, duly enumerated, and clearly defined circumstances) and *limited* (to a select group of "others," considerably smaller than the totality of humanity and, most important, narrower and thus more easily manageable that the indefinite sum total of "others" who may eventually awaken in the subjects the sentiments of inalienable, and boundless, responsibility). Using the vocabulary of Knud Løgstrup (a thinker remarkably close to Levinas's viewpoint who, like Levinas, insists on the primacy of ethics over realities of life-in-society and calls the world to account for failing to rise to the standards of ethical responsibility), we would say that society is an arrangement for rendering the otherwise stubbornly and vexingly, harrowingly silent (because unspecific) ethical command audible—that is, specific and codified—and thereby reducing the infinite multitude of options such a command may imply to a much narrower, manageable range of obligations.

It so happened, however, that the advent of the liquid-modern society of consumers sapped the credibility and persuasive power of both cases for the ineluctability of societal imposition. Each was diminished in a different way, though for the same reason: for the ever more evident dismantling of the system of normative regulation, and thereby the releasing of ever larger chunks of human conduct from coercive patterning, supervision, and policing, and relegating ever larger numbers of previously socialized functions to the realm of individual "life politics." In the deregulated and privatized setting focused on consumerist concerns and pursuits, the summary responsibility for choices—for the action that follows the choice and for the consequences of those actions—is cast squarely on the individual actors' shoulders. As Pierre Bourdieu had already signaled two decades ago, coercion is being replaced by stimulation, forceful imposition of behavioral patterns by seduction, policing of conduct by PR and advertising, and the normative regulation, as such, by the arousal of new needs and desires. Apparently, the advent of consumerism has stripped the Hobbesian case of quite a lot of its credibility, as the catastrophic consequences it predicted for any retreat or emaciation of the socially administered normative regulation have failed to materialize.

The new profusion and unprecedented intensity of interindividual antagonisms and open conflicts that followed the progressive deregulation and privatization of the previously societal functions are widely recognized and provide focus for ongoing debate, but the deregulated and privatized society of consumers is still far from the terrifying vision of Hobbes's *bellum omnium contra omnes*. Freud's case for the necessarily coercive nature of civilization fared no better. It seems likely (even if the jury is still out) that once exposed to the logic of commodity markets and left to their own choices, consumers found the power relationship between pleasure and reality principles reversed. It is now the "reality principle" that has been forced to go on the defense; it is daily compelled to retreat, self-limit, and compromise in the face of renewed assaults by the "pleasure principle." What the powers of the consumerist society seem to have discovered—and turned to their advantage—is that there is little to be gained from servicing the inert, hard-and-fast "social facts" deemed indomitable and irresistible at the time of Emile Durkheim, whereas catering to the infinitely expansible pleasure principle promises infinitely extendable commercial profits. The already blatant and still growing "softness," flexibility, and brief life expectancy of liquid-modern "social facts" help to emancipate the search for pleasure from its past limitations and fully open it to profitable exploitation by the markets.

As to the case composed and advanced by Levinas and Løgstrup, the task of cutting down the suprahuman boundlessness of ethical responsibility to the capacity of an ordinary human's sensitivity, an ordinary human's power of judgment and ability to act, tends now (except in a few selected areas) to be "subsidiarized" to individual men and women. In the absence of an authoritative translation of the "unspoken demand" into a finite inventory of prescriptions and proscriptions, it is now up to each individual to set the limits of her or his responsibility for other humans and to draw the line between the plausible and the implausible among moral interventions—as well as to decide how far she or he is ready to go in sacrificing personal welfare for the sake of fulfilling moral responsibility to others. As Alain Ehrenberg convincingly argues, most common human sufferings tend to grow nowadays from the surfeit of *possibilities,* rather than from the profusion of *prohibitions* as they used to in the past.[14] If the opposition between the possible and the impossible has taken over from the antinomy of the allowed and the forbidden as the cognitive frame and essential criterion for evaluating life choices and strategies, it is only to be expected that the depressions arising from the terror of *inadequacy* would replace the neuroses caused by the horror of *guilt* (that is, from the charge of *nonconformity* following the breach of rules) as the most characteristic and widespread psychic afflictions among the denizens of the consumer society.

Once shifted over (or abandoned) to individuals, the task of ethical decision making becomes overwhelming, as the stratagem of hiding behind a recognized and apparently indomitable authority, one that vouches to remove the responsibility (or at least a significant part of it) from their shoulders, is no longer a viable or reliable option. Struggling with so daunting a task casts the actors into a state of permanent uncertainty. All too often, it leads to harrowing and demeaning self-reprobation.

And yet the overall result of the privatization and subsidiarization of responsibility proves somewhat less incapacitating for the moral self and moral actors than Levinas, Løgstrup, and their disciples—myself included—would have expected. Somehow, a way has been found to mitigate the potentially devastating impact on individuals and limit the damage. There is, it appears, a profusion of commercial agencies eager to take up the tasks abandoned by the "great society" and to sell their services to the bereaved, ignorant, and perplexed consumers.

Under the deregulated/privatized regime, the formula for "relief from responsibility" has remained much the same as it was in the earlier stages of modern history: a measure of genuine or putative clarity is injected into a hopelessly opaque situation by replacing (more correctly, covering up) the mind-boggling complexity of the task with a set of straightforward must-do and mustn't-do rules. Now, as then, individual actors are pressed, nudged, and cajoled to put their confidence in authorities trusted to decide and spell out what exactly the unspoken demand commands them to do in this or that situation, and just how far (and no further) their unconditional responsibility obliges them to go under those situations. In the pursuit of the same stratagem, however, different tools now tend to be deployed.

The concepts of responsibility and responsible choice, which used to reside in the semantic field of ethical duty and moral concern for the Other, have moved or have been shifted to the realm of self-fulfillment and calculation of risks. In the process, the Other as the trigger, the target, and the yardstick

for a responsibility accepted, assumed, and fulfilled has all but disappeared from view, having been elbowed out or overshadowed by the actor's own self. "Responsibility" means now, first and last, *responsibility to oneself* ("You owe this to yourself," as the outspoken traders in relief from responsibility indefatigably repeat), while "responsible choices" are, first and last, such moves as serve well the interests and satisfy the desires of the actor and stave off the need to compromise.

The outcome is not much different from the "adiaphorizing" effects of the stratagem practiced by solid-modern bureaucracy.[15] That stratagem was the substitution of the "responsibility to" (to a superior person, to an authority, to a cause and its spokesmen that originate an action) for the "responsibility for" (for the welfare, autonomy, and dignity of another human at the receiving end of the action). However, adiaphorizing effects (that is, rendering actions ethically neutral and exempting them from ethical evaluation and censure) tend to be achieved these days mostly through replacing responsibility for others with responsibility *to* oneself and responsibility *for* oneself rolled into one. The collateral victim of the leap to the consumerist rendition of freedom is the Other as object of ethical responsibility and moral concern.

Faithfully following the convoluted itinerary of the "public mood" in her widely read and highly influential book *The Cinderella Complex,* Colette Dowling declared the desire to be safe, warm, and taken care of to be a "dangerous feeling."[16] She warned the Cinderellas of the coming age to beware of falling into its trap: in the impulse to care for others and the desire to be cared for by others looms the awesome danger of dependency, of losing the ability to select the tide most comfortable for surfing and of swiftly moving from one wave to another the moment the tide turns. As Arlie Russell Hochschild comments, "Her fear of being dependent on another person evokes the image of the American cowboy, alone, detached, roaming free with his horse . . . On the ashes of Cinderella, then, rises a postmodern cowgirl."[17] The most popular of the empathizing, self-help best sellers of the day "whisper[ed] to the reader: 'Let the emotional investor beware' . . . Dowling cautions women to invest in the self as a solo enterprise," writes Hochschild. "The commercial spirit of intimate life is made up of images that prepare the way for a paradigm of distrust . . . by offering as ideal a self well defended against getting hurt . . . The heroic acts a self can perform . . . are to detach, to leave, and to depend on and need others less . . . In many cool modern books, the author prepares us for people out there who don't need our nurturance and for people who don't or can't nurture us."

The possibility of populating the world with more caring people and inducing people to care more does not figure in the panoramas painted in the consumerist utopia. The privatized utopias of the cowboys and cowgirls of the consumerist era show instead vastly expanded "free space" (free for *my* self, of course)—a kind of empty space of which the liquid-modern consumer, bent on solo performances and solo performances only, never has enough. The space that liquid-modern consumers need and are advised from all sides to fight for can be conquered only by evicting other humans—and particularly the kind of humans who care for others or may need care themselves.

The consumer market took over from the solid-modern bureaucracy the task of adiaphorization: the task of squeezing the "being for" poison away from the "being with" booster shot. It is just as Emmanuel Levinas adumbrated, when musing that rather than being a contraption making peaceful and friendly human togetherness achievable for inborn egoists (as Hobbes suggested), society may be a stratagem for making a self-centered, self-referential, egotistic life attainable for inborn moral beings, through cutting down the responsibilities for others that go together with the presence of the Face of the Other, indeed, with human togetherness.

According to Frank Mort, who researched the quarterly reports of the Henley Centre for Forecasting, at the top of the list of pleasures preferred and most coveted by the British for the last two decades were such pastimes as are "principally made available through market-based forms of provision: personal shopping, eating out, DIY [do-it-yourself projects] and video watching. Right at the bottom of the list came politics; going to a political meeting ranked on a par with a visit to the circus as one of the British public's least likely things to do."[18]

In *The Ethical Demand,* Løgstrup aired an optimistic view of humans' natural inclination. "It is a characteristic of human life that we normally encounter one another with natural trust," he wrote. "Only because of some special circumstance do we ever distrust a stranger in advance . . . Under normal circumstances, however, we accept the stranger's word and do not mistrust him until we have some particular reason to do so. We never suspect a person of falsehood until after we have caught him in a lie."[19] Let me emphasize that the author's judgments are not intended as phenomenological statements but as empirical generalizations. If most of Levinas's ethical theses enjoy the immunity of phenomenological status, this is not the case with Løgstrup, who induces his generalizations from daily interactions with his co-parishioners.

The Ethical Demand was conceived of by Løgstrup during the eight years following his marriage to Rosalie Maria Pauly, when they lived in the small and peaceful Danish parish of Funen Island. With due respect to the friendly and sociable residents of Aarhus, where Løgstrup was later to spend the rest of his life teaching theology at the local university, I doubt whether such ideas could have gestated in Løgstrup's mind after he had settled in that town and then had to face point-blank the realities of the world at war, living under German occupation as an active member of the Danish resistance.

People tend to weave their images of the world out of the yarn of their experience. The present generation may find Løgstrup's sunny and buoyant image of a trusting and trust-worthy world rather far-fetched, if not sharply at odds with what they themselves learn daily and what is insinuated by the common narratives of human experience they hear every day. They would more likely recognize themselves in the acts and confessions of the characters on the recent wave of hugely popular television shows of the *Big Brother, Survivor,* and *The Weakest Link* type, which (sometimes explicitly but always implicitly) convey quite a different message: that strangers are *not* to be trusted. The *Survivor* series, for instance, bears a says-it-all subtitle—"Trust No One"—to which every successive installment of *Big Brother* also adds ample and vivid illustrations. Fans and addicts of these "reality" shows (and this means a large part, possibly a substantive majority, of our contemporaries) would reverse Løgstrup's verdict on human society and decide that it is a characteristic of human life that we encounter one another with *natural suspicion*.

These TV spectacles that have taken millions of viewers by storm and immediately captured their imagination are public rehearsals of the concept of the *disposability* of humans. They carry an indulgence and a warning rolled into one story, their message being that no one is indispensable, no one has the right to his or her share in the fruits of joint effort just because he or she has added at some point to the group's growth—let alone because of being, simply, a member of the team. Life is a hard game for hard people, so the message goes. Each game starts from scratch, past merits do not count, you are worth only as much as the results of your last duel. Each player in every moment is playing for herself (or himself), and to progress, not to mention to reach the top, one must (alas!) cooperate first in excluding those many others eager to survive and succeed who are blocking the way, and then outwit, one by one, all those with whom one has cooperated—after squeezing out their last drop of usefulness—and leave them behind. The others are first and foremost competitors; they are always scheming, as all competitors do, digging holes, laying ambushes, itching for us to stumble and fall.

The assets that help the winners to outlive their competitors, and thus to emerge victorious from the cutthroat battle, are of many sorts, ranging from blatant self-assertiveness to meek self-effacement. Whatever stratagem is deployed, however, and whatever are the assets of the survivors and liabilities of the defeated, the story of survival is bound to develop in the same monotonous way: *In the game of survival, trust, compassion, and mercy* (the paramount attributes of Løgstrup's "sovereign expression of life") *are suicidal.* If you are not tougher and less scrupulous than all the others, you will be done in by them, with or without remorse. We are back to the somber truth of the Darwinian world: it is the fittest who invariably survive—or, rather, surviving for longer than others do is the ultimate proof of fitness.

Were the young people of our times also readers of books, and particularly of old books not currently on the best-seller list, they would be likely to agree with the bitter, not at all sunny picture of the world painted by the Russian exile and philosopher at the Sorbonne, Leon Shestov: "*Homo homini lupus* is one of the most steadfast maxims of eternal morality. In each of our neighbours we fear a wolf . . . We are so poor, so weak, so easily ruined and destroyed! How can we help being afraid! . . . We see danger, danger only."[20] They would insist, like Shestov suggested they should and as the *Big Brother* shows have promoted to the rank of common sense, that this is a tough world, meant for tough people. It is a world of individuals left to rely solely on their own cunning, trying to outwit and outdo each other. Meeting a stranger, you need vigilance first, and vigilance second and third. Coming together, standing shoulder to shoulder, and working in teams make a lot of sense so long as they help you to get your way, but there is no reason for such teamwork to continue once it brings no more benefit, or brings less benefit than would shedding those commitments and canceling the obligations.

Bosses tend nowadays to dislike having employees who are burdened with personal commitments to others—particularly those with firm commitments and especially the firmly long-term commitments. The harsh demands of professional survival all too often confront men and women with morally devastating choices between the requirements of their career and caring for others. Bosses prefer to employ unburdened, free-floating individuals who are ready to break all bonds at a moment's notice and who never think twice when "ethical demands" must be sacrificed to the "demands of the job."

We live today in a global society of consumers, and the patterns of consumer behavior cannot but affect all other aspects of our life, including work and family life. We are all now pressed to consume more, and on the way, we become ourselves commodities on the consumer and labor markets.

In the words of J. Livingstone, "The commodity form penetrates and reshapes dimensions of social life hitherto exempt from its logic to the point where subjectivity itself becomes a commodity to be bought and sold in the market as beauty, cleanliness, sincerity and autonomy."[21] And as Colin Campbell puts it, the activity of consuming "has become a kind of template or model for the way in which citizens of contemporary

Western societies have come to view all their activities. Since . . . more and more areas of contemporary society have become assimilated to a 'consumer model' it is perhaps hardly surprising that the underlying metaphysics of consumerism has in the process become a kind of default philosophy for all modern life."[22]

Arlie Hochschild encapsulates the most seminal "collateral damage" perpetrated in the course of the consumerist invasion in a succinct and poignant phrase, to "materialize love": "Consumerism acts to maintain the emotional reversal of work and family. Exposed to a continual bombardment of advertisements through a daily average of three hours of television (half of all their leisure time), workers are persuaded to 'need' more things. To buy what they now need, they need money. To earn money, they work longer hours. Being away from home so many hours, they make up for their absence at home with gifts that cost money. They materialize love. And so the cycle continues."[23]

We may add that their new spiritual detachment and physical absence from the home scene makes male and female workers alike impatient with the conflicts, big, small, or downright tiny and trifling, that mixing daily under one roof inevitably entails.

As the skills needed to converse and to seek mutual understanding dwindle, what used to be a challenge meant to be confronted head-on and patiently negotiated increasingly becomes a pretext for individuals to break communication, to escape and burn bridges behind them. Busy earning more to buy things they feel they need in order to be happy, men and women have less time for empathy and the intense, sometimes tortuous and painful but always lengthy and energy-consuming negotiations, let alone resolutions, of their mutual misapprehensions and disagreements. This sets in motion another vicious cycle: the more they succeed in "materializing" their love relationship (as the continuous flow of advertising prompts them to do), the fewer opportunities they have left to achieve the mutually sympathetic understanding that the notorious power/care ambiguity of love calls for. Family members are tempted to avoid confrontation and seek respite (or better still, permanent shelter) from domestic infighting; then the urge to "materialize" love and loving care acquires further impetus because the time- and energy-consuming relationship negotiations have become even less attainable—just when that work is more and more needed because of the steadily growing number of grudges to be smoothed over and disagreements clamoring for resolution.

While highly qualified professionals—the apples of the company director's eye—are often offered a workplace designed to serve as an agreeable substitute for the cozy homeyness missing at home (as Hochschild notes, for these employees the traditional division of roles between workplace and family homestead tends to be reversed)—nothing is offered for the employees who are lower in rank, the less skilled and easily replaceable. If some companies, notably Amerco, which was investigated in depth by Hochschild, "offer the old *socialist utopia* to an *elite* of knowledge workers in the top tier of an increasingly divided labour market, other companies may increasingly be offering *the worst of early capitalism* to *semi-skilled and unskilled workers.*" For the latter, "neither a kin network nor work associates provide emotional anchors for the individual but rather a gang, fellow drinkers on the corner, or other groups of this sort."[24]

The search for individual pleasures articulated by the commodities currently on offer, a search guided and constantly redirected and refocused by successive advertising campaigns, provides the sole acceptable (indeed, badly needed and welcome) substitute for both the uplifting solidarity of workmates and the glowing warmth of caring for and being cared for by those near and dear in the family home and its immediate neighborhood.

Whoever calls to resuscitate the seriously wounded "family values"—and is serious about what such calls imply—should begin by thinking hard about the consumerist roots of, simultaneously, the wilting of social solidarity in the workplace and the fading of the caring-sharing impulse in the family home.

Having spent several years closely observing the changing patterns of employment in the most advanced sectors of the American economy, Hochschild noted and documented trends strikingly similar to those found in France and all over Europe and described in great detail by Luc Boltanski and Eve Chiapello as the "new spirit of capitalism."[25] The strong preference among employers for unattached, flexible, ultimately disposable, and "generalist" employees (Jack-of-all-trades types, rather than specialists with narrowly focused training) has been the most seminal among the findings.

In our allegedly reflection-addicted society, trust is unlikely to receive much empirical reinforcement. Sober scrutiny of life's evidence points in the opposite direction, repeatedly revealing the perpetual fickleness of rules and the frailty of bonds. Does this mean, however, that Løgstrup's decision to invest his hope of morality in the spontaneous, *endemic tendency to trust* has been invalidated by the *endemic uncertainty* saturating the world of our times?

One would be entitled to say yes—if not for the fact that it was never Løgstrup's view that moral impulses arise out of reflection. On the contrary, in his view the hope of morality is vested precisely in its *prereflexive spontaneity:* "Mercy is spontaneous because the least interruption, the least calculation, the least dilution of it in order to serve something else destroys it entirely, indeed turns it into the opposite of what it is, unmercifulness."[26]

Emmanuel Levinas is known for insisting that the question "Why should I be moral?" (that is, arguments and protests such as, "What is there in it for me?" "What did she do for me to justify my care?" "Why should I care, if so many others don't?" and "Couldn't someone else do it instead of me?") is not the *starting point* of moral conduct but a signal of its imminent *demise*—just as all amorality began with Cain's question, "Am I my brother's keeper?" Løgstrup, with his reliance on spontaneity, impulse, and the urge to trust, rather than on calculating reflection, seems to agree.

Both philosophers also seem to agree that "the *need* of morality" (that expression is an oxymoron; whatever answers a "need" is something other than morality) or just "the advisability of morality" cannot be discursively established, let alone proved. Morality is nothing but an innately prompted manifestation of humanity—it does not serve any "purpose" and most surely is not guided by the expectation of profit, comfort, glory, or self-enhancement. It is true that objectively good—helpful and useful—deeds have been time and again performed out of the actor's calculation of gain, be it Divine grace, public esteem, or absolution from mercilessness shown on other occasions; these deeds, however, cannot be classified as genuinely *moral* acts precisely because of having been so *motivated*.

In moral acts, "ulterior motive is ruled out," Løgstrup insists.[27] These spontaneous expressions are *radical* precisely thanks to the absence of ulterior motives—both amoral *and* moral. This is one more reason why the ethical demand, that "objective" pressure to be moral emanating from the very fact of being alive and sharing the planet with others, is and must stay silent. Since obedience to the ethical demand can easily turn (be deformed and distorted) into a motive for conduct, the ethical demand is at its best when it is forgotten and not thought of: its radicalism consists in its demand to be super-fluous. Immediacy of human contact is sustained by the immediate expressions of life, and it needs, and indeed tolerates, no other supports. Levinas would wholeheartedly agree with Løgstrup on this. As Richard Cohen, the translator of Levinas's conversations with Philippe Nemo, summed it up: "Ethical exigency is not an ontological necessity. The prohibition against killing does not render murder impossible. It renders it evil." The "being" of ethics consists solely in "disturbing the complacency of being."[28]

In practical terms, it means that however much a human may resent being left alone to (in the last account) his or her own counsel and responsibility, it is precisely that loneliness that contains the hope of a morally impregnated togetherness. Hope—not certainty, and especially not a guaranteed certainty.

The spontaneity and sovereignty of life expressions do not ensure that the resulting conduct will be the ethically proper and laudable choice between good and evil. The point is, though, that blunders *and* the right choices arise from the same condition—as do the craven impulses to run for cover that authoritative commands obligingly provide, *and* the boldness to accept one's own responsibility. Without bracing oneself for the possibility of wrong choices, little can be done toward persevering in the search for the right choice. Far from being a major threat to morality (and so an abomination to ethical philosophers), *uncertainty is the home ground of the moral person and the only soil in which morality can sprout and flourish.*

But, as Løgstrup rightly points out, it is the immediacy of human contact that is sustained by the immediate expressions of life. I presume that this connection and the mutual conditions go both ways. "Immediacy" seems to play in Løgstrup's thinking a role similar to the "proximity" in Levinas's writings. The "immediate expression of life" is triggered by proximity, or by the immediate presence of the other human being—who is weak and vulnerable, suffering and needing help. We are challenged by what we see, and we are challenged *to act*—to help, to defend, to bring solace, to cure or save.

Let me repeat: The world today seems to be conspiring against trust. Trust may remain, as Knud Løgstrup suggests, a natural outpouring of the "sovereign expression of life"—but once released it seeks in vain a place to anchor itself. Trust has been sentenced to a life of frustration. People (singly, severally, conjointly), companies, parties, communities, great causes, and the patterns and routines we invest with the authority to guide our lives all too often fail to repay trust's devotion. At least, they are seldom paragons of consistency and long-term continuity. There is hardly a single reference point on which attention could be reliably and securely fixed, absolving the beguiled guidance seekers from the irksome duty of constant vigilance and the incessant retraction of steps already taken or as yet merely intended. No available orientations seem to have a longer life expectancy than the orientation seekers themselves, however abominably short their own corporeal lives might be. Individual experience stubbornly points to the self as the most likely focus for the duration and continuity we avidly seek.

These tendencies are starkly evident today particularly in the big cities, those ever-growing, sprawling conurbations in which, in a few years' time, more than half of the planet's population will live, and in which the high density of human interaction, combined with insecurity-born fears, provides especially fertile ground for *ressentiment,* and for the search for objects on which it might be focused.

As Nan Ellin, a most acute researcher and insightful analyst of contemporary urban trends, points out, protection from danger was "a principal incentive for building cities whose borders were often defined by vast walls or fences, from the ancient villages of Mesopotamia to medieval cities to Native American settlements."[29] The walls, moats, or stockades marked the boundary between "us" and "them," order and wilderness, peace and warfare: enemies were those left on that other side of the fence and not allowed to cross over. "From being a relatively safe place," writes Ellin, in the past hundred years or so the city has become associated "more with danger than with safety."

Today, in a curious reversal of their historical role and in defiance of the original intentions of city builders and the expectations of city dwellers, our cities are turning swiftly from shelters against dangers into the dangers' principal source. Diken and Laustsen go as far as to suggest that the millennia-old "link between civilization and barbarism is reversed. City life turns into a state of nature characterised by the rule of terror, accompanied by omnipresent fear."[30]

It seems that the sources of danger have now moved almost wholly into the urban areas and settled there. Friends—and also enemies, and above all the elusive and mysterious *strangers* who veer threateningly between the two extremes—now mix and rub shoulders on the city streets. The war against insecurity, and particularly against dangers and risks to personal safety, is now waged *inside* the city, and inside the city the battlefields are set and front lines are drawn. Heavily armed trenches (impassable approaches) and bunkers (fortified and closely guarded buildings or building complexes) aimed at separating, keeping strangers away and barring their entry, have fast become one of the most visible aspects of contemporary cities, though they take many forms and their designers try hard to blend these creations into the cityscape, thereby "normalizing" the state of emergency in which urban residents, safety-addicted yet perpetually unsure of their safety, dwell daily.

"The more we detach from our immediate surroundings, the more we rely on surveillance of that environment . . . Homes in many urban areas around the world now exist to protect their inhabitants, not to integrate people with their communities," observe Gumpert and Drucker.[31] Separation and keeping distance has become the most common strategy in the urban struggle for survival. The continuum along which the results of the struggle are plotted stretches between the poles of voluntary and involuntary urban ghettos. Residents without means, and therefore viewed by the rest of the residents as potential threats to their safety, tend to be forced away from more benign and agreeable parts of the city and crowded in separate, ghetto-like districts. Resourceful residents buy into separate, also ghetto-like areas of their choice and bar all others from settling there; in addition, they do whatever they can to disconnect their own daily world from the worlds of the rest of the city's inhabitants. Increasingly, their voluntary ghettos turn into outposts or garrisons of extraterritoriality.

The waste products of the new physical extraterritoriality of these privileged urban spaces inhabited and used by the global elite, whose "internal exile" is achieved through, manifested in, and sustained by means of "virtual connectedness," are the disconnected and abandoned spaces, the "ghost wards," as they have been called by Michael Schwarzer, places where "dreams have been replaced by nightmares and danger and violence are more commonplace than elsewhere."[32] If the areas surrounding the privileged spaces are to be kept impassable, to stave off the danger of leakage and contamination of the regional purity, a policy of zero tolerance toward the homeless—banishing them from the spaces where they can make a living but are also obtrusively and disturbingly visible, and confining them to such abandoned, off-limits spaces where they can do neither—comes in handy. "Prowlers," "stalkers," "loiterers," "beggars," "travelers," and other kinds of trespassers become sinister characters in the nightmares of the elite. They are also the walking avatars of the hidden dangers of life on a densely populated planet—and the principal targets of *ressentiment*.

It seems that the "spontaneous expression of life" is in its current embodiment more likely to lead toward mistrust and "mixophobia" than to trust and care. "Mixophobia" is a highly predictable and widespread reaction to the mind-boggling, spine-chilling, and nerve-racking variety of human types and life-styles that meet and jostle for space in the streets of the contemporary cities—not only in the officially proclaimed (and thus avoided) rough districts or "mean streets" but also in the ordinary (read: unprotected by "interdictory spaces") living areas. As the multivocality and cultural variegation of urban environments in the globalization era sets in—a condition that is likely to intensify in the course of time—the tensions arising from the vexing, confusing, irritating unfamiliarity of the setting will probably go on prompting segregationist urges.

The factors precipitating mixophobia are banal—not at all difficult to locate, easy to understand though not necessarily easy to forgive. As Richard Sennett suggests, "The 'we' feeling, which expresses a desire to be similar, is a way for men" and women "to avoid the necessity of looking deeper into each other." It promises, we might say, some spiritual comfort: the prospect of making togetherness easier to bear by cutting off the effort to understand, to negotiate, to compromise that living amidst and with difference requires. "Innate to the process of forming a coherent image of community is the desire to avoid actual participation. Feeling common bonds without common experience occurs in the first place because men are afraid of participation, afraid of the dangers and the challenges of it, afraid of its pain."[33]

The drive toward a "community of similarity" is a sign of withdrawal, not just from the otherness *outside* but also from the commitment to the lively yet turbulent, invigorating yet cumbersome interaction *inside*. The attraction of the community of sameness is that of an insurance policy against the risks with which daily life in a polyvocal world is fraught. Immersion in sameness does not decrease or stave off the risks that prompted it. Like all palliatives, it may at most promise only shelter from some of the risks' most immediate and most feared effects.

Choosing the escape option as the cure for mixophobia has an insidious and deleterious consequence of its own: once adopted, the allegedly therapeutic regime becomes self-propelling, self-perpetuating, and self-reinforcing the more it is ineffective. Sennett explains why this is (indeed must be) the case: "Cities in America during the past two decades have grown in such a way that ethnic areas become relatively homogeneous; it appears no accident that the fear of the outsider has also grown to the extent that these ethnic communities have been cut off."[34] Once the territorial separation takes hold, and the longer people stay in their uniform environments—in the company of others "like them" with whom they can "socialize" perfunctorily and matter-of-factly, without the risk of miscomprehension and without struggling with the vexing need for the (forever risky) two-way translations between distinct universes of meaning—the more one is likely to "delearn" the art of negotiating shared meanings and an agreeable *modus covivendi*.

The territorial wars waged on both sides of the barricade separating the well- and the ill-off cannot but deepen the communication breakdown. As the willing and unwilling soldiers in the permanent territorial wars fail to acquire the skills necessary for living a gratifying life amid difference, there is little wonder that those who practice "escape therapy" view with rising horror the prospect of confronting strangers face to face. "Strangers" (that is, people on the other side of the barrier) tend to appear ever more frightening as they become increasingly alien, unfamiliar, and incomprehensible, as the dialogue and interaction that could eventually assimilate their "otherness" to one's own world fade out, or never take off in the first place. The drive to find a homogeneous, territorially isolated environment may be triggered by mixophobia, but the *practicing* of territorial separation is mixophobia's lifeline and food source; it gradually becomes its principal reinforcing agent.

Alongside open, friendly, trustful "sovereign expressions of life," Løgstrup names their powerful adversaries—the "constrained" expressions, expressions externally induced and so heteronomous instead of autonomous; or, rather (in an interpretation probably better attuned to Løgstrup's intention) expressions whose motives (once represented, or rather misrepresented, as *causes*) are projected on the outside agents.

As examples of the constrained expressions, offense, jealousy, and envy are named—all those sentiments that we saw earlier lurking behind the phenomenon of *ressentiment*. But, as Løgstrup suggests, in each case the striking feature of conduct is the self-deception designed to disguise the genuine springs of action. For instance, the individual has too high an opinion of himself to tolerate the thought of having acted wrongly, and so imputation of an offense by an-Other is called for to deflect attention from his own misstep. We take satisfaction in being the wronged party, Løgstrup points out, and so we must invent wrongs to feed this self-indulgence. The autonomous nature of action is thereby concealed; it is the *other party*, charged with the original misconduct, with the starting-it-all felony, that is cast as the true actor in the drama. The self thereby stays wholly on the receiving side; the self is a *sufferer of the other's action* rather than an actor in his own right.

Once embraced, this vision seems to be self-propelling and self-reinforcing. To retain credibility, the outrage imputed to the other side must be ever more awesome and, above all, ever less curable or redeemable, and the resulting sufferings of its victim must be declared ever more abominable and painful, so that one may go on justifying harsher and harsher measures undertaken by the self-declared victim as a "just response" to the committed offense or as a defense against offenses yet to be committed (or even, as quite recently in the new military doctrine of the Pentagon, as "preemptive"—that is, to stave off offenses that merely can be committed, even if there is no evidence of an intention to commit them). Constrained actions need constantly to *deny* their autonomy. It is for that reason that they constitute the most radical obstacle to the admission of the self's sovereignty and to the self's acting in a fashion resonant with such an admission. We may surmise that they are also the major obstacles to mitigating *ressentiment;* they are instead instrumental in creating *ressentiment*—what in Robert Merton's terminology constitutes a "self-fulfilling prophesy." The initial grudge, so to speak, is "justified" and "confirmed" by the actions of those who hold it.

Overcoming self-imposed constraints by unmasking and discrediting the self-deception on which they rest emerges, therefore, as the preliminary, indispensable condition of giving free rein to the sovereign life's expression—the expression that manifests itself, first and foremost, in trust, compassion, and mercy.

We know, roughly, what must be done to neutralize, defuse, even disarm the temptation of *ressentiment* and thereby defend human togetherness against the practices it prompts. This does not mean, alas, that we know how to achieve it. And even if we knew, we would still have to confront the daunting task of discovering (or inventing) the resources and means that the task would require.

Ressentiment is a discharge, a by-product, of social settings that set interests in conflict and those who hold those interests at loggerheads. We have traced three types of relationships that are particularly prone to produce it: humiliation (denial of dignity), rivalry (status competition), and fearful ambivalence. All three are social products, not individual ones; all three, therefore, can be approached and tackled only through rearrangement of the social settings that are their sources. Fighting *ressentiment* and preventing its germination and proliferation cannot but be projects for the long haul.

And finally: the ethical challenge of "globalization," or, more precisely, globalization as an ethical challenge.

Whatever else "globalization" may mean, it means that we are all dependent on each other. Distances matter little now. Something that happens in one place may have global consequences. With the resources, technical tools, and know-how humans have acquired, their actions can span enormous distances in space and time. However local their intentions might be, actors would be ill-advised to leave out of account global factors, since they could decide the success or failure of their actions. What we do (or abstain from doing) may influence the conditions of life (or death) for people in places we will never visit and of generations we will never know.

This is the situation in which, knowingly or not, we make our shared history these days. Though much—perhaps everything or almost everything—in that unraveling history depends on human choices, the conditions under which choices are made are not themselves a matter of choice. Having dismantled most of the space-time limits that used to confine the potential of our actions to the territory we could survey, monitor, and control, we can no longer shelter either ourselves or those at the receiving end of our actions from the global web of mutual dependency. Nothing can be done to arrest, let alone reverse, globalization. One can be "in favor of" or "against" the new planetwide interdependency, but the effect will be similar to that of supporting or resenting the next solar or lunar eclipse. However, much does depend on our consent or resistance to the lopsided form the globalization of the human plight has thus far taken.

Half a century ago Karl Jaspers could still neatly set apart "moral guilt" (the remorse we feel when causing harm to other humans—either by what we have done or by what we've failed to do) from "metaphysical guilt" (the guilt we feel when a human being is harmed, even if the harm was in no way connected to our action). With the progress of globalization, that distinction has since been stripped of its meaning. As never before, John Donne's words, "Never send to know for whom the bell tolls; it tolls for thee," represent the genuine solidarity of our *fate;* the point is, however, that the new solidarity of fate is as yet nowhere near being matched by the solidarity of our feelings, let alone our actions.

Within the world's dense network of global interdependence, we cannot be sure of our moral innocence whenever other human beings suffer indignity, misery, or pain. We cannot declare that we do not know, nor can we be certain that there is nothing we could change in our conduct that would avert or at least alleviate the sufferers' fate. We might be impotent individually, but we could do something together, and "togetherness" is made of and by the individuals. The trouble is—as another great twentieth-century philosopher, Hans Jonas, complained—although space and time no longer limit the effects of our actions, our moral imagination has not progressed much beyond the scope it had acquired in Adam-and-Eve times. The responsibilities we are ready to assume do not venture as far as the influence that our daily conduct exerts on the lives of ever more distant people.

The globalization process has thus far produced a network of interdependence penetrating every nook and cranny of the globe, but little else. It would be grossly premature to speak of even a global society or global culture, not to mention a global polity or global law. Is there a global social system emerging at the far end of the globalization process? If there is such a system, it does not as yet resemble the social systems we have learned to consider the norm. We used to think of social systems as totalities that coordinated and adjusted or adapted all aspects of human existence—most notably economic mechanisms, political power, and cultural patterns. Nowadays, though, what used to be coordinated at the same level and within the same totality has been set apart and placed at radically disparate levels. The planetary reach of capital, finances, and trade—the forces that decide the range of choices and the effectiveness of human action, the way humans live and the limits of their dreams and hopes—has not been matched on a similar scale by the resources that humanity developed to control those forces that control human lives.

Most important, that planetary dimension has not been matched by democratic control on a similarly global scale. We may say that power has "flown" from the historically developed institutions that used to exercise democratic control over uses and abuses of power in the modern nation-states. Globalization in its current form means a progressive disempowerment of nation-states and (so far) the absence of any effective substitute.

A similar Houdini act has been performed by economic actors once before, though obviously on a more modest scale. Max Weber, one of the most acute analysts of the logic (or illogicality) of modern history, noted that the birth-act of modern capitalism was the separation of business from household; the "household" standing for the dense web of mutual rights and obligations sustained by the village and township communities, parishes or craftsmen's guilds, in which families and neighborhoods were tightly wrapped. With that separation (better named, with a bow to the famed Menenius Agrippa's ancient allegory, "secession") business ventured into a genuine frontier, a virtual no-man's-land, free of all moral concerns and legal constraints and ready to be subordinated to the business's own code of behavior. As we know, the unprecedented moral extraterritoriality of economic activities led in time to the spectacular advance of industrial potential and growth of wealth. We know as well, though, that for almost the whole of the nineteenth century the same extraterritoriality rebounded in a lot of human misery and poverty, and a mind-boggling polarization of living standards and opportunities. Finally, we also know that the emergent modern states reclaimed the no-man's-land that business had staked out as its exclusive property. The rule- and norm-setting agencies of the state invaded that land and eventually, though only after overcoming ferocious resistance, annexed and colonized it, thereby filling the ethical void and mitigating its most unprepossessing consequences for the life of its subjects/citizens.

Globalization may be described as "Secession Mark Two." Once more, business has escaped the household's confinement, though this time the household left behind is the modern "imagined household," circumscribed and protected by the nation-states' economic, military, and cultural powers topped with political sovereignty. Once more, business has acquired an "extraterritorial territory," a space of its own where it can roam freely, sweeping aside minor hurdles erected by weak local powers and steering clear of the obstacles built by the strong ones. It can pursue its own ends and ignore or bypass all others as economically irrelevant and therefore illegitimate. And once more we observe social effects similar to those that met with moral outrage at the time of the first secession, only now (like the second secession itself) on an immensely greater, global scale.

More than a century and a half ago, in the midst of the first secession, Karl Marx charged with the error of "utopianism" those advocates of a fairer, equitable, and just society who hoped to achieve their purpose by stopping the advance of capitalism in its tracks and returning to the starting point, to the premodern world of extended households and family workshops. There was no way back, Marx insisted, and on this point, at least, history proved him right. Whatever kind of justice and equity stand a chance of taking root in social reality must now, as then, start from where the irreversible transformations have already brought the human condition. This ought to be remembered when the options endemic to the second secession are contemplated.

A retreat from the globalization of human dependency, from the global reach of human technology and economic activities is, in all probability, no longer in the cards. Responses like "Circle the wagons" or "Back to the tribal (national, communal) tents" won't do. The question is not how to turn back the river of history but how to fight against its pollution by human misery and how to channel its flow to achieve a more equitable distribution of the benefits it carries.

And another point to remember: Whatever form the postulated global control over global forces may take, it cannot be a magnified replica of the democratic institutions developed in the first two centuries of modern history. Such institutions were cut to the measure of the nation-state, then the largest all-encompassing "social totality," and they are singularly unfit to be inflated to the global size. To be sure, the nation-state was not an extension of communal mechanisms either. It was, on the contrary, the end product of radically novel modes of human togetherness and new forms of social solidarity. Nor was it an outcome of negotiation and a consensus achieved through hard bargaining among local communities. The nation-state that in the end provided the sought-after response to the challenges of the "first secession" implemented it in spite of the die-hard defenders of communal traditions and through further erosion of the already shrinking and emaciated local sovereignties.

An effective response to globalization can only be global. And the fate of such a global response depends on the emergence and entrenchment of a global (as distinct from international or, more correctly, interstate) political arena. It is such an arena that is today most conspicuously missing. The existing global players are singularly unwilling to set it up. Their ostensible adversaries, trained in the old yet increasingly ineffective art of interstate diplomacy, seem to lack the ability and the necessary resources. New forces are needed to reestablish and reinvigorate a truly global forum adequate to the globalization era—and they may assert themselves only through bypassing *both* kinds of players.

This seems to be the only certainty—all the rest being a matter of our shared inventiveness and political trial-and-error practices. After all, few if any thinkers could envisage in the midst of the first secession the form that the damage-repairing operation would ultimately take. What they were sure of was that some operation of that kind was the paramount imperative of their time. We are all in debt to them for that insight.

Lacking the resources and institutions needed for collective effort, we are baffled by the question "Who is able to do it?"—even if we guess what there is to be done. But here we are, and there is no other place available at the moment. *Hic Rhodos,* as the ancients used to say: *hic salta.*

No one could claim to record better the dilemmas we face when climbing those stairs than with the words put in Marco Polo's mouth by the great Italo Calvino in his *Città invisibili:* "The inferno of the living is not something that will be: if there is one, it is what is already here, the inferno where we live every day, that we form by being together. There are two ways to escape suffering it. The first is easy for many: accept the inferno and become such a part of it that you can no longer see it. The second is risky and demands constant vigilance and apprehension: seek and learn to recognize who and what, in the midst of the inferno, are not inferno, then make them endure, give them space."[35]

I guess that neither Levinas nor Løgstrup would decline to add his signature to that advice.

◆

CHAPTER TWO

Categorial Murder, or the Legacy of the Twentieth Century and How to Remember It

◆

AT THE THRESHOLD of the modern era, nature was viewed as the major source of uncertainty that haunted human life. Floods and droughts, famines that struck without warning, and contagious diseases that came unannounced, unspeakable dangers lurking in the "wilderness"—spaces yet untouched by humans' ordering zeal and often starting just a few yards beyond the farm fence—were the main repositories of the fearsome unknown. Even the dangers threatened by other people were seen as side effects of the drawbacks in taming nature. The ill will, malice, and uncouth conduct of the neighbors next door, or on the next street, or beyond the river, that made people fear and tremble in anticipation of imminent disaster, were classified on the side of nature, as distinct from the man-made part of the world. They were viewed as the regrettable results of the warlike instincts, "natural aggression," and resulting inclination to *bellum omnium contra omnes* that were seen as the "natural state" of mankind, as the legacy and relics of raw "nature" that needed to be and duly would be eradicated, reformed, or repressed through the patient, laborious, and painstaking effort of the "civilizing process." The confidence-building myth of the modern era was the story of humans lifting themselves by their own wits, acumen, determination, and industry, those refined versions of Baron von Münchhausen's bootstraps, out of the mire of the "natural," "precivilized" condition. The corollaries of that myth were the unshakeable trust in the human ability to improve on nature and the belief in the superiority of reason over "blind natural forces"—which humans, with reason's help, can harness to more useful tasks, or shackle in case they prove too obstreperous. By far the most repulsive and intolerable feature of all things natural—that is, objects and states unprocessed by purposeful and reason-guided human labor—was that their haphazard, random conduct defied expectations, evaded human control, and so exploded human designs.

The idea of "civilized order" was a vision of the human condition from which everything that was not allowed to be a part of that order was prohibited and eliminated. Once the civilizing process completed its job, there would be no dark corners left, no black holes of ignorance, no gray areas of ambivalence, no vile dens of vicious uncertainty. Hobbes hoped (memorably, thanks to the generations of his loyal disciples) that society (identified with the state as the carrier of sovereign power) would eventually provide the much needed and universally coveted shelter from uncertainty—by defending its subjects against the fearsome powers of nature and against their own inborn wickedness and base instincts, which they are too weak to conquer on their own. Many years later, in the middle of the twentieth century, Carl Schmitt summarized if not the reality, then at least the intention of the modern state by defining "the

Sovereign" as he who decides on the state of exception. Commenting on Schmitt's definition, Giorgio Agamben recently suggested that the constitutive feature of the sovereign state was the "relation of exception," through which "something is included solely through its exclusion," and that the rule asserts itself by setting the limits to its application.[1] The modern state, indeed, was about managing human affairs through the exclusion of everything unmanageable and thereby undesirable. I might add that uncertainty, and all that caused it and contributed to it (all that was resistant to management, evaded categorization, was underdefined, category-crossing, ambiguous, and ambivalent), was the major, most toxic pollution of the would-be man-made order that had to be excluded. The modern state was about the activity of cleansing and the purpose of purity.

I suggest that this tendency of the modern state culminated in the middle of the past century—after a good part of that century had passed under the aegis of the imminent end of history as known that far: history as a free play of unbridled, discoordinate forces.

In the 1940s, when rumors of the mass murder of Jews throughout Nazi-occupied Europe leaked across the front line, the biblical term "holocaust" was recalled and redeployed to name it. The act had no precedent in recorded history and thus no established dictionary name. A new name had to be coined for the act of "categorial murder"—for the physical annihilation of men, women, and children for reason of their belonging (or having been assigned) to a category of people unfit for the intended order and on whom, for that reason, a death sentence was summarily passed. By the 1950s, the old/new term "holocaust" came to be widely accepted as the proper name of the meant-to-be-total destruction of European Jews perpetrated in the years 1940 through 1945 on the initiative of the Nazi leadership.

In subsequent years, though, the usage of the term has been extended to cover the numerous cases of mass murder aimed against ethnic, racial, or religious groups, and to the cases in which a disempowering or expulsion of the targeted group, rather than its total annihilation, was the proclaimed or tacit objective. Because of the enormous emotional load of the term and an almost universal ethical condemnation of the actions it stood for, naming of a suffered harm as a case of another "holocaust" was widely sought. The kind of damages inflicted by one human group on another that deserve to be branded as one more holocaust have been stretched over the years much beyond their original field. The term "holocaust" has become an "essentially contested" concept, used in numerous ethnic and other violent group conflicts as a charge raised against the conduct or intentions of the adversary to justify one's own group's hostility.

In popular speech, "holocaust" tends to be these days interchangeable with "genocide"—another linguistic novelty of the twentieth century. In 1993 Helen Fein noted that between 1960 and 1979 "there were probably at least a dozen genocides and genocidal massacres—cases include the Kurds in Iraq, southerners in the Sudan, Tutsi in Rwanda, Hutus in Burundi, Chinese . . . in Indonesia, Hindus and other Bengalis in East Pakistan, the Ache in Paraguay, many peoples in Uganda . . ."[2] Since those words were written, the list has been considerably extended, and as I'm writing these words, it shows no signs of nearing the end. Genocide, in Frank Chalk and Kurt Jonassohn's definition, "is a form of one-sided mass killing in which a state or other authority intends to destroy a group, as that group and membership in it are defined by the perpetrators."[3] In genocide, the power over life intertwines with the power to define (or more precisely, the power to exempt). Before the wholesale extermination of a group comes the classification of groups into categories and the definition of the assignment to a certain category as a capital crime. In many an orthodox war, the number of casualties exceeded many times the numbers of many a genocide's victims. What sets the genocide apart, however, from even the most violent and gory conflicts is not the number of its victims but its *monological nature*. In genocide, the prospective targets of violence are *unilaterally* defined and denied a right to response. The victims' conduct or the qualities of the condemned category's individual members are irrelevant to their preordained fate. The sufficient proof of the capital offense, of the charge from which there is no appeal, is the fact of having been accused.

If this is the true nature of genocidal acts, the current meaning of the word "holocaust," by and large synonymous and so exchangeable with that of the term "genocide," bears only an oblique relation to the meaning carried by the term appearing in Leviticus, in the Greek translation of the Old Testament, from which it has been derived. That ancient term was recalled and invoked as a metaphor for the Nazi extermination of the Jews probably because of its suggestion of the *thoroughness of the destruction*. The Greek term ὁλόκαυστος was a literal translation of the Hebrew for "wholly burned," a requirement that the offerings brought to the Temple had to be destroyed by fire *in their entirety*.

What sets the original and the metaphorical meanings of the term wide apart, however, is the fact that the "wholly burned" referred to by the ancient term was full of religious meaning: it was meant to symbolize the completeness of human surrender to God and the unconditionality of human piety. The objects of sacrifice had to be the most valuable, proud possessions of the faithful: specially chosen young bullocks or male lambs, specimens without blemish, as perfect in every detail as was the

human reverence for God and human dedication to the fulfillment of Divine commands. Following this track of metaphorical extension, "sacrifice" came to mean, according to the
Oxford English Dictionary, the "surrender of something valued
or desired for the sake of something having a higher or more
pressing claim."

If this is what sacrifice is about, the Holocaust was anything
but a sacrifice. The victims of the Holocaust, and more generally victims of all genocides, are not people "sacrificed" in the
name of a greater value. The object of genocide that follows
the pattern introduced by the Nazi Holocaust is, in Giorgio
Agamben's terms, *homo sacer*—one "who may be killed and yet
not sacrificed." The death of *homo sacer* is devoid of religious
significance; *homo sacer* is not just a person of a lesser value
but an entity devoid of any value, be it sacred or profane, divine or mundane. What is annihilated is a "bare life," stripped
of all value. "In the case of *homo sacer* a person is simply
set outside human jurisdiction without being brought into the
realm of divine law." He is an object "of a double exception,
both from the *ius humanum* and from the *ius divinum*."[4]

We may say that before they were rounded up, deported to
the death camps, shot, or suffocated, the Jews of Germany and
other countries of Nazi-occupied Europe (alongside the Roma
and Sinti) had been, so to speak, declared a collective *homo
sacer*—a category whose life was devoid of all positive value
and whose murder therefore had no moral significance and
commanded no punishment. Theirs was *unwertes Leben*—life
unworthy of living—along with the lives of Gypsies, homosexuals, and the mentally ill and mentally disabled, according to the
Nazi vision of the *Neue Ordnung;* or, in the words of a Swedish
government report of 1929, they were people "with regard to
whom it is in the interest of society that their numbers are as
few as possible."[5] What all those categories had in common
was their unfitness for the new and better order that was

planned to replace the present messy realities—the social order purified of all undesirable admixtures, blemishes, and imperfections that the sovereign rulers set out to build.

It was the vision of a perfect order that supplied the criteria for setting apart the "fit" from the "unfit"—subjects whose lives deserved to be defended and enhanced from those who could render no conceivable service to the strength of the new order but were bound instead to impair its harmony. The sovereign power (a power exercised over humans reduced to "bare bodies") enabled the builders of the new order to admit their subjects into the order or to exempt them from it at will. Claiming the right to include or exclude from the realm of legal rights and ethical obligations was the essence of the modern state's sovereignty—and the Holocaust (alongside the massive purges of "class aliens" in Stalinist Russia) was by common consent the most extreme and radical manifestation of that claim.

Mass murders have accompanied humankind throughout its history. But the peculiar variety of categorial mass murder called the Holocaust would be inconceivable outside the frame of modern society. Systematic murder, conducted over a long period of time, required enormous resources and the frequent adjustment of procedure. It would hardly be possible without such typically modern inventions as industrial technology; bureaucracy, with its meticulous division of labor; the strict hierarchy of command and discipline, as well as the neutralization of personal (and ethical) convictions; and the managerial ambition to subordinate social reality to a rationally designed model of order—innovations that happened to be, as well, the prime causes of the modern era's spectacular successes. "Consider the numbers," observed John P. Sabini and Mary Silver:

> The German state annihilated approximately six million Jews. At the rate of 100 per day [this was the number of

victims of the infamous Kristallnacht, the Nazi-organized pogrom of German Jews] this would have required nearly 200 years. Mob violence rests on the wrong psychological basis, on violent emotion. People can be manipulated into fury, but fury cannot be maintained for 200 years. Emotions, and their biological basis, have a natural time course; lust, even blood lust, is eventually sated. Further, emotions are notoriously fickle, can be turned. A lynch mob is unreliable, it can sometimes be moved by sympathy—say by a child's suffering. To eradicate a "race" it is essential to kill the children.[6]

To eradicate a "race" or a "class" that transmits its destructive potential through generations, it is necessary to suppress human emotions and other manifestations of human individuality, and submit human conduct to the uncontested rule of instrumental reason. *Modernity made the Holocaust possible, whereas it was the totalitarian rule* (that is, a total and absolute sovereignty) *that implemented the possibility.*

To acclaim that reached far beyond the boundaries of the land he ruled, Hitler announced the arrival of the Thousand Years Reich, which would start with the elimination of the last *unwertes Leben*. To the joy of his enthusiasts worldwide, Stalin proclaimed the end of injustice, together with the end of class oppression and class wars, to be just around the corner—merely waiting for the unmasking and executing of the last enemy of the society, whose classlessness would assert itself by shooting or starving to death all who stood out and didn't fit in. Using Schmitt's concept as popularized by Agamben, we can say that both forms of twentieth-century totalitarianism explored the limits (or limitlessness?) of the sovereign power of exclusion. Auschwitz and Kolyma were laboratories in which the limits of human pliability were researched and, most important, the most effective means of cleansing society of its disorderly, uncertainty-generating contaminations were experimented with and put to practical tests.

In totalitarian regimes the tendency of modern state sovereignty (described at the threshold of the century by Max Weber, and later by Norbert Elias, as a "monopoly of the means of coercion") was given free rein and allowed to run berserk, with the hope that it would find its own limits (or rather that it would demonstrate its transcend-ability in the face of all extant and future limits). The totalitarian adventure was not an aberration, an "accident of history" that can be explained away and dismissed as a cancerous deformation of the otherwise healthy modern political body, but was a sustained effort to stretch that body's fitness to its ultimate potential.

During the last century, approximately six million Jews and by some accounts close to a million Gypsies, accompanied by many thousands of homosexuals and mentally disabled persons, were shot, poisoned, and burned by the builders of the Nazi-designed New World Order—because they did not fit the order about to be built.

They were not the only casualties of the innumerable construction sites spattered all over the globe—not by a long shot—even if they have turned out to be the most notorious and most widely spoken-about victims of the building zeal. Before them, a million and a half Armenians were killed for being the wrong people in the wrong place, followed by ten million genuine or alleged kulaks, wealthy farmers, in Ukraine, who were starved to death for being the wrong sort of people to be admitted to the brave new world of classless conformity. After them, millions of Muslims were annihilated for being a blot on a uniformly Hindu landscape, and millions of Hindus lost their lives for soiling the landscape of the Muslims. Millions were destroyed for standing in the way of the Chinese great leap forward or of the tranquil, unperturbed and simple, graveyard-style harmony with which the Khmer Rouge resolved to replace the messy, noisy, and unclean world of raw humanity. All continents of the globe have had their local Hutus who have massacred their Tutsi neighbors, while everywhere native Tutsi have repaid their persecutors in kind. All continents have had their fill of Darfurs, Sudans, Sierra Leones, East Timors, and Bosnias.

Let me repeat: all such and similar slaughters have stood apart from innumerable past explosions of human cruelty, not just (or not even necessarily) for the number of their victims but for being *categorial murders*. In these cases, men, women, and children were exterminated for having been assigned to a category of beings that was meant to be exterminated.

What made all such cases into categorial murders was, first, the fact that only the acts of their assignment and sentencing, both performed unilaterally by their prospective murderers, sealed the fate of the victims—no other proof of the victims' "guilt" was called for. The assignment was oblivious to the diversity of personal qualities of the assigned, as well as to the degree of danger that the individual members of the condemned category could individually present. It was therefore irrelevant, from the point of view of the murderous *categorial* logic, how old or young, strong or weak, genial or malevolent the victims were. Prospective victims did not need to have committed a punishable crime for the verdict to be pronounced and the execution performed. Nor was it relevant to the verdict that their wrongdoing had been proved, let alone measured to permit the matching of the apportioned punishment against the gravity of the assumed wrongdoing. Conversely, nothing of what the victims did or did not do could earn them salvation—nothing could bring exemption from the fate common to the category to which they belonged. As Raul Hilberg famously observed, the fate of the European Jews had been decided and sealed the moment the Nazi officials completed their Jewish registers separate from the rosters of "ordinary" German subjects, and stamped the letter "J" on their passports.

Second, what makes the piling up of corpses an instance of categorial murder is its one-directionality. Categorial murder is the very opposite of combat, of a confrontation between two forces, *both* bent on destroying the adversary, even if one of them has been prompted by self-defense only, having been provoked, attacked, and drawn into conflict by the hostility of the other side. Categorial murder is from start to finish a *one-sided affair.* Precautions are taken to make sure that the victims are on and stay on the receiving side of the operation, which is fully designed and administered by the perpetrators. In the course of categorial murder, the lines dividing the subjects from the objects of actions, the right to initiative from bearing its consequences, "doing" from "suffering," are all clearly drawn, closely guarded, and made impassable. Categorial murder is meant to deprive the appointed human targets of their lives—but also, and a priori, to expropriate them from their humanity, of which the right to subjectivity, to the self-guided action, is an indispensable, indeed a constitutive, ingredient.

For having been committed in the heart of Europe, which deemed itself at the time to be the pinnacle of historical progress and the guiding light for the rest of the human species less civilized or less prone to civilizing; for having been conducted with extraordinary resolve, methodically and consistently over a long period of time; for mustering the help and commanding throughout the cooperation of "the best" in science and technology, that crowning achievement and pride of modern civilization; for spawning a mind-boggling number of corpses, while scattering far and wide an unprecedented moral devastation through transforming most Europeans into silent witnesses of a horror that would go on haunting their conscience for many years to come; for having left behind an inordinately large volume of written and recorded evidence of cruelty, depravity, degradation, and humiliation; for having earned and been given more worldwide publicity and insinuating itself into the world consciousness more deeply than any other case of categorial murder; for all these reasons, and probably for more reasons yet—the Jewish Holocaust has acquired in the awareness of the age an iconic place, a place entirely of its own. One could say that it stands out as the paragon of, or the archetype of, or the shorthand for categorial murder as such. One could go on and say that it has become thereby a *generic name* for the homicidal tendencies ubiquitously present and repeatedly exploding with awesome regularity in the course of modern history.

It was hoped fifty or sixty years ago that the gruesome knowledge of the Holocaust would shock humanity out of its ethical somnolence and make further genocides impossible. This did not happen. The legacy of the Holocaust proved to be a temptation to try other "final solutions" as much as it inspired repulsion from such solutions. More than half a century later, the problem of making society immune to genocidal temptations remains wide open.

This said, one would have dearly wished to add that, because of its unspeakable horror and the revulsion that followed its revelation, the Jewish Holocaust started off a more civilized and humane era in human history, that it ushered us into a safer and more ethically alert world; that even if the homicidal tendency has not dried up completely, the fuses needed to explode it will from now on be in shorter-than-ever supply, perhaps withdrawn from production altogether. Alas, one cannot say all this. The legacy of the Holocaust has proved much too complicated to allow this to be said with any degree of conviction. The logic of human cohabitation does not follow the precepts of the logic of moral conscience, and the two logics spawn widely different rationalities.

No doubt the Holocaust did change the condition of the world, though not necessarily in the way it was expected and could be hoped that it would. The Holocaust added considerably to our collective knowledge of the world we collectively inhabit, and that new knowledge cannot but change the way we inhabit it and the way we think of and narrate the past experience and the prospects of shared habitation. Before it was undertaken, the Holocaust was unimaginable. To most people, it remained inconceivable when already well under way. Today, it is difficult to conceive of a world that does not contain a possibility of a holocaust, or even a world securely fortified, let alone insured against the implementation of such possibility. We all have been alerted, and the alert has never been called off.

What does it mean, though, to live in a world forever pregnant with the kind of horrors that the Holocaust has come to stand for? Does the memory of the Holocaust make the world a better and safer place, or a worse and more dangerous one?

Martin Heidegger explained that Being (*Sein*) is tantamount to a process of continuous *Wiederholung*—recapitulation—of the past. There is no other way for Being to be, and this applies to human *groups* as much as it does to human *individuals*. The two aspects of (individual and/or collective) identity distinguished by Paul Ricoeur, *l'ipséité* (the difference bordering on uniqueness) and *la mêmeté* (continuity of the self, identity with itself over time), intertwine to the point of being inseparable, neither of the two being able to survive on its own.

Once Heidegger's and Ricoeur's observations have been put together, the seminal role played by the retention of the past in shaping the individual (or collective) present is evident. It has become by now a commonplace to propose that groups that lose their memory thereby lose their identity—that losing the past leads inextricably to losing the present and the future. If the preservation of a group is at stake, being a value that needs to be defended to be cherished, then the success or failure of the struggle hangs on the effort to keep the memory alive.

This may be true—but this, most certainly, is not the whole truth, because memory is a *mixed* blessing. More precisely, it is a blessing and a curse rolled into one. It may "keep alive" many things of sharply unequal value for the group and its neighbors. The past is a bagful of events, and memory never retains them all; whatever it retains or recovers from oblivion it never reproduces in its "pristine" and "original" form (whatever that may mean). The "whole past," the past *wie es ist eigentlich gewesen,* as it really happened (how, as Ranke suggested, it should be retold by the historians), is never recaptured by memory—and if it were, memory would be a liability rather than an asset to the living. Memory *selects* and *interprets*—and *what* is to be selected and *how* it needs to be interpreted is moot and a matter of continuous contention. The resurrection of the past, keeping the past alive, can be attained only through the active, choosing, reprocessing, and recycling work of memory. To remember is to *interpret* the past—or, more correctly, to tell a story meant to *stand for* the course of past events. The status of the "story of the past" is ambiguous and bound to remain that way.

On the one hand, stories are *told.* There are not and cannot be stories without story*tellers,* and the tellers, like all humans, are admittedly given to erring and to flights of fancy. To be human means to err. On the other hand, however, the idea of "the past" stands for a stubborn, once-and-for-all, unalter-able, irreversible, and solid "thing," the very epitome of "real-ity" that can be neither revoked nor wished away. Storytellers hide their human frailty behind the majestic grandiosity of the past—which, unlike the fickle present and the as-yet-shapeless future, can be (contrary to the facts, as it were) hal-lowed for admitting no contention. The past tends to be pos-ited (if counterfactually) as the sole solid rock in a whirlwind of brittle, transient, shifty, elusive opinions only supposed to be true. Invoking the authority of their subject matter, the tellers of the story of the past may divert attention from the repro-cessing job that had to be performed before the past could turn into a story. Invocation of the past's authority ensures inter-pretation against uninvited inquisition, resented as meddle-some and vexing. Truth does not necessarily benefit, but the "feel good"—the comfort from the belief of being in the right—is, for a time at least, saved.

The dead have no power to guide—let alone monitor and correct—the conduct of the living. In a raw state, *wie es ist eigentlich gewesen,* their own lives could hardly teach; to be-come lessons, they first have to be made into *stories* (Shake-speare, unlike many other storytellers and even less their lis-teners, knew this when he made Hamlet, before dying, instruct his friend Horatio: "Tell my story"). The past does not inter-fere with the present directly: all interference is mediated by a story. What course that interference will ultimately take is decided on the battlefield of memory, where stories are the troops and storytellers are the shrewd or hapless commanders of the fighting forces. The lessons to be drawn from the past are the prime stakes of the battle.

The contest of interpretations in the course of which the past is reforged into visible contours and in the lived-through significance of the present, and then recycled into designs for the future, is conducted, as Tzvetan Todorov recently pointed out, in the narrow passage between the two traps of *sacralization* and *banalization.*[7] The degree of danger that each of these traps contains depends on whether the individual or the group memory is at stake.

Todorov concedes that a degree of sacralization (an operation that makes a past event into a unique event, held to be "unlike any event experienced by others," incomparable with events experienced by others and at other times, and that therefore condemns all such comparisons as sacrilegious) is called for, indeed is unavoidable, if the memory is to fulfill its role in the self-assertion of the *individual* identity. Indeed, some areas of inwardness resistant to communication, certain irreducible, insoluble, and ineffable core subjective experiences unfit for interpersonal transmission, are indispensable for the sustenance of the *ipséité* of the self. Without such a core, there would be no chance of genuine individuality. Contrary to the insinuation of innumerable TV chat shows and of the public confessions they inspire, personal experience is indeed *personal:* as such, it is "nontransferable." Refusal of communication, or at least a certain degree of communicational reticence, may be a condition sine qua non for individual autonomy.

Groups, however, are not "like individuals, only bigger." Reasoning by analogy would ignore the crucial distinction: unlike the self-asserting individuals, groups live by communication, dialogue, exchange of experience. Groups are constituted by *sharing* memories, not by holding them back and barring access to strangers. The true nature of the experience of categorial murder (and so of categorial victimhood) consists in its having been shared, and in its memory's being meant to be shared and made into common property; in other words, in its being defended against the temptation of sacralization. In the case of shared memory of a shared experience, and particularly the memory of shared victimhood, sacralization effectively staves off the chance of communication, and so of adding to the collective wisdom of those alive. As Todorov put it, "Sacralization obstructs the drawing of generally valid lessons from particular cases, and so the communication between the past and the present."[8]

Refusing other groups the benefit they may derive from learning and memorizing the experience of others, sacralization protects, on the face of it, the interests of the sacralizers. But appearances mislead: the ostensible selfishness of sacralization is *misconceived,* and in the end counterproductive and harmful to the sacralizing group's own interests. If common lessons contained in the group's experience and discoverable only in the course of communicative exchange are ignored or not attended to properly, the group's future conditions will be poorly protected. After all, the group's survival and well-being depend more on the principles that rule (or do not rule, as the case may be), and on the network of dependencies in which the group is embedded, than on whatever the group may do to itself and the rest of the network on its own.

Banalization ostensibly follows a route directly opposite of that pursued by sacralization, yet it ends up with much the same results: it refutes, even if only obliquely, all originality of the group's experience and so deprives its message, a priori, of the unique value that may justify the need for intergroup dialogue. As in the case of sacralization, though on the strength of an allegedly opposite reason, such banalization offers no desire or encouragement to invite, or join, a conversation. If the phenomenon known to one group from its experience keeps repeating itself with dull monotony in almost everybody else's experience, there is little or nothing that one group can learn from another. The cases lose that enlightening potency that rests in their particularity. Among the multitude of similar or identical cases, the peculiarity from which something genuinely general and universally important can be learned, precisely because of its uniqueness, is lost. Worse still, there is nothing that the groups can learn from sharing experiences of their cohabitation, since the ubiquity and repetitiveness of experiences suggest, wrongly, that the causes of each group's fate (sufficient causes of the fate, or causes sufficient to explain its course) could be explored and revealed while the search is focused solely on the group's own actions or neglect. Paradoxically, banalization plays into the hands of the sacralizers. It boosts sacralization, corroborates its wisdom and logic, and inspires yet more sacralizing zeal.

Both sacralization and banalization set groups apart and at loggerheads. Both commit them to inwardness, since both play down or deny the survival value of intergroup dialogue and of sharing group experiences that tend to be lived through separately while group members remain irretrievably intertwined. Both make the road to such togetherness as could render the group's survival secure—and so categorial murder in all its varieties redundant—more rough and forbidding, perhaps impassable.

Sacralization goes hand in hand with banalization. Todorov discusses the case of Richard Holbrooke, representing the U.S. State Department in Yugoslavia, who agreed to talk with the Belgrade authorities already accused of conducting "another holocaust" in Bosnia and cited the precedent of Raul Wallenberg, who, under Nazi rule, put aside his personal well-being in order to save lives. Todorov points out that while Wallenberg risked his life when he resolved to serve the victims and to resist, to achieve that purpose, the all-powerful perpetrators of the crime, Holbrooke, in the name and at the behest of the world's most formidable hyperpower, went to command and bring to book people being daily showered by that hyperpower with smart missiles and bombs. Clinton justified the military intervention in Bosnia by quoting Churchill's warning against appeasing Hitler. But what was the worth of such a comparison? asks Todorov. Was Milosevic a threat to Europe comparable to Hitler?

Banalization comes in handy when coercion against a weaker adversary is contemplated and needs to be sold to the public as a noble self-sacrifice rather than an act of power politics. Spreading thinly the horror and revulsion prevents people from spotting in the lost peculiarity of the banalized crime the principles of justice, the ethical rules, and the political ideals that would be salient if it were properly remembered. Without banalization, the peculiarity of the crime would be found to be ethically pregnant. The chance for drawing universally valid ethical principles has been lost if Moshe Landau, who in 1961 presided over Eichmann's trial, could twenty-six years later chair the commission that legalized the use of torture against "similar" Jew-haters, the Palestinians of the occupied territories.

Banalization substitutes an illusory similarity of the enemy's treachery (or even more simply, a similarity of enmity: all enemies tend to look "like each other," and also to act treacherous like each other, once they have been cast as enemies) for the similarity that truly counts if a lesson from past experience is sought: the similarity of power relations and the morality (or immorality) of acts. Whenever and wherever an omnipotent force stifles the voices of the weak and the hapless instead of listening to them, it stays on the wrong side of the ethical divide between good and evil; banalization is a desperate (but successful for a time, so long as the strong stay stronger and the weak stay weaker) attempt to deny that truth. Only on the grounds of ethical universality may one condemn the French general Paul Aussaresses for the atrocities he authorized and encouraged against the Algerian rebels, or Bob Kerrey (former U.S. senator and then university president), who was accused after many years by a former comrade-in-arms of perpetrating hideous mass executions in Vietnam when he was there with the U.S. expeditionary force.[9] "Justice that is not equal to all does not deserve its name," Tzvetan Todorov reminds us.[10] And so long as there is no prospect of punishing the slaughterers in Chechnya, or the American inspirers, sponsors, and paymasters of the violations of human rights in Salvador, Guatemala, Haiti, Chile, or Iraq, or those guilty of the maltreatment of the Palestinians, and indeed those in authority guilty of "an expansive endorsement of the harshest interrogation techniques ever used by the Central Intelligence Agency," the right of the state to persecute its own citizens or the residents of dependent territories is confirmed (and seen as confirmed), after apportioning to the victims, for whom no appeal is allowed, the evil intentions that justify and absolve the state for ill deeds committed, but most of all for such as are likely to be committed.[11] This is the same right that, when stretched to its limits and squeezed of the last drop by the Nazi rulers, rebounded in the catastrophe of the Holocaust.

Alas—the right of the strong to do whatever they wish to the weak is also a lesson of the age of genocides. A gruesome, frightening lesson to be sure, but no less eagerly learned, appropriated, and applied for that reason. To be ready for adoption, it must be first thoroughly stripped of all ethical connotations, right to the bare bones of a zero-sum game of survival. "The stronger lives." "Who strikes first, survives." "So long as you are strong, you may get away, unpunished, with whatever you have done to the weak"—at least so long as they stay weak.

The fact that the dehumanization of the victims dehumanizes—morally devastates—their victimizers is dismissed as a minor irritant, if it is recognized at all. What counts is to get on top and stay on top. Surviving, staying alive, is a value untarnished by the inhumanity of life and worth pursuing for its own sake, however high the costs paid by the defeated and however deeply this may deprave and degrade the victors.

This terrifying and most inhuman among the genocide (and genocidal) lessons comes complete with the inventory of pains one may inflict on the weak in order to assert one's own strength. Rounding up, deporting, locking away in concentration camps or forcing whole populations to submit to a plight close to the concentration camp model, demonstrating the futility of the law through executing suspects on the spot, imprisoning without trial and a set term of confinement, spreading the terror that random and unaccounted for punishment spawns—have all been amply proved to be effective and so "rational." The list may be, and is, extended as time goes by. "New and improved" expedients are tried and added to the inventory if successfully tested—like razing single homes or whole residential districts, uprooting olive groves, plowing crops under, setting fire to workplaces, cutting a farm off from the house by building a wall and otherwise destroying sources of the farmer's already miserable livelihood. All such measures display the self-propelling and self-exacerbating propensity to inflict harm and to victimize others. As the list of the committed atrocities grows, so does the need to apply them ever more resolutely to prevent the victims from making their voices not only heard but also listened to. And as old stratagems become routine and the horror they have sown among their targets wears off, new and more painful and horrifying contrivances need to be feverishly sought.

Lessons of the genocide inspired by sacralization and

banalization prompt and perpetuate more separation, suspicion, hatred, and hostility, and so make the likelihood of a new catastrophe greater than it otherwise would be. In no way do they diminish the sum total of violence. Nor do they bring any closer the moment of ethical reflection upon the faults and the preferred shape of human cohabitation. Worse still, they divert attention from anything beyond the immediate, current concerns of group survival, in particular the deep sources of categorial murder that could be revealed, understood, and counteracted only if the narrow group-bound horizon were transcended.

The Holocaust was indeed an event of tremendous importance for the future shape of the world—but its significance lies in its role as a laboratory in which certain otherwise diluted and scattered potentials of humankind's modern, widely shared forms of cohabitation were condensed, brought to the surface and into view. If that significance is not acknowledged, the most important lesson of the Holocaust, revealing the genocidal potential endemic to our forms of life, and the conditions under which that potential may bear its lethal fruits, is bound to remain, to everyone's peril, unlearned.

The sacralized/banalized readings of the Holocaust's message are wrong and dangerous for the double reason that they direct our concerns away from genuinely danger-diminishing strategies, while simultaneously making the strategy selected instead counterproductive to the purpose it is supposed and hoped to serve. These readings trigger "schismogenetic" chains (like "force needs to be replied to by force and fought with a yet greater force") that multiply and magnify the genocidal dangers that set them in motion in the first place.

Gregory Bateson, one of the most perceptive and insightful anthropologists of the past century, pondered the nature of the schismogenetic chain, knotted into a sinister circle of human animosity. Once entangled and locked in that vicious cycle of challenge and response, the antagonists excite, prod, and spur each other into acts of frantic militancy, ever more militancy, and ever more dogged and passionate and, in the end, unscrupulous militancy. Militancy acquires its own momentum and feeds on its own fury, with each successive act of hostility providing all the reason that the next act needs; as time goes on, the original cause of the antagonism counts ever less and may well be forgotten—conflict develops just because it develops.

There are two kinds of schismogenetic chains. One is "complementary." First, one person or group forces another person or group to do something that they dislike doing and would not do unless coerced. Then, having learned the hard lesson of their wrong-doer's hostile intentions and also their superior power, the frightened victims manifest their meekness and declare their obedience, hoping to avoid another blow. The sight of their docility, however, only beefs up the arrogance of the oppressor—and the next blow is more painful than the first. That makes the victims even more submissive, and emboldens their tormentors further. You can imagine the rest of the story. Blows and pains will succeed each other with increasing speed, gaining in force each time. Unless the chain is broken, only the total destruction of the victims will bring it to its end.

The other schismogenetic chain is "symmetrical." Here, both sides play the same game. Eye for eye, tooth for tooth, blow for blow. Offense can be repaid only by offending the offender, harm by harming the harmer. Whatever you do, I'll do as much and more, and with greater passion and severity. The exchange of blows turns into a competition—in ruthlessness, mercilessness, cruelty. Both sides believe that the more hard-hearted and bloodthirsty their acts are, the greater the chance that the adversary will think twice before risking another blow and in the end will throw in the towel. And both sides believe that toning down or weakening their responses (not to mention abstaining from response altogether) will only encourage the adversary to deliver yet more humiliating blows. You can imagine the rest of the story. With two sides sharing this belief, the chances of breaking the chain are virtually nil. Only the mutual destruction of the adversaries or their total exhaustion may bring the contest to its end.

There are no good prospects for humanity so long as these two vicious chains are in operation. One wonders, rather, how come the human species, equipped with such disastrous inclinations, has survived until now? But it has survived. So alongside the dangers, there must be hope. There must be a way of cutting schismogenetic chains short, mustn't there?

At the very beginning of Europe's long, convoluted, and turbulent history, that question was asked—in the Oresteian Trilogy by Aeschylus. In one of the plays, encouraged by the chorus ("to shed blood for blood shed," "evil for evil . . . is no impiety!"), Electra seeks vengeance for her father, murdered by her mother's lover, and calls her brother Orestes to kill the killers: "Let those who killed taste death for death . . . My curse to match their curse, wickedness for wickedness." The chorus is delighted: "Let hatred get hatred in turn, let murderous blow meet blow that murdered"; "the gods ordain that blood by murder shed cries from the ground for blood to flow again." Another massacre follows—closing one account of unrepaid wrongs only to open another. At the end of the play, confused and brokenhearted, the chorus cries: "When shall the ancestral curse relent, and sink to rest, its fury spent?" But, alas, there is no one left to answer. It is only in the next part of the trilogy that the answer is forthcoming, from Athena, the Goddess of Wisdom: "Fair trial, fair judgment, ended in an even vote, which brings to you neither dishonour nor defeat." "Then quench your anger: let no indignation rain pestilence on our soil, corroding every seed till the whole land is sterile desert."[12]

Not that Athena's verdict was obeyed through more than two millennia of subsequent history. On countless occasions it was disregarded, on many was it blatantly violated. And yet it hovered above Europe's history as a painful reproach of conscience whenever Athena's advice was not followed. Slowly, and not without deviations and retreats, the trail from the rule of vengeance to the rule of law and justice, as the way of breaking the shackles of the schismogenetic chains, was blazed. "Fair trial, fair judgment," one that "brings neither dishonor nor defeat" and so allows the adversaries to put aside their grudges and live together in peace, eventually cuts short the otherwise endless chain of retaliation and revenge.

Ryszard Kapuściński, the indefatigable explorer of the best known, less known, and altogether overlooked sites of gory inflammation and human misery, and an uncannily perceptive researcher of the conflicts that ripped apart the incipient humanity of our fast globalizing world, summed up the challenge that we jointly confront and the gruesome consequences of our failure to respond: "Is not the reductionism that consists in describing each case of genocide separately, as if it was detached from our cruel history and particularly from power deviations in other parts of our planet, a means to evade the questions most brutal and fundamental for our world and the dangers that threaten it? When they are described and fixed on the margins of shared history and memory, genocidal episodes are not lived as collective experience, as a shared test that may unite us."[13]

When the successive outbursts of the categorial murder frenzy are sacralized as a private tragedy of the victims, of the victims' descendants and their exclusively owned heritage, while banalized by all the rest of mankind as a regrettable yet ubiquitous manifestation of human iniquity or irrational folly, shared reflection on the sources of that frenzy and shared action aimed at blocking them turn out to be all but impossible. Following Kapuściński's advice and warning is a most urgent task, an imperative that can be dismissed solely at our joint peril.

We may start from an attempt to comprehend the many and varied cases of categorial murder as manifestations of two by no means idiosyncratic, but on the contrary common and widespread, indeed typical, varieties of instrumental rationality, that quality of thought and action that our modern world, far from resisting, actively promotes, providing ample means to mobilize human emotions in its service. Their peculiarities notwithstanding, all contemporary cases of categorial murder can be seen as following two kinds of logic, which for lack of better names we may identify deploying Ferdinand Tönnies's distinction between *Gesellschaft* (the contractual and impersonal aggregates) and *Gemeinschaft* (primordial unities) as "societal" and "communal."

Neither of the two types of totalities distinguished and juxtaposed by Tönnies more than a century ago is nowadays "natural" or simply "given" (though "givenness" was, according to Tönnies, the distinctive feature of *Gemeinschaft* in opposition to *Gesellschaft*). In our world of liquid modernity, of fast disintegration of social bonds and their traditional settings, both totalities are first *postulated* and then need to be *built,* and their construction is a task that, unless confronted, consciously embraced, and resolutely seen through, would not start, let alone be completed, on its own momentum. In the contemporary world, communities as much as societies can be only achievements: artifices of a productive effort. Categorial murder is nowadays a by-product, side effect, or waste product of their production.

The *societal* logic of categorial murder is that of the order-building (I tried to describe that logic at length in *Modernity and the Holocaust* and a number of subsequent studies). In designing the "greater society" meant to replace the aggregate of no more effectively self-reproducing local orders, certain sections of the population are inevitably classified as "leftovers," for whom no room in the future, rationally constructed order can be found—just as when, in designing a harmonious pattern in a garden, certain plants need to be assigned to the "weeds" category, earmarked for destruction. Categorial murder, like weeding (or, more generally, all and any "cleaning up," "purifying" activities) is a *creative* destruction. Through eliminating everything out of place and unfitting (like "aliens" or *unwertes Leben*), order is created or reproduced. The classless order of a communist society called for the destruction of the carriers of class inequality; the race-clean order of the Thousand Years Reich needed a thorough cleansing from the building site of the racially impure and race-polluting substances. The vocabulary serving genocide might have varied from one place to another, but the basic pattern has been repeated many times over in modern history, whenever the accelerated construction of a "new and improved" order happened to be undertaken by some resourceful and overwhelmingly strong powers of the modern state, and whenever that state exercised full and undivided, unobstructed rule over the population of its sovereign territory (for instance in Pol Pot's Cambodia, Mao's China, or Suharto's Indonesia).

The *communal* logic, much like the societal one, is a fully legitimate offspring of the modern condition, even if the family resemblance may be at first difficult to detect. With all the established and familiar frameworks used to underpin the self-confidence of action, the security of social position, and the safety of the body and its extensions fast melting and sent floating, one of the possible and quite probable reactions is a feverish search for a steady point—a shelter from the anxiety fed by the unreliable, erratic setting of life. Amid the cacophony of signals and kaleidoscopic mutability of vistas, with everything around us shifting, drifting, and changing face on short notice or without notice, such a shelter seems to reside in the uniformity of sameness. In the absence of a clear-cut hierarchy of values, which has been replaced by the cut-throat competition of short-lived purposes, the shelter seems to lie in the undivided loyalty making null and void all other taxing and confusingly numerous responsibilities. Once everything else has become blatantly artificial, conspicuously "man-made" (and so admittedly amenable to being "man-unmade"), the shelter seems to dwell in a company "no man can tear apart" because of its "natural," primordial presence, immune to all human choices and set to survive them. The modern era, and particularly the liquid-modern era, is a time of intense though inconclusive (intense *because* inconclusive, and all the more desperate and dedicated for that reason) community building. It inspires categorial murders of its own. Their cases proliferate at an accelerating pace, from Bosnia and Kosovo to Rwanda to Sri Lanka.

As argued and convincingly demonstrated by René Girard, there is hardly anything that unites and cements a freshly patched-together "community" more solidly than the sharing of complicity in a crime, and so the categorial murder of the communal type differs in a number of striking features from the societal type.[14] In stark opposition to the societal type of categorial murder as exemplified by the Holocaust, the emphasis in genocidal acts inspired by community building is on the "personal" nature of the crime, on killing in broad daylight, with the murderers known by face and name to their victims and the victims being the murderers' kith and kin, acquaintances and next-door neighbors. When it comes to a categorial murder in the name of community building, "suspension of emotions" is neither required nor approved; the excuse of "acting under orders" is thereby denied. It must be clear to everyone that only the postulated community about to be constructed will stand between the perpetrators and the war-crime tribunal, that solely the continuous solidarity and loyalty to the communal cause may defend the perpetrators from the charge of crime. The appointed victims are but the tools of community building; the genuine and most avidly spied-on and most mercilessly chased enemies are the whistle-blowers, turncoats, or those just lukewarm among the individuals designated (with or without their knowledge and consent) as community brethren.

Societal and communal varieties of categorial murder have been here presented as "pure types," so to speak. In practice, most cases of categorial murder contain a mixture of the two, in varying proportions, and need to be plotted somewhere between the "ideal-typical" extremes. Ideal types have been deployed here as analytical devices, to assist comprehension of the principal sources of genocidal threats in our liquid-modern society. It is my main contention in this chapter that the need to pay close attention to such sources and take concerted action to block them is the single most important lesson to be drawn from the legacy of the Holocaust. The urgency of this task is indeed the core of that legacy—the ethical obligation bequeathed by the genocide victims to all of us, the living.

Indeed: to *all* of us. Division, separation, and exclusion have been and remain the paramount instruments of categorial murder and by no stretch of the imagination can they be proposed as the means of its prevention. Cutting the roots of the genocidal tendency calls for the inadmissibility of double standards, differential treatment, and the separation that lays the groundwork for the battle of survival waged as a zero-sum game. Whatever precepts of human cohabitation are drawn from the long record of categorial murders, they can be only *universal*. They cannot be applied selectively, lest they be transformed into another apology for the right of the stronger (whoever happens to be stronger at the moment the apology is recited). This seems to be an imperative—though not a comforting one. In the world today, which is undergoing fast yet uncoordinated globalization, mutual dependency has already reached a global extent, which, however, has not been matched, nor is likely to be matched soon, by a similarly worldwide society, or institutions of political control, or law, or binding ethical code. Solidarity of fate has not generated thus far solidarity of sentiment and action, and it is far from clear what needs to be done and can be done to induce it to do so. And so the imperative comes without instructions for use and instruments that such use may require. That sorry circumstance does not make it less essential or urgent, though, and for a moral person, uncertainty about a realistic path of action is not an excuse for doing nothing or for seeking comfort by adopting the posture of a bystander.

We may only (should, rather?) repeat after Kapuściński: "Since there are no mechanisms, no legal, institutional or technical barriers able to repulse effectively new acts of genocide, our sole defense against them rests in the moral elevation of individuals and societies alike. In spiritually vivid conscience, in powerful will to do good, in constant and attentive listening to the commandment: 'love your neighbor as yourself.'"[15]

To a skeptical reader who would doubt the efficacy of the commandment as set against modern tanks, helicopters, time bombs, and smart missiles, and the intoxicating temptation they arouse in their proud owners, we may say that one lesson that the story of categorial murder has taught beyond reasonable doubt is that loving one's neighbor and inducing the neighbor to love you is (apart from its other—for instance, moral—virtues) the only reasonable, effective, and long-lasting service that individuals and groups can render their self-love.

"Fair trial, fair judgment" means the rule of law—an equal law for all, a nonpartisan and uncorrupt law. People tend to live in peace and refrain from resorting to violence when they can address their complaints and grudges to a power whose incorruptibility and fairness they may trust. But on our fast and chaotically globalizing planet, such power is conspicuous only by its absence. Such power is present inside the boundaries of politically sovereign states—but most painful damage, targeted or "collateral," is delivered nowadays from that "outer space" outside all boundaries, from that no-man's-land, Wild West–style land, where there is no "right" without "might," only the stronger sit in judgment, and only the weaker are punished for their deeds. In our globalizing world, power no longer resides with politics. Coercive power—economic and military—has broken its political shackles and roams free over the planetary space, while politics that could bridle its antics (and which did attempt to bridle them, with some success, inside the boundaries of nation-states) stays local, as before.

In such a world, no one, nowhere, feels safe or secure. Once more, schismogenetic chains take hold of human fate. They are *global* now, they wrap the planet around and render the cutting tools developed over the centuries sorely inadequate for the task. Once more, the Electras today call on their brothers to avenge the wrongs they suffered and redress the injustice done to their near and dear, because they seek—in vain—the powers that could assure fair trials and judgments. The heavenly voice of Athena still waits, hopefully yet in vain, to be heard on the globalized Earth.

Unrestrained competition in violence (ever more exorbitant and outrageous violence) feeds on the same world disorder on which the unrestrained competition for profits (ever more exorbitant and outrageous profits) thrives, adding yet more chaos to the disorderly planet. Allegedly engaged in a war of attrition, the two competitions are close allies; both have a vested interest in the perpetuation of planetary disorder, without which they would not last long, and both resent the prospect of political control and the rule of law, the advent of which they would not survive.

On a globalizing planet, neither of the two planetwide schismogenetic chains can be cut locally. There are no local solutions to globally rooted problems. The causes of survival and justice, often at loggerheads in the past, now point in the same direction, call for similar strategies, and tend to converge into one; and that unified cause cannot be pursued, let alone fulfilled, locally and by local-only efforts. Global problems have only global solutions. On a globalizing planet, human problems can be tackled and resolved only by solidary humanity.

♦

CHAPTER THREE

Freedom in the Liquid-Modern Era

♦

THE GAME GOES ON, whatever we do, noted Günther Anders first in 1956, though he kept repeating it until the end of the century in successive editions of *Die Antiquiertheit des Menschen:* "Whether we play the game or not, it is being played with us. Whatever we do or abstain from doing, our withdrawal will change nothing."[1]

Half a century later, we hear the same concerns expressed by leading minds of our times. Pierre Bourdieu, Claus Offe, and Ulrich Beck may differ considerably in their descriptions of that world which plays games with us, compelling us by the same token to play the make-believe game of "free" players—but what they all struggle to grasp in their descriptive efforts is the same paradox: the greater our individual freedom, the less it is relevant to the world in which we practice it. The more tolerant the world becomes of the choices we make, the less the game, our playing it, and the way we play it are open to our choice. No longer does the world appear amenable to kneading and molding; instead, it seems to tower above us—heavy, thick, and inert, opaque, impenetrable and impregnable, stubborn and insensitive to any of our intentions, resistant to our attempts to render it more hospitable to human coexistence. The face it shows us is mysterious and inscrutable, like faces of the most seasoned poker players. To that world, *there seems to be no alternative.* No alternative, at any rate, that we the players, by our deliberate efforts, singly, severally, or all together, could put in its place.

Amazing. Baffling. Who would have expected it? One can only say that for the past two or three centuries since that great leap to human autonomy and self-management variously called "Enlightenment" or "the advent of the modern era," history has run in a direction no one planned, no one anticipated, and no one wished it to take. What makes this course so astonishing and such a challenge to our understanding is that these two to three centuries started with the human resolve to take history under human administration and control—deploying for that purpose reason, believed to be the most powerful among human weapons (indeed, a flawless human facility to know, to predict, to calculate, and so to raise the "is" to the level of the "ought")—and were filled throughout with zealous and ingenious human effort to act on that resolve.

In the April 1992 issue of the *Yale Review,* Richard Rorty remembered Hegel's melancholy confession that philosophy is, at its utmost, "its time held in thought." I might add: this is at any rate what philosophy tries hard to do—to hold its time, to contain its restless and capricious jolts in a riverbed carved in rock with the sharp chisel of logic firmly held in the hilt of reason. "With Hegel," Rorty suggested, "the intellectuals began to switch over from fantasies of contacting eternity to [the] fantasy of constructing a better future." I might add: they hoped first to learn where the river of time was flowing, and they called it "discovery of the laws of history." Disappointed and impatient with the slowness of the current and the twists and turns of the river, they later resolved to take the decision into their own hands: to straighten the course of the river, to encase the riverbanks in concrete to prevent overflow, to select the estuary and lay out the trajectory that the river of time should follow. They called it "designing and building a perfect society." Even when pretending humility, philosophers could hardly hide their self-confidence. From Plato to Marx, Rorty suggests, they believed that "there just *must* be large theoretical ways of finding out how to end injustice, as opposed to small experimental ways."[2]

We believe this no longer, and few of us would be prepared to swear that they still do, though many seek desperately to cover up the humiliating discovery that we, the intellectuals, may after all be no better than our fellow citizens at holding our time in thought. The discovery that time stubbornly refuses to stay obediently in the riverbed carved by reason, that it would surely tear to pieces any thought container in which it was supposed to be held, that no map has been charted nor is likely to be charted showing its direction, and that there is no lake called "perfect society" at the far end of its flow—if, that is, there is an end to that flow.

Rorty, for once, rejoices in that loss of the intellectuals' self-assurance and welcomes the new modesty that is bound to follow. He wishes the intellectuals to admit—to others and to themselves—that there is "nothing in particular that we know that everybody else doesn't know." He wants them "to rid themselves of the idea that they know, or ought to know, something about deep, underlying forces—forces that determine the fates of human communities." And he wants them to recall Kenneth Burke's remark that "the future is really disclosed by finding out what people can sing about"—but also to remember Václav Havel's sober, salutary warning that in any given year one will probably not be able to guess which songs will be on people's lips in the year to come.

If there ever was, as Jürgen Habermas insists, a "project of modernity," it was an intention to replace collective and individual human *heteronomy* with collective and individual *autonomy* (autonomy of the human species toward hazards and contingencies of nature and history, and autonomy of human persons toward external manmade pressures and constraints). That double-pronged autonomy was hoped and anticipated to produce and ensure a similarly two-level freedom of self-assertion, simultaneously species-wide and individual. The two front lines in the war for autonomy were meant to be closely interdependent. The autonomy of humanity was to secure and protect the autonomy of the individuals, while the individuals, once they became truly autonomous and free to deploy their powers of reason, would see to it that humanity jealously guarded its newly acquired autonomy and exploited it to promote and safeguard autonomy of the individuals.

If ever there was a project of Enlightenment, it was wrapped around the idea of *emancipation*. Before freedom had the chance to usher humankind and all its members into the world of autonomy and self-assertion, humanity needed to be liberated from tyranny. To untie its hands and enable it to celebrate the match of human reason and human history, humanity had to be liberated from physical and spiritual slavery—from the *physical* slavery that prevented humans from doing what they would otherwise do, if allowed to wish freely and to freely follow their wishes, and from the *spiritual* slavery that prevented humans from being guided in their wishing by reason, and from wishing, therefore, what they should have wished (that is, wishing for what served best their interests and human nature). Have the courage to serve your own understanding! This is the motto of the Enlightenment, wrote Kant. The maxim of thinking on one's own—this is Enlightenment. For Denis Diderot, the ideal human was someone who dared to think for himself, trampling over prejudice, tradition, antiquity, popular beliefs, authority—in short over everything that enslaves the spirit. And Jean-Jacques Rousseau called his readers to act according to the maxims of their own judgment. It was thought that once these calls to spiritual freedom were heard, listened to, and obeyed, the demise of physical slavery would follow, but that the condition of listening to and obeying the calls to spiritual autonomy was the abolition of physical slavery. And so the fight against the infamy of prejudice and superstition must proceed hand in hand with the struggle against the outrage of political despotism.

On that second front, citizenship, republic, and democracy are the main weapons. In Alexis de Tocqueville's summary of the political chapter of Enlightenment-inspired emancipation, liberating individuals from the arbitrary rule of a despot while leaving them to their own, private concerns and devices (a condition described by Isaiah Berlin as *negative* freedom) simply won't do; what is needed more than anything else is *positive* freedom: their right and willingness to associate with their co-citizens, to participate in the affairs of their shared polity, in particular the law making. Collective autonomy means obeying no rules except those that have been decided upon and made binding by those who are expected to obey them. The double victory on both fronts would usher in—or at least this is what all quoted spiritual fathers of modernity believed—a transparent, predictable, and manageable user-friendly world, one hospitable to the humanness of humanity.

This is not, however, what actually happened. Two to three centuries later, the world we inhabit is still anything but transparent and predictable. Nor is it a secure home for the human species, let alone its humanity. One is ready to agree with Habermas that the project of Enlightenment remains unfinished. But the incompleteness of the project is not, to be sure, a novel discovery. A genuine novelty is that today we no longer believe that project to be finishable. And yet another novelty is that *many of us*, perhaps *most of us*, do not particularly care. It is because of these two novelties that *some of us* worry that freedom, understood as the autonomy of a society of autonomous individuals, has fallen on hard times—uncomfortable and unprepossessing times.

Half a century ago, Anders worried that, quite possibly, his contemporaries were busy building a world from which they would find no exit, and a world no longer within their power to comprehend, imagine, and emotionally absorb. It is now possible that what half a century ago could be treated as an inordinately, and probably also excessively, dark premonition, has since acquired the rank of a statement of fact and commands ever wider, if not universal, support.

When first proclaimed amid the gathering revolutionary excitement in France, the slogan *Liberté, Égalité, Fraternité* was a succint statement of a life philosophy, a declaration of intent, and a war cry, all rolled into one. Happiness is a human right, whereas the pursuit of happiness is a natural and universal human inclination—so went the tacit, matter-of-fact assumption of the philosophy—and to achieve happiness, humans needed to be free, equal, and indeed brotherly, since for brothers, mutual sympathy and the succor and help of siblings are birth rights, not perquisites that need to be earned and shown to have been earned before being granted. As John Locke memorably argued,[3] even if "there is only one" path to *eternal* happiness that may be chosen and pursued by men (the path of piety and virtue, leading to eternity in heaven, as the centuries of memento mori groomed people to believe), "in [the] great variety of ways that men follow it [it] is still doubted which is the right one. Now neither the care of the commonwealth, nor the right of enacting laws, does discover this way that leads to heaven more certainly to the magistrate, than every private man's search and study discovers it unto himself."

Locke's insistence on the pursuit of happiness as the principal purpose, simultaneously, of individual life efforts *and* of association of individuals in a commonwealth was hardly ever questioned throughout the modern era. For most of that time, mankind did not question, either, the idea that freedom, equality, and brotherhood were all that men needed in order to be able to pursue their happiness unhampered and undisturbed. To pursue happiness, that is—though not necessarily to attain it; Locke's vision was to a great extent an earthly, mundane, this-worldly version of Luther's or Calvin's uncertainty of the ultimate resolution of the salvation-versus-damnation dilemma. But whether in its otherworldly or this-worldly rendition, it was the *pursuit* of felicity itself, rather than a certain *summum bonum* (the greatest good) lurking at the far—and for all we know stubbornly underdetermined—end of the road that gave genuine happiness. Happiness equaled *freedom of experimentation*: liberty to take right *and* wrong steps, freedom to succeed *and* to fail, to invent, try, and test ever new varieties of pleasurable and gratifying experience, to choose and to take the risk of erring. Unhappiness meant being barred from that freedom; being deprived of the right to choose freely, and instead being, by hook or by crook, by force or by deceit, "protected from" wrong choices.

Two tacit (since viewed as self-evident), axiomatic assumptions underpinned the tripartite design. The program of freedom, equality, and brotherhood implied matter-of-factly that it was the duty of the commonwealth to provide and to guard the conditions favorable to the pursuit of happiness so understood. Pursuit of happiness was an individual affair, concern, destiny, and duty, it was to be conducted individually, by each and any individual deploying individually possessed and managed resources, but the call to seek happiness was addressed to individuals *and* society alike; whether it would be answered properly depended on the shape of the "commonwealth"—society understood as the shared home and joint concern and product of *les hommes et les citoyens,* humans/citizens. The other unspoken yet accepted axiomatic assumption was the necessity to conduct the battle for happiness on two fronts. While individuals needed to acquire and develop the art of living a happy life, the powers that shaped the conditions under which that art could be effectively practiced had to be themselves reshaped into something more "practitioner-friendly." Pursuit of happiness stood no chance of rising to the rank of a genuinely universal right unless those powers took proper care of the parameters of "good society"—equality and fraternity being the most prominent and decisive among them.

It is those assumptions of the intimate and unbreakable link between the quality of the commonwealth and the chances of individual happiness that have lost, or are fast losing, their axiomatic hold on the popular thinking as well as on the products of its intellectually sublimated recycling. And it is perhaps for that reason that the assumed conditions of individual happiness are being shifted away from the supraindividual sphere of Politics with a capital *P* and toward the domain of individual life-politics, postulated as the field of primarily individual undertakings in which individually commanded and managed resources are mainly, if not exclusively, deployed. The shift reflects the changing living conditions resulting from liquid-modern processes of deregulation and privatization (that is, "subsidiarizing," "outsourcing," "contracting out," or otherwise renouncing the successive functions previously assumed and performed by the commonwealth institutions). The presently emerging formula for the (unchanged) purpose of pursuing happiness may be best expressed as shifting from *Liberté, Égalité, Fraternité* to *Sécurité, Parité, Réseau* (Security, Parity, Network).

The trade-off called "civilization" has come full circle since 1929, when Sigmund Freud, in *Das Unbehagen in der Kultur*, first noted the tug-of-war and logrolling between the two equally indispensable and cherished values, which were vexingly resistant to reconciliation. In less than a century, the continuous progress toward individual freedom of expression and choice has reached the point at which the price of that progress, the loss of security, has begun to be seen by a rising number of liberated individuals (or individuals forced loose without being asked for consent) as exorbitant—unendurable and unacceptable. Risks involved in the individualization and privatization of the pursuit of happiness, coupled with the gradual yet steady dismantling of the societally designed, built, and serviced safety nets and societally endorsed insurance against misfortune, have proved to be enormous, and the resulting fear-excreting uncertainty daunting. The value of "security" is the value that elbows out liberty. A life imbued with a bit more certainty and safety, even if paid for by somewhat less personal freedom, has suddenly gained in attractiveness and seductive power.

"Modern Time," as Albert Camus pointed out, "begins with the crash of falling ramparts."[4] And as Dostoyevsky's Ivan Karamazov suggested (following and bringing to a summation the legacy of a long chain of thinkers, starting at least from Pico della Mirandola, the Renaissance herald of the divine omnipotence of Man), with the Divine creation declared faulty and immortality a nebulous notion, the "new man" is permitted, exhorted, and nudged "to become God." Rehearsals of that new role proved to be inconclusive, however, and above all much less enjoyable than expected. Groping in the dark with no reliable compass or authoritatively endorsed map appeared to be fraught with acute discomforts hardly recompensed by sporadic, brief, and brittle joys of self-assertion. And so the Great Inquisitor of another Dostoyevsky tale found out that men prefer freedom from responsibility to the freedom to tell and set apart good from evil. The further that human freedom, with its requisites of risk and responsibility, progressed, the more intense grew human resentment of rising insecurity and indetermination; and as security gained in perceived attraction and ascribed value, the perks of freedom lost much of their luster. Freud would probably reverse his century-old verdict and ascribe the present psychological ailments and disorders to the consequences of trading an excessively large measure of security for the sake of greater freedom.

In the constellation of conditions (and so also the hoped-for prospects) for decent and agreeable life today, the star of parity shines ever brighter, while that of equality fades. "Parity" is, most emphatically, not "equality"; or rather it is an equality stripped down to equal entitlement to recognition, to the right to be and the right to be left alone. The idea of leveling up wealth, well-being, life comforts, and life prospects, and, even more, the idea of having equal shares in the running of life in common and in the benefits that life in common has to offer, are disappearing from politics' agenda of realistic postulates and objectives. All varieties of liquid-modern society are increasingly reconciled to the permanence of economic and social inequality. The vision of uniform, universally shared life conditions is being replaced by that of principally unlimited diversification, and the right to become equal is being replaced by the right to be and remain different without being denied dignity and respect for that reason.

While the *vertical* disparities in access to the universally approved and coveted values tend to grow at a constantly accelerating pace, encountering little resistance and triggering at best only sporadic, narrowly focused, and marginal remedial action, *horizontal* differences multiply, vociferously lauded, celebrated, and all too often actively promoted by the political and commercial, as well as the ideational, powers that be. Wars for recognition take the place once occupied by revolutions; at stake in ongoing struggles is no longer the shape of the world to come but having a tolerable and tolerated place in that world; no longer are the rules of the game at stake but solely admission to the table. This is what "parity," the emergent avatar of the idea of fairness, is ultimately about: recognition of the right to partake of the game, quashing a verdict of exclusion, or staving off the chance of such a verdict's being carried in future.

Finally, the network. If "brotherhood" implied a preexisting structure that predetermined and predefined the rules binding conduct, attitudes, and principles of interaction, "networks" have no previous history: networks are born in the course of action and are kept alive (or rather continually, repetitively recreated/resurrected) solely thanks to successive communicative acts.

Unlike a group or any other kind of "social whole," a network is individual-ascribed and individually focused—the focal individual, the hub, being its sole permanent and irremovable part. Each individual is presumed to carry his or her unique network on or around his or her own body, like a snail carries its home. Person A and person B may both belong to the network of C, though A does not belong to B's network and

B does not belong to A's—a circumstance disallowed in the case of totalities, such as nations, churches, or neighborhoods.

The most consequential feature of networks is, however, the unusual flexibility of their reach and the extraordinary facility with which their composition may be modified: individual items are added or removed with no greater effort than it takes to type in or delete a telephone number in a cellular phone's directory. Eminently breakable bonds connect the network units, as fluid as the identity of the network's "hub," its sole creator, owner, and manager. Through networks, "belonging" becomes a (soft and shifting) sediment of identification. Belonging is transferred from the "before" to the "after" of identity and follows promptly, and with little resistance, the identity's successive renegotiations and redefinitions. By the same token, relations set by and sustained by network-type connectedness come close to the ideal of a "pure relationship": one based on easily dissolvable one-factor ties, with no determined duration, no strings attached, and unburdened by long-term commitments. In sharp opposition to the "groups of belonging," whether ascribed or joined, a network offers its owner/manager the comforting (even if ultimately counterfactual) feeling of total and unthreatened control over his or her obligations and loyalties.

One of the most acute and insightful observers and analysts of intergenerational change and particularly of the emergent life-styles, Hanna Swida-Ziemba, has noted that "people of past generations situated themselves in the past as much as in the future." For the new, contemporary young person, however, she says only the present exists: "The young people to whom I talked during the research conducted in 1991–1993 asked: why is there so much aggression in the world? Is it possible to achieve full happiness? Such questions are no longer important."[5]

Swida-Ziemba was speaking of Polish youth. But in our fast-globalizing world she would find very similar trends in whatever land or continent on which she focused her inquiry. The data collected in Poland, a country just emerging from long years of an authoritarian rule that had artificially conserved modes of life elsewhere left behind, only condensed and telescoped the worldwide trends, making them steeper and therefore more salient and somewhat easier to note.

When you ask, "Where does aggression come from?" what probably prompts you to ask is an urge to do something about it; it is because you feel strongly about it, wish to stem aggression or fight it back, that you desire to learn where the roots of aggression lie. Presumably, you are keen to reach those places where the impulses of aggression or aggressive schemes breed and flourish, in order to incapacitate and destroy them. And if this guess is correct, then you must resent the fact that the world is infused with aggression, and view it as uncomfortable or downright unfit for human life, and for that reason iniquitous and undesirable; but you must also believe that such a world *could* be made more hospitable and friendly to humans—and that if you tried, as try you should, *you* might become a part of that force destined and able to make it into such a world. Also, when you ask whether full happiness can be attained, you probably believe in attaining, singly or severally, a more agreeable, worthy, and satisfying way of living your life—and are willing to undertake such effort (perhaps even bear such sacrifice) as any worthy cause calls for. In other words, when you ask such questions you imply that, rather than accepting things meekly, since they seem at present to be showing little or no sign of changing, you are inclined to measure your strength and ability by the standards, tasks, and goals you've set for your life yourself, not the other way around.

You surely must have had, and followed, such assumptions. Otherwise you wouldn't be bothered by such questions. For such questions to occur to you, you first need to believe that the world around you is not "given" once and for all, that it can be changed, and that you yourself can be changed while applying yourself to the job of changing it. You must assume that the state of the world could be different than it is now, and that how different it may eventually become depends on what you do; that no less than the state of the world—past, present, and future—may depend on what you do or desist from doing. In other words: you believe that you are, simultaneously, an artist able to create and shape things, and the product of such creation and shaping.

As Michel Foucault suggested, only one conclusion follows from the proposition that identity is not given: we need to *create it,* just as works of art are created. For all practical intents and purposes, the question, "Can the life of every human individual become a work of art?" is rhetorical; we can do without an elaborate argument. Assuming the positive answer to be a foregone conclusion, Foucault asks: If a lamp or a house can be a work of art, why not a human life?[6] I surmise that both the "new young" and the "past generations" that Swida-Ziemba compares would have agreed wholeheartedly with Foucault's suggestions, but I also guess that members of each of the two age cohorts would have something else in mind when thinking of "works of art."

Those of the past generations would probably think of an artwork as something of lasting value and imperishable, resistant to the wear of time and caprices of fate. Following the habits of old masters, they would meticulously prime their canvas before applying the first brushstroke, and would equally carefully select the solvents—to make sure that the layers of paint wouldn't crumble when drying and would retain their freshness of color over many years to come, if not for eternity. The younger generation, though, would seek to imitate the patterns and practices of currently celebrated artists—in the art world's popular "happenings" and "installations." With happenings, one knows only that no one (not even their producers and prime actors) can be sure what course they will eventually take, that their trajectories are hostage to ("blind," uncontrollable) fate, that as they unravel, anything *may* happen but nothing is certain to happen. And with installations—put together of brittle and perishable, preferably self-degradable elements—everyone knows that the works won't survive the close of the exhibition, that to fill the gallery with the next batch of exhibits, it will need to be cleared of the (now useless) bits and pieces—remnants of the old. The young may also associate works of art with the posters and other prints they put up all over the wallpaper in their rooms. They know that the posters, like the wallpaper, are not meant to adorn their rooms forever. Sooner or later they will need to be "updated"—torn down to make room for the likenesses of the next latest idols.

Both generations (past and new) imagine works of art after the patterns of their particular world, the true nature and meaning of which one presumes and hopes the arts will lay bare and make available to scrutiny. One expects the world to be made more intelligible, perhaps even fully understood, thanks to the labors of artists; but well before that happens, the generations that "live through" that world know it from "autopsy," so to speak: from examining their personal experience and from the stories commonly told to report their experience and make it meaningful. No wonder, then, that in stark opposition to previous generations, the new young believe that one can't really navigate one's life along a route designed before the voyage started, and that random fate and accident decide, in the last account, its itinerary. Of some of the Polish young people interviewed by Swida-Ziemba, for instance, she says that "they note that a mate climbed high in the firm, was repeatedly promoted and reached the top, until the company went bankrupt and he lost everything he had gained. It is for that reason that they may quit the studies that went very well and go to England to work on a building site." The others don't think of the future at all ("It's a waste of time, isn't it?") and don't expect life to reveal any logic but instead look for the occasional stroke of luck (possibly) and banana skins on the sidewalk (equally probably)—and for that reason "want every moment to be pleasurable." Indeed: *every* moment. An unpleasurable moment is a moment wasted. Since it is impossible to calculate which sort of future profits, if any, a present sacrifice may bring, why should one surrender the instant pleasure that could be squeezed out of the here and now and enjoyed on the spot?

The "art of life" may mean different things for the members of older and younger generations, but they all practice it and can't possibly not. The course of life and the meaning of its every successive episode, as well as life's "overall purpose" or "ultimate destination," are nowadays presumed to be do-it-yourself jobs, even if they consist only in selecting and assembling the right type of flat-packed IKEA-style kit. Each and any practitioner of life is expected, just as the artists are, to bear full responsibility for the outcome of the job, and to be praised or blamed for its results. These days each man and each woman is an artist not so much *by choice* as, so to speak, *by the decree of universal fate.*

"Being artists by decree" means that nonaction also counts as action; swimming and navigating as much as allowing oneself to drift with the waves are, a priori, assumed to be acts of creative art and will be retrospectively recorded as such. Even people who refuse to believe in the logical succession, continuity, and consequentiality of choices, decisions, and undertakings, and in the feasibility and plausibility of taming fate—in overruling providence or destiny and keeping life on a predesigned and preferred course—even they do not sit on their hands; they still need to "assist fate" by seeing to the endless little tasks that fate decreed they will perform (as if following the drawings attached to the ready-to-assemble kit). Just like those who see no point in delaying satisfaction and decide to live "for the moment," people who care about the future and are wary of undermining their chances yet to come are convinced of the volatility of life's promises. They all seem to be reconciled to the impossibility of making foolproof decisions, of predicting exactly which one of the successive steps will prove to be the right one, or which of the scattered seeds of the future will bring plentiful and tasty fruit and which flower buds will wilt and fade before a sudden gust of wind or a wasp on an accidental visit can pollinate them. And so whatever else they believe, they all agree that one needs to hurry; that doing nothing, or doing something slowly and lackadaisically, is a grave mistake.

This is particularly true for the young: as Swida-Ziemba noted, they collect experiences and credentials "just in case." The young Poles say może; the English of their age would say "perhaps," the French peut-être, the German vielleicht, the Italians forse, the Spanish tal vez—but they would all mean much the same thing: who can know, while there is no knowing, whether one or the other ticket will win in the next drawing in life-lotto?

Myself, I belong to one of those "past generations."

As a young man, together with most of my contemporaries, I read attentively the instructions of Jean-Paul Sartre concerning the choice of a "life project"—that choice meant to be the "choice of choices," the metachoice that would determine, once and for all, from beginning to end, all the rest of our (subordinate, derivative, executive) choices. To every project (so we learned reading Sartre's instructions), there would be a road map attached and a detailed briefing on how to follow the itinerary. We had no difficulty understanding Sartre's message and found it compatible with what the world around us appeared to announce or imply. In Sartre's world, as in the world shared by my generation, maps aged slowly if at all (some of them even claimed to be "definitive"), roads were laid once and for all (they could, though, be resurfaced from time to time, to enable yet greater speed), and they promised to lead to the same destination each time they were taken; the signs at the crossroads were time and again repainted, but their messages never changed.

I (though again in the company of other young people my age) also listened patiently, with no murmur of protest let alone rebellion, to the lectures in social psychology that were founded on the laboratory experiments with hungry rats in a maze, seeking the one and only correct and proper succession of turns—that is, the one and only itinerary with a coveted morsel of lard at the end—in order to learn and memorize it for the rest of their lives. We did not protest at this because, in the plight and concerns of the laboratory rats, as much as in Sartre's advice, we heard echoes of our own life experiences.

Most young people of today, however, are likely to view the need to memorize the track out of the maze as the rats' worry but not their own. They would shrug their shoulders if advised by Sartre to fix their life's destination and to plot in advance the moves ensuring that it will be reached. Indeed, they would object: How do I know what the next month, let alone next year, will bring? I can be certain of one thing only, that the next month or year, and most certainly the years that will follow them, will be unlike the time I am living in now; being different, they will invalidate much of knowledge and know-how that I am currently exercising (though there is no guessing which of its many parts); much of what I've learned I'll have to forget, and I'll have to get rid of many (though there is no guessing which) things and inclinations I now display and boast about having; choices deemed today to be most reasonable and praiseworthy will be decried tomorrow as silly and disgraceful blunders. What follows is that the sole skill I really need to acquire and exercise is *flexibility*—the skill of promptly getting rid of useless skills, the ability to quickly forget and to dispose of the past assets that have turned into liabilities, the skill of changing tacks and tracks at short notice and without regret, and of avoiding oaths of life-long loyalty to anything and anybody. Good turns, after all, tend to appear suddenly and from nowhere, and equally abruptly they vanish; woe to the suckers who by design or default behave as if they were to hold to them forever.

It seems these days that though one can still dream of *scripting* a full-life scenario in advance, and even try to make the dream true—to *hold on* to any scenario, even to the most glorious, seductive, and apparently foolproof of scenarios, is risky and may prove suicidal. The scenarios of yore can date even before the play goes into rehearsals, and if they survive at all to the opening night, the run of the play may prove abominably brief. And then, having the stage of life committed to such a scenario for a considerable time ahead will be equal to forfeiting the chance for many (there is no knowing how many) more up-to-date and for that reason successful productions. Opportunities, after all, keep knocking, and there is no telling on which door and when they will knock.

Take the case of Tom Anderson. Having studied art, he probably did not acquire much engineering know-how and had little notion of how the technological wonders work. Like most of us, he was just a user of modern electronics, and like most of us, he must have spent little time meditating on what is inside the computer box and why this rather than something else popped up on the screen when he pressed this and not that key. And yet all of a sudden, probably to his own great surprise, Tom Anderson was acclaimed in the computing world as the creator and pioneer of "social networking" and the originator of what was promptly dubbed "the second Internet revolution." His blog, perhaps mostly a private pastime in its intention, in less than a couple of years evolved into the company MySpace, swarmed by young and very young Internauts (older Web users, if they heard of the company at all, probably played it down or derided it as another passing fad or another silly idea with the life expectancy of a butterfly). The "company" was still bringing in no profit to speak of, and Anderson had no idea how (and probably no strong intention, either) to make it financially profitable. Then in July 2005, Rupert Murdoch, unsolicited, offered $580 million for MySpace, which was then operating on not much more than a shoestring. Murdoch's decision to buy "opens sesames" in this world much more surely than the magic of the most ingenious and sophisticated spells. No wonder that fortune hunters invaded the Web in search of more uncut diamonds. Yahoo bought another Web site of the social-networking category for a billion dollars, and in October 2006 Google set aside $1.6 billion to obtain yet another, called YouTube—started up just a year and a half earlier, in purely cottage-industry fashion, by another pair of amateur enthusiasts, Chad Hurley and Steve Chene. On 8 February 2007 the *New York Times* reported that for their felicitous idea, Hurley was paid in Google shares worth $345 million, while Chene received shares with a market value of $326 million.

"Being found" by fate, embodied in the person of a high and

mighty protector or a resourceful patron searching for as-yet-unrecognized or just not duly appreciated talents, has been since the late Middle Ages and early Renaissance a popular motif in the biographical folklore about painters, sculptors, and musicians. (This was not true in the ancient world, though, where art was seen as the way to obediently and faithfully depict the magic of Divine creation: the Greeks "could not reconcile the idea of creation under the auspices of divine inspiration with monetary reward for the work created."[7] Being an artist was then associated more with renunciation and poverty, "being dead to the world," than with any kind of worldly, let alone pecuniary, success.) An etiological myth of being discovered by the high and mighty was probably invented at the threshold of the modern era, to account for the (still few and far between) unprecedented cases of individual artists who suddenly rose to fame and riches in a society that made birth a no-appeal-allowed life sentence and had no room for the idea of "self-made men" (and even less, of course, for self-made women)—and to account for such extraordinary cases in a way that would reaffirm rather than undermine the norm— the mundane order of power, might, and the right to glory. Being of lowly origin, if not downright outcasts, future masters of the arts found as a rule (at least this was what the myth insinuated) that even the greatest talent coupled with uncommonly dogged determination and genuinely extraordinary and inexhaustible missionary zeal was still not enough to fulfill their destiny, unless a benevolent and powerful hand was stretched forth to fetch them into the otherwise unreachable land of fame, wealth, and admiration.

Before the advent of modernity, the legend of "meeting with fate" was confined almost exclusively to artists; and no wonder, given that the practitioners of fine arts, like painters or composers, were almost the only people who managed to rise above their original lowly station and end up supping with princes and cardinals, if not kings and popes. As modernity progressed, however, the ranks of class-barrier-breakers stretched. As the numbers of parvenus multiplied, the stories inspired by their meetings with fate were democratized. These stories now inform the expectations of any and all "life artists," the mundane practitioners of the mundane art of mundane life; and this means all of us, or almost all. We have all been decreed owners of the right to "meet with fate," and through that fateful meeting to taste success and enjoy a life of happiness. And once a right is decreed to be universal, in no time it turns into a universal duty.

True, it is mainly the artists (or more precisely, the people whose practices, courtesy of their sudden acquisition of celebrity status, have been with no further argument classified as fine art) whose trials and tribulations are plotted in the fables of a miraculous rise from rags to riches, and who are promptly cast in the limelight and publicly celebrated. (For instance, we have the notorious story of the girl who was selling, for two-pounds apiece, fifty-pence glass ashtrays adorned with pop idols' photographs cut from newspapers and glued, slapdash, on the bottom. She was biding her time in a little shop on a drab little street in East London—until one day in front of that shop stopped a limousine carrying a great patron of art, destined to transform the girl's long-unmade bed into a priceless work of high art in the manner of Cinderella's fairy godmother, who conjured up a gold-dripping carriage out of a pumpkin.) Stories of successful artists (or more precisely of boys and girls magically transformed into such) have the advantage of falling onto ground well prepared by the centuries-old storytelling tradition; they also, however, fit particularly well the mood of our liquid-modern times, because unlike the early-modern stories—for instance the legend of a shoeshine boy who became a millionaire—they omit the thorny and rather off-putting issues of patience, hard work, and self-sacrifice that success in life most commonly requires. Stories of celebrated visual and performing artists play down the issues of which kind of activity one should choose and pursue to become worthy of public attention and esteem, and how one should make this choice (anyway, in a liquid-modern world one expects, and with good reason, that few if any worthy activities are likely to retain their worthiness for long). It is, rather, a general principle on which the typical liquid-modern stories focus: that in a compound with benevolent fate, any ingredient may cause the glittering crystals of success to sediment from the murky solution called life. *Any* ingredient: not necessarily the drudgery, self-denial, and self-sacrifice that the classic-modern stories of success suggested.

Considering such conditions, the invention of computerized networks came in eminently handy. One of the many virtues of the Internet (and one of the principal causes of its mind-boggling rate of growth) is that it puts paid to the awkward necessity of taking sides when faced with the ancient, now out-of-fashion and barely comprehended opposition between work and leisure, exertion and rest, purposeful action and idleness, or indeed application and sloth. The hours spent in front of your computer when zapping your way through the thicket of Web sites—what are they? Work or entertainment? Labor or pleasure? You cannot tell, you do not know, yet you must be absolved of your sin of ignorance, since the reliable answer to this dilemma won't come and can't come before fate shows its cards.

There is little wonder, therefore, that by 31 July 2006, 50 million blogs had been counted on the World Wide Web, and that by latest calculations their numbers have since grown, on average, by 175,000 a day. On what do those blogs inform the

"Internet public"? They inform us on everything that may occur to their owners/authors/operators, whatever may enter their heads—since there is no knowing what, if anything, may attract the attention of the Rupert Murdochs or Charles Saatchis of this world.

Creating a "personal site," a blog, is just another variety of the lottery: you go on, as it were, buying tickets just in case, with or without the illusion that there are rules that enable you (or anyone else, for that matter) to predict the winning ones—at least the kind of rules you could learn and remember to observe faithfully and effectively in your own practice. As Jon Lanchaster, who examined a large number of blogs, reported, one blogger recorded in great detail what he had consumed for breakfast, another described the joys he got from the previous evening's game, a she-blogger complained of the intimate bedroom shortcomings of her partner, another blog contained an ugly photograph of the author's pet dog, yet another meditated on the discomforts of a policeman's life, and another still collated the tastier sexual exploits of an American in China.[8] And yet one trait was found to be shared by all blogs: an unashamed sincerity and straightforwardness in displaying, in public, the most private experiences and most intimate adventures—brutally speaking, a burning zeal and evident lack of inhibition in putting oneself (or at least some parts or aspects of one's self) on the market. Perhaps one bit or another would prod the interest and inflame the imagination of prospective "buyers"—perhaps even some rich and powerful buyers—or if not, just some ordinary folks, but numerous enough to attract the attention of the powerful few, to inspire them to make the blogger an offer he or she wouldn't refuse and push sky-high his or her market price. Public confession (the juicier the better) of the most personal and meant-to-be-secret affairs is a sort of substitute currency, even if an inferior one: a currency to which we may resort when we can't afford the currencies routinely used by more "serious" (read: more resourceful) investors.

Many eminent art critics suggest that the arts have now conquered the whole world of the living. The allegedly idle dreams of the past century's avant-garde have been fulfilled—though not necessarily in the form the avant-garde artists wished and hoped such a victory would take. In particular, and most frustrating: it looks today as though, once they are victorious, the arts may no longer need the artworks to manifest their existence.

Not so long ago, and most certainly in the avant-garde's halcyon days, the arts struggled to prove their right to exist by documenting their usefulness to the world and its inhabitants; they needed solid and durable, tangible and possibly irremovable and indestructible, eternal proof of the valuable services they render. Now, however, not only do they manage well without leaving solid traces of their presence, but they also seem to avoid leaving traces so deep as to prevent their speedy and expedient effacement. Artists today appear to specialize mostly in assembling and promptly dismantling their creations; at least they treat the activities of assembling and disassembling as equally valid, worthy, and indispensable variants of artistic creativity. One great American artist, Robert Rauschenberg, put on sale sheets of paper on which drawings had once been made by another great American artist, Willem de Kooning, but from which they had been thoroughly erased; Rauschenberg's own creative contribution, for which the collectors were expected to pay, was the bleak, illegible traces of his rubbing-off action. In this way Rauschenberg promoted *destruction* to the rank of artistic *creation;* it was the act of *annihilating* the traces left on the world, not *imprinting* them, that his gesture was aimed to represent as the valuable service that the arts offer their contemporaries. In sending such a message, Rauschenberg was by no means alone among the most prominent and influential contemporary artists. Obliteration of traces, covering up of tracks, was and continues to be placed on the level heretofore occupied solely by their embossing or engraving (for eternity, it was hoped)—perhaps even on an even higher, superior level, where the most urgently needed tools of life are experimented with and the gravest challenges of the human existential condition are located, confronted, and dealt with.

Everything said thus far about the recent transformation of fine arts applies in full to the arts' most common, universally practiced genre: the art of life. In fact, the fateful departures that occurred in fine arts seem to have resulted from the artists' efforts to catch up with changes in the art of life, at least in its most ostentatiously displayed varieties. As in so many other fields, so in this case art replicates life; in most cases, changes in fine arts lag behind changes in the mode of life, though the artistic creators do their best to anticipate these changes and sometimes succeed in inspiring or facilitating a change and smoothing its entry and settlement into daily life practices. Before the artists discovered it, "creative destruction" was already widely practiced and entrenched in mundane life as one of its most common, indeed routinely applied, expedients. Rauschenberg's gesture could therefore be interpreted as an attempt to update the meaning of "representative painting." Whoever wishes to lay bare, put on display, and render intelligible human experiences (in both their *Erfahrungen* and *Erlebnisse* forms), whoever wants her or his oeuvre to faithfully represent those experiences, ought to follow Rauschenberg's example in unmasking, making salient and available to scrutiny the intimate connections between creation and destruction.

To practice the art of life, to make one's life a work of art, amounts in our liquid-modern world to being in a state of permanent transformation, to perpetually redefining oneself through *becoming* someone other than one has been thus far; and "becoming someone else" amounts to *ceasing* to be what one has been, to breaking and shaking off one's old form, as a snake does its skin or a shellfish its carapace—rejecting and hoping to wipe out, one by one, the used-up, worn-out, too-tight, or just not as satisfying personae, as they are revealed to be in comparison with new and improved opportunities and offers. To put a new self on public display and to admire it in front of a mirror and in the eyes of others, one needs to remove the old self from one's own and the others' sight and possibly also from one's own and their memory. When "self-defining" and "self-asserting," we practice creative destruction. Daily.

To many people, particularly to the young ones who leave behind only few and mostly shallow traces, apparently easy to obliterate, this new edition of the art of life may well appear attractive and likeable. Admittedly, this is not without good reason. This new kind of art offers a long string of joys—apparently infinitely long. It promises, in addition, that those who seek this joyful, satisfying life will never suffer an ultimate, definitive, irrevocable defeat, that after every setback there will be a chance to recover, that they will be allowed to cut their losses and start again, "begin from the (new) beginning"—and thus win back or be fully recompensed for what has been lost through being "born again" (that is, through joining another—and, one hopes, more user-friendly and lucky—"only game in town"), so that the destructive bits in the successive acts of creative destruction can be easily forgotten and their bitter aftertaste quashed by the sweetness of new vistas and their yet untested promises.

Pressures are most difficult to resist, fight back, and repel when they do not resort to blatant coercion and do not threaten violence. A command—"You must do it (or you mustn't do it), or else . . ."—prompts resentment and breeds rebellion. In comparison, a suggestion—"You want it, you can get it, so go for it"—panders to the *amour de soi* constantly hungry for compliments, nourishes self-esteem, and encourages one to try—according to one's own will and for one's own pleasure.

In our society of consumers, the urge to replicate the style of life currently recommended by the latest market offers and praised by the markets' hired and voluntary spokespersons (and by implication, the compulsion to perpetually overhaul one's identity and public persona) has ceased to be associated with external (and thus offensive and annoying) coercion; the urge tends to be perceived, on the contrary, as another manifestation and proof of personal freedom. Only if one tries to opt out and retreat from the chase after elusive, forever unfinished identity—or if one is blackballed and chased away from the chase (a truly horrifying scenario) or refused admission a priori—will one learn just how powerful are the forces that manage the racetrack, guard the entries, and keep the runners running—and only then will one find out how severe is the punishment meted out to the hapless and insubordinate. That this is the case is known all too well to those who, for the lack of bank account and credit cards, can't afford the price of entry to the stadium. For many others still, all of this may be intuited from the dark premonitions that haunt them at night after a busy shopping day—or from the warning that goes off when their bank account falls into the red and their unused credit reaches zero.

Road signs marking life's trajectory appear and vanish nowadays with little or no warning; maps of the territory that the trajectory is likely to cross at some point are updated almost daily (albeit irregularly and without warning). Maps are printed and put on sale by many publishers and are available at any newsagent's in profusion, but none of them is "authorized" by an office credibly claiming control over that future; whichever map you choose, you are responsible and you choose at your own risk. In short, the life of the identity seekers/constructors/reformers is anything but short of troubles; their particular art of life demands much money, unremitting effort, and, on many an occasion, nerves of steel. No wonder, then, that despite all the joys and blissful moments it promises and time and again delivers, quite a few people do not view this life as a kind of life that they themselves, given genuine liberty of choice, would wish to practice.

It is often said of such people that they are indifferent if not downright hostile to freedom, or that they have not yet grown up and matured enough to enjoy it. Which implies that their nonparticipation in the style of life dominant in the liquid-modern society of consumers tends to be explained by either ideologically aroused resentment of freedom or the inability to practice it. Such an explanation, however, is at best only partially true. The frailty of all and any identities (even their insufficiently trustworthy solidity) burdens the identity seekers with the duty of attending to the job daily and intensely. What might have started as a conscious undertaking can turn, in the course of time, into a no-longer-reflected-upon routine, whereby the endlessly and ubiquitously repeated assertion that "you *can* make yourself into someone other than you are" is rephrased as "you *must* make yourself into someone other than you are."

It is this "must" that for many people does not sound tantamount to freedom, and it is for that reason that they resent this "must" and rebel against it. As the pressure of the "must" remains steady and overpowering, whether or not you possess the resources that "doing what you must" would require, the "must" sounds more like slavery and oppression than any imaginable avatar of liberty. One reader complained, in a letter to a highly regarded and widely read British daily, that "the four key items that are a must-have" for a respectable man in Spring 2007, recommended in the paper's "fashion" section (khaki trench, collarless shirt, V-neck sweater, and navy jacket), would cost a total of 1,499 pounds sterling. So—meal for some, poison for some (many? most?) others? If "to be free" means to be able to act on one's wishes and pursue the chosen objectives, the liquid-modern, consumerist version of the art of life may promise freedom to all, but it delivers it sparingly and selectively.

"As the need for public services has increased, American voters have come to favor reducing the supply of care that government provides, and many favor turning to the beleaguered family as a main source of care," notes Arlie Hochschild.[9] They find themselves, however, falling out of the frying pan into the fire.

The same consumerist pressures that associate the idea of "care" with an inventory of consumer commodities like orange juice, milk, frozen pizza, and microwave ovens strip the families of their social-ethical skills and resources and disarm them in their uphill struggle to cope with the new challenges—challenges aided and abetted by the legislators, who attempt to reduce state financial deficits through the expansion of the "care deficit" (cutting funds for single mothers, the disabled, the mentally ill, and the elderly).

A state is "social" when it promotes the principle of *communally endorsed,* collective insurance against individual misfortune and its consequences. It is primarily this principle—declared, set in operation, and trusted to be working—that recasts the otherwise abstract idea of "society" into the experience of a felt and lived community by replacing the "order of egoism" (to deploy John Dunn's terms), bound to generate an atmosphere of mutual mistrust and suspicion, with the confidence- and solidarity-inspiring "order of equality." It is the same principle that lifts members of society to the status of *citizens*—that is, makes them stakeholders in addition to being stockholders, beneficiaries but also actors—the wardens as much as wards of the "social benefits" system—individuals with an acute interest in the common good, which is understood as the network of shared institutions that can be trusted, and realistically expected, to guarantee the solidity and reliability of the state-issued "collective insurance policy."

The application of such a principle may, and often does, protect men and women from the plague of poverty; most important, however, it can become a profuse *source of solidarity,* able to recycle "society" into a common good, shared, communally owned, and jointly cared for, thanks to the defense it provides against the twin horrors of *misery* and *indignity*—that is, of the terrors of being excluded, of falling or being pushed overboard from a fast-accelerating vehicle of progress, of being condemned to "social redundancy," denied the respect owed to humans and otherwise designated to "human waste."

A "social state" was to be, in its original intention, an arrangement to serve precisely such purposes. Lord Beveridge, to whom we owe the blueprint for the postwar British welfare state, believed that his vision of comprehensive, collectively endorsed insurance for *everyone* was the inevitable consequence, or rather indispensable complement, of the Liberals' idea of individual *freedom,* as well as a necessary condition of *democracy.* Franklin Delano Roosevelt's declaration of war on fear was based on the same assumption. The assumption was reasonable: after all, freedom of choice can't but come together with uncounted and uncountable risks of failure, and many people are bound to find such risks unbearable, fearing that they may exceed their personal ability to cope. For many people, freedom of choice will remain an elusive phantom and idle dream, unless the fear of defeat is mitigated by the insurance policy issued in the name of community, a policy they can trust and rely on in case of personal failure or a freak blow of fate.

If freedom of choice is granted in theory but unattainable in practice, the pain of *hopelessness* will surely be topped with the ignominy of *haplessness*—as the daily test of one's ability to cope with life's challenges is the very workshop in which individuals' self-confidence and also their sense of human dignity and self-esteem are cast or melted away. Besides, without the collective insurance there would hardly be much stimulus for political engagement—and certainly not for participation in a democratic ritual of elections, as indeed no salvation is likely to arrive from a political state that is not, and refuses to be, a *social* state. Without social rights *for all,* a large and in all probability growing number of people would find their political rights useless and unworthy of their attention. If political rights are necessary to set *social* rights in place, social rights are indispensable to keep *political* rights in operation. The two rights need each other for their survival; that survival can be only their joint achievement.

The social state is the ultimate modern embodiment of the idea of community: that is, it is an institutional incarnation of the idea of community in its modern form—an abstract, imagined totality woven of reciprocal dependence, commitment, and solidarity. Social rights—rights to respect and dignity—tie that imagined totality to the daily realities of its members and base that imagined view on the solid ground of life experience; those rights certify, simultaneously, the veracity and realism of mutual trust *and* of the trust in the shared institutional network that endorses and validates collective solidarity.

The sentiment of "belonging" translates as trust in the benefits of human solidarity and in the institutions that arise out of that solidarity and promise to serve it and ensure its reliability. Quite recently, all those truths were spelled out in the Swedish Social Democratic Program of 2004:

> Everyone is fragile at some point in time. We need each other. We live our lives in the here and now, together with others, caught up in the midst of change. We will all be richer if all of us are allowed to participate and nobody is left out. We will all be stronger if there is security for everybody and not only for a few.

Just as the carrying power of a bridge is measured not by the average strength of its pillars but by the strength of the weakest pillar, and is built up from that strength, the confidence and resourcefulness of a society are measured by the security, resourcefulness, and self-confidence of its weakest sections, and it grows as they grow. Contrary to the assumption of the "third way" advocates, social justice and economic efficiency, loyalty to the social state tradition and the ability to modernize swiftly (and, most significantly, with little or no damage to the social cohesion and solidarity), need not be and are not at loggerheads. Rather, as the social-democratic practice of the Nordic countries amply demonstrates and confirms, "The pursuit of a more socially cohesive society is the necessary precondition for modernization by consent."[10]

Contrary to the grossly premature obituaries of what was promoted and heralded as the third way, the Scandinavian pattern is nowadays anything but a relic of past and now-frustrated hopes, or a blueprint dismissed by popular consent as outdated. One can see just how topical and how alive its underlying principles are, and how strong are its chances of inflaming human imagination and the inspiration to act, in the recent triumphs of the emergent or resurrected social states in Venezuela, Bolivia, Brazil, and Chile, which are gradually yet indefatigably changing the political landscape and popular mood of the Latin part of the Western Hemisphere, and are bearing all the marks of that "left hook" with which, as Walter Benjamin pointed out, all truly decisive blows have tended to be delivered in human history. However hard it may be to perceive this truth in the daily flow of consumerist routines, this is the truth nevertheless.

To avoid misunderstandings, let it be clear that the social state in the society of consumers is neither intended nor practiced as an alternative to the principle of consumer freedom—just as it was not meant, nor did it act, as an alternative to the work ethic in the society of producers. The countries with firmly established social-state principles and institutions in the society of consumers also happen to be the countries with impressively high levels of consumption, just as the countries with firmly established social-state principles and institutions in the societies of producers were also countries with thriving industry.

The purpose of the social state in the society of consumers is, just as it was in the society of producers, to defend society against the "collateral damage" that the guiding principle of life would cause if not monitored, controlled, and constrained. It is meant to protect society against the multiplying of the ranks of "collateral victims" of consumerism—the excluded, the outcasts, the underclass. Its task is to salvage human solidarity from erosion and to keep the sentiments of ethical responsibility from fading.

CHAPTER FOUR

Hurried Life, or Liquid-Modern Challenges to Education

◆

AN INFLUENTIAL AND widely read fashion handbook for the autumn-winter 2005 season offers "half a dozen key looks" "for the coming months" "that will put you ahead of the style pack." This promise is aptly, skillfully calculated to catch our attention: in a brief, crisp sentence it manages to address all the anxieties and urges bred by the society of consumers and born of the consuming life.

First, to be and to stay ahead (of the "style pack," that is, of those "significant others," the others who count, and whose approval or rejection draws the line between success and failure).[1] *Being* ahead is the sole trustworthy recipe for the style pack's acceptance, while *staying* ahead is the only way to make sure the supply of respect is comfortably ample and continuous. The offer promises, therefore, a guarantee of safety resting on self-confidence, of certainty or near certainty of "being in the right"—the kind of sensation that the consuming life most conspicuously, and painfully, misses, despite being guided by the desire to acquire it. The reference to being and staying ahead of the style pack promises belonging—being approved and included. "Ahead" implies safety from falling by the way-side: avoiding exclusion, abandonment, loneliness.

Second, the promise comes with a use-by date: you have been warned that it holds solely "for the coming months." The latent message is, "Hurry up—there is no time to waste." There is also an assumption of yet greater import: whatever your gain from promptly following the call, it won't last forever. Whatever insurance for safe sailing you acquire will need to be *renewed* once the "coming months" pass. So watch this space. As Milan Kundera observed in the novel appropriately called *Slowness,* there is a bond between speed and forgetting: "The degree of speed is directly proportional to the intensity of for-getting." Why so? Because if "taking over the stage requires keeping other people off it," taking over the stage that is public attention—the attention of the public earmarked to be recycled into consumers—requires keeping other objects of attention off it. "Stages," Kundera reminds us, "are floodlit only for the first few minutes."

Third, since there is not one look on offer but "half a dozen," you are free (that is, free to *choose* between *these* six). You can pick and choose your look. Choosing a look is not at issue (choosing as such, and bearing responsibility for your choice, you can't avoid), nor are the options you must choose from (there are no other options; all possibilities have already been discovered and preselected). But never mind the pressure of time, the necessity to curry the favor of the style pack, and the limited number of choices you can make (only half a dozen). What matters is that *it is you who are now in charge.* And be in charge you must: Choice is yours, but making choices is obliga-tory, and the limits on what you are allowed to choose are non-negotiable.

All three messages together announce the state of emergency. Emergency itself is no news, to be sure (only the assurances that the vigilance, the constant readiness to go where one must go, the money spent, and the labors done are sure to be right and proper are added to reassure the anxious). Alert signals (orange? red?) are switched on and announce that new beginnings full of promise lie ahead, along with new risks full of threats. The point is, now as before, never to miss the moment for action, lest one find oneself behind instead of ahead of the style pack. And that taking action while relying on implements and routines that worked in the past won't do. The consuming life is a life of *rapid learning—and swift forgetting.*

Forgetting is as important as learning, if not more. There is a "must not" for every "must," and which of the two reveals the true objective of the breathtaking pace of renewal/removal, and which one is but an auxiliary measure to ensure that the objective is attained, is a moot question at best. The kind of information and instruction likely to crop up most profusely in this fashion handbook and in the scores of similar ones is that "the destination *this autumn* is 1960s Carnaby Street," or that "the current trend for gothic is perfect *for this month.*" This autumn is, of course, not last summer, and *this* month is not like *past* months, and so what was perfect last month is no longer perfect for this one, just as last summer's destination is no longer this autumn's destination. "Ballet pumps?" "Time to put them away." "Spaghetti straps?" "They have no place this season." "Biros?" "The world is a better place without them." The call to "open up your makeup bag and take a look inside" is likely to be followed with an exhortation such as, "*The coming season* is all about rich colors," followed closely by the warning that "beige and its safe-but-dull relatives have had their day . . . Chuck it out, *right now.*" Obviously, "dull beige" can't be pasted on the face simultaneously with "deep rich colors," and one of the palettes must give way.

But what is all this about? Must you "chuck out" the beige in order to make your face ready to receive deep rich colors, or are the deep rich colors bursting from the supermarket shelves and cosmetics counters in order to make sure that the bagful of unused beige supplies is indeed chucked out right away? The millions chucking the beige out and refilling their bag with deep rich colors would most probably say that the beige consigned to the rubbish heap is a sad side-effect, or "collateral casualty," of makeup progress. Yet some of the thousands who restock the supermarket shelves might possibly admit in a moment of truth that overflowing the shelves with rich deep colors was prompted by the need to shorten the beige's useful life and so to keep the economy going. Both explanations will be right. Is not GNP, the official index of the nation's well-being, measured by the amount of money changing hands? Is not economic growth propelled by the energy and activity of *consumers?* Is not a "traditional consumer," a shopper who shops only to meet his or her "needs" and stops once those needs have been met, the greatest danger to the consumer markets? Is not the bolstering of *demand,* rather than the satisfying of needs, the prime purpose and the flywheel of consumerist prosperity? In a society of consumers and in the era of life politics' replacing Politics with a capital *P,* the true economic cycle, the one that truly keeps the economy going, is the cycle of "buy it, use it, chuck it out."

The fact that two such ostensibly contradictory answers may both be right at the same time is precisely the greatest feat of the society of consumers and the key to its astounding capacity to reproduce and expand itself.

The consuming life is not about acquiring and possessing. It is not even about getting rid of what had been acquired the day before yesterday and was proudly paraded a day later. It is, first and foremost, about *being on the move.* If Max Weber was right and the ethical principle of the producing life was (and is, whenever a life wishes to become a producing life) the delay of gratification, the ethical principle of the consuming life (if its ethics could be at all frankly articulated) would be about the *fallaciousness of resting satisfied.* The major threat to a society that announces "customer satisfaction" to be its motive and purpose is a satisfied consumer. To be sure, the "satisfied consumer" would be a catastrophe to herself or himself as grave and horrifying as it would be to the consumerist economy. Having nothing more to desire? Nothing to chase after? Left to what one has (and so what one is)? Nothing vies any longer for a place on the stage of attention, and so there is nothing to push the memory off the stage and clear the site for "new beginnings." Such a condition—hopefully short-lived—would be called boredom. The nightmares that haunt *Homo consumens* are memories outstaying their welcome and cluttering the stage.

Rather than the creation of *new needs* (some call them "artificial needs"—though wrongly, since a degree of artificiality is not a unique feature of "new" needs; while using natural predispositions as their raw material, all needs in any society are given form by the "artifice" of sociocultural patterns and pressures), it is the playing down, derogation, ridicule, and uglification of *yesterday's needs* (beige makeup, the sign of last season's boldness, is not just out of fashion now, but dull and indeed shameful, since cowardly: "This is not makeup—it's a security blanket") and, even more, the discrediting of the idea that the consuming life ought to be guided by the satisfaction of needs, that constitutes the major preoccupation and, as Talcott Parsons would have said, the "functional prerequisite" of the society of consumers. In that society, those who go solely by what they believe they need, and are activated only by the urge to satisfy those needs, are *flawed consumers* and so also *social outcasts.*

The secret of every durable—that is, successfully self-repro-ducing—social system is the recasting of "functional prerequi-sites" into behavioral motives for actors. To put it a different way: the secret of all successful "socialization" is making the individuals *wish to do* what the system *needs them to do* for it to reproduce itself. This may be done explicitly—by muster-ing popular support for, and in direct reference to, the declared interests of a "whole," like a state or a nation, through a pro-cess variously dubbed "spiritual mobilization," "civic educa-tion," and "ideological indoctrination"—as it was commonly done in the solid phase of modernity, in the society of produc-ers. Or this may be done obliquely, through an overt or covert imposition or drilling-in of appropriate behavioral patterns. And also through problem-solving patterns, which once ob-served (as observed they must be, because of the receding and vanishing of alternative choices and of the skills needed to practice them), sustain the system—as it is done in the liquid phase, in the society of consumers.

The explicit way of tying together systemic prerequisites and individual motives typical of the society of producers re-quired the devaluation of the "now"—in particular, immediate satisfaction, and more generally, enjoyment (or rather, the de-valuation of what the French entail in the virtually untranslat-able concept of *jouissance*). By the same token, that way also necessarily had to enthrone the precept of delayed gratifica-tion—that is, the sacrifice of specific present rewards in the name of imprecise future benefits, as well as the sacrifice of in-dividual rewards for the benefit of the "whole" (be it society, state, nation, class, gender, or just a deliberately underspecified "we")—that would secure in due course a better life for all. In a society of producers, the long term is given priority over the short term, and the needs of the whole over the needs of its parts—and thus the joys and satisfactions derived from "eternal" and "supraindividual" values are cast as superior to fleeting individual raptures, and the happiness of a greater number is put above the plight of a smaller one. These are seen as, in fact, the only *genuine and worthy* satisfactions amid the multitude of seductive but false, deceptive, *contrived,* and *degrading* "pleasures of the moment."

Wise after the fact, we (men and women whose lives are conducted in the liquid-modern setting) are inclined to dismiss that way of dovetailing systemic reproduction with individual motivation as wasteful, exorbitantly costly, and, above all, abominably oppressive because it goes against the grain of the "natural" human proclivity and propensity. Sigmund Freud was one of the first thinkers to note this; though gathering his data, as he had to, from a life lived on the rising slope of the society of mass industry and mass conscription, even that exquisitely imaginative thinker was unable to conceive of an alternative to the coercive suppression of instincts.[2] To what he observed, Freud ascribed the generic status of necessary and unavoidable features of all and any civilization—of civilization "as such."

Freud concluded that the demand of instinct-renunciation would not be willingly embraced. A great majority of humans, he insisted, obey many of the cultural prohibitions (or precepts) "only under the pressure of external coercion"—and "it is alarming to think of the enormous amount of coercion that will inevitably be required" to promote, instill, and make safe the necessary civilizing choices such as, for instance, work ethics (that is, a wholesale condemnation of leisure coupled with the commandment to work for the work's sake, whatever the

material rewards), or the ethics of peaceful cohabitation pre-
scribed by the commandment, "Thou shalt love thy neighbor
as thyself." ("What is the point of a precept enunciated with
so much solemnity," Freud asks rhetorically, "if its fulfilment
cannot be recommended as reasonable?") The rest of Freud's
case is too well known to be restated here in any detail: civilization must be sustained by repression, and repeated re-
bellions, as well as continuous efforts to hold them down, or
preempt them, are inescapable. Dissent and mutiny cannot be
avoided, since all civilization means constraint and all constraint is repulsive. "The replacement of the power of the individual by the power of community constitutes the decisive step
of civilization. The essence of it lies in the fact that the members of the community restrict themselves in their possibilities
of satisfaction, whereas the individual knew no such restric-
tion."

Let's leave aside the caveat that "the individual" who is not
already a "member of the community" may be an even more
mythical figure than Hobbes's presocial savage of the *bellum
omnium contra omnes,* or be just a rhetorical device "for the
sake of argument" (like the famous "original patricide" that
would crop up in Freud's later work). For whichever reason
the particular wording of the message was chosen, the substance of the message is that putting the interests of a
supraindividual group above the individual inclinations and
impulses, as well as placing the long-term effects above the immediate satisfactions in the case of work ethics, is unlikely to
be willingly acknowledged, embraced, and obeyed by the hoi
polloi; and that the civilization (or, for that matter, peaceful
and cooperative human cohabitation with all its benefits) that
deploys such precepts to legitimate its demands must rest on
coercion, or at least on a realistic threat that coercion would be
applied if the restrictions imposed on instinctual urges were

not punctiliously observed. If civilized human togetherness is to persist, the "reality principle" must be, by hook or by crook, assured an upper hand over the "pleasure principle."

Freud reprojects that conclusion on all types of human togetherness (retrospectively renamed "civilizations")—presenting it as a universal law of life in society. But whatever answer is given to the question of whether or not the repression of instincts was indeed coterminous with the history of humanity, one can credibly suggest that it could have been discovered, named, put on record, and theorized upon only at the dawn of the modern era; more to the point, only following the disintegration of the ancien régime that immediately preceded it, that sustained a by-and-large monotonous (indeed, sufficiently unproblematic to remain unnoticed and perhaps unnoticeable) reproduction of the customary rights and duties. It was the failure of such reproduction that laid bare the human-made artifice hiding behind the idea of the "natural" or "Divine" order, and so forced the reclassification of that order from the category of the "given" to the category of "tasks," thus re-representing the *logic* of *Divine* creation as an *achievement* of *human* power.[3]

"Power of community" did not have to *replace* "the power of the individual" to make human cohabitation feasible and viable; power of community was in place long before its necessity, let alone its urgency, was discovered. Indeed, the idea that such replacement was a task yet to be performed by one or the other power holder, collective or individual, would hardly occur to either the individual or the community so long as that was the case. Community, as it were, held power over the individual (a total, "everything included" kind of power) so long as it remained *unproblematic,* and not a task (as all tasks) in which it could succeed or fail. To put it in a nutshell, community held individuals in its grip so long as it remained *unaware* of "being a community."

Turning the subordination of individual powers to those of a community into a need waiting to be met reversed the logic of modern development. At the same time, however, by "naturalizing" what was in fact a historical process, it generated in one fell swoop its own legitimation and an etiological myth of the ancient, presocial collection of free-floating, solitary individuals who, once upon a time, came to be transmogrified, through civilizing effort, into a community bidding for the authority to trim and repress such individual predispositions as had been revealed and declared to be contrary to the requirements of secure cohabitation.

Community might be as old as humanity, but the idea of "community" as a condition sine qua non for humanity could be born only through the experience of its crisis. That idea was patched together out of the fears emanating from the disintegration of the self-reproducing social settings retrospectively called the ancien régime and recorded in the social-scientific vocabulary under the rubric of "traditional society." The *modern* "civilizing process" (the only process calling itself by that name) was triggered by the state of uncertainty for which the falling apart and impotence of "community" was one of the suggested explanations.

"Nation," that eminently modern innovation, was visualized in the likeness of community: it was to be "like the community," or a new community—but a community-by-design, a community expanded and stretched to unprecedented volume, made to the measure of the newly extended network of human interdependencies and exchanges. What was later to be named the "civilizing process" (at the time when the developments to which that name referred were grinding to a halt or apparently shifting into reverse!) was a steady attempt to re-pattern and re-regularize, by new means pursued by new strategies, the human conduct no longer subjected to the homogenizing pressures of self-reproducing premodern institutions. Ostensibly, that process was focused on individuals: the new capacity for self-control in the newly autonomous *individual* was to take over the job done before by the no-longer-available *social* controls. But what was genuinely at stake was the deployment of the self-controlling capacity of individuals in the service of re-enacting or reconstituting the "community" at a new, much higher level.

Just as the ghost of the lost Roman Empire hovered over the formation of feudal Europe, the specter of lost community soared over the constitution of modern nations. Nation building was accomplished with patriotism, an induced (taught/learned) readiness to sacrifice individual interests to the interests shared with other individuals ready to do the same, as its principal raw material. As Ernest Renan famously summed up the strategy: a nation is (or rather can live only by) the daily plebiscite of its members.

When setting about restoring the historicity absent from Freud's extemporal model of civilization, Norbert Elias explained the birth of the modern self (that awareness of one's own "inner truth," coupled with the acceptance of one's own responsibility to assert it) by the internalization of external constraints and their pressures. The nation-building process was inscribed in the space extending between supraindividual panoptic powers and the individual's capacity to accommodate him- or herself to the necessities that those powers set in place. The newly acquired individual *freedom of choice* (including the choice of self-identity) resulting from the unprecedented underdetermination of social placement caused by the demise or advanced emaciation of traditional bonds was to be deployed, paradoxically, in the service of the *suppression of choices* deemed detrimental to the "new totality": the community-like nation-state.

Whatever its pragmatic merits, the panopticon-style, "discipline, punish, and rule" way of achieving the needed/intended manipulation and routinization of behavioral probabilities was, however, cumbersome, costly, and conflict-ridden. It was also inconvenient, and surely not the best choice for the power holders, as it imposed severe and nonnegotiable constraints on the rulers' freedom of maneuver; as it transpired later, alternative and less-awkward strategies could be devised through which systemic stability, better known under the name "social order," could be achieved and made secure. It was because they had identified "civilization" as having a centralized system of coercion and indoctrination (later reduced, under Michel Foucault's influence, to its coercive wing) that social scientists were left with little choice except to, misleadingly, describe the advent of the "postmodern condition" (which coincided with the entrenchment of the society of consumers) as a product of the "de-civilizing process." What in fact happened was the discovery, invention, or emergence of an *alternative* method of civilizing (a less cumbersome, less costly, and relatively less conflict-ridden method, but above all, one that gives more freedom, and so more power, to the power holders)—an alternative way of manipulating the behavioral probabilities necessary to sustain the system of domination represented as social order. Another variety of the civilizing process, an alternative and apparently more convenient way in which the task of that process can be pursued, was found and set in place.

This new variety of the civilizing process, practiced by the liquid-modern society of consumers, arouses little if any dissent, resistance, or rebellion as it represents the *obligation* to choose as *freedom* of choice; by the same token, it overrides the opposition between "pleasure" and "reality" principles. Submission to the stern demands of reality may be experienced as an exercise of freedom, and indeed as an act of self-assertion. Punishing force, if applied, is seldom naked; it comes disguised as the result of a false step or lost (overlooked) opportunity, and far from bringing into the light the limits of individual freedom, it hides them yet more securely by obliquely entrenching individual choice in its role as the main, perhaps even the only, "difference that makes a difference" between victory and defeat in the individual pursuit of happiness.

The "totality" to which the individual should stay loyal and obedient no longer enters individual life in the shape of obligatory sacrifice (of the universal-conscription kind—of a duty to surrender individual interests, including one's own survival, to the survival and welfare of a "whole," of the country and the national cause), but in the form of highly entertaining, invariably pleasurable and relished festivals of communal togetherness and belonging, held on the occasion of a soccer World Cup or a cricket test. Surrendering to the "totality" is no longer a reluctantly embraced, discomforting, cumbersome, and often onerous duty but an avidly sought and eminently enjoyable entertainment.

Carnivals, as Mikhail Bakhtin memorably suggested, tend to be interruptions in the daily routine, the brief exhilarating intervals between successive installments of dull quotidianity, a pause in which the mundane hierarchy of values is temporarily reversed, most harrowing aspects of reality are for a brief time suspended, and the kinds of conduct considered shameful and prohibited in "normal" life are ostentatiously and with delight practiced and brandished in the open. If, during the old-style carnivals, it was the individual liberties denied in daily life that were put unashamedly on public display and ecstatically enjoyed, now it is a time to shelve the burdens and quash the anguishes of individuality through dissolving oneself in a "greater whole" and joyously abandoning oneself to its rule, while submerging in the tide of an undifferentiated sameness. The function (and seductive power) of the liquid-modern carnival lies in the momentary resuscitation of sunk-in-a-coma togetherness. Such carnivals are akin to "rain dances" and séances during which people join hands and summon the ghost of deceased community. Not an insignificant part of their charm is the awareness that the ghost will pay but a fleeting visit and will promptly go away, out of sight, once the séance is over.

All this does not mean that the "normal," weekday conduct of the individuals has become random, unpatterned, and uncoordinated. It means only that the nonrandomness, regularity, and coordination of individually undertaken actions can be, and as a rule are, attained by means other than the solid-modern contraptions of enforcement, policing, and chain of command, of a totality bidding for being "greater than the sum of its parts" and bent on training or drilling its "human units" into discipline.

The consumerist economy lives by the turnover of commodities and is booming when more money changes hands. Money changes hands whenever consumer products are hauled to the dump. Accordingly, in a society of consumers the pursuit of happiness tends to be refocused from *making* things or *acquiring* them to *disposing of* them—just as it should if one wants the gross national product to keep growing. For the consumerist economy, the first and now abandoned focus of consumption (appeal to the needs) portends ill: the suspension of shopping. The second (appeal to forever-elusive happiness) bodes well: it augurs another round of shopping.

Big companies specializing in selling "durable goods" have accepted that much. These days they seldom charge their customers for *delivery*—much more frequently they demand payment for the *disposal* of the customers' old "durable goods," converted by the new and improved durable goods from a source of joy and pride into an eyesore, a blot on the homescape, and altogether a stigma of shame. It is getting rid of such burdens that promises to make one happy, and happiness needs to be paid for. Just think of disposing of the waste in transit from the UK, where the volume, as Lucy Siegle reports, will soon pass 1.5 million metric tons.[4]

Big companies specializing in selling "personal services" focused on the client's body have followed suit. What they advertise most avidly and sell for the largest financial gains are the services of excision, removal, and disposal: of body fat, face wrinkles, acne, body odors, post-this or post-that depressions, the oodles of yet unnamed mysterious fluids or undigested leftovers of past feasts that settle illegitimately inside the body and won't leave unless forced, and whatever else can be detached or squeezed and disposed of. As to the big firms specializing in bringing people together, such as the America Online (AOL) Internet dating service, they tend to stress the facility with which clients who use their services can get rid of unwanted company, or prevent that company from becoming difficult to dispose of. When offering their go-between assistance, they stress that the "online dating experience" is "safe"—while warning that "if you feel uncomfortable about a member, stop contacting them. You can block them so you will not get unwanted messages." AOL supplies a long list of "arrangements for a safe offline date." Such appeals and promises are clearly in tune with the spirit of the time: as Helen Haste, professor of psychology at the University of Bath, found out, a third of questioned boys and nearly a fourth of girls saw nothing wrong in ending a relationship with a mobile-telephone text mes-sage.[5] These numbers, as one would guess, are bound to have grown further since: the number of mobile-telephone mes-sages that make cumbersome face-to-face negotiations redun-dant shot up in the UK from zero to 2.25 million per month in a matter of five years. Increasingly, it appears, text messages are being recognized as the most convenient way of preventing the chore and agony of breaking up from turning acrimonious and too time- and labor-intensive.

It seems to be but a small step for a man, though a gigan-tic one for mankind, that leads from the here and now to which the hurried, emergency culture of consumerist society has already brought us, to the exporting of *human* waste (or, so to speak, "wasted humans"): transporting the undesirable—that is, the humans charged with the guilt or crime of un-desirability—to faraway places, where they can be safely tor-tured until they confess that they have been indeed guilty as charged.[6]

In a book with a says-it-all title, Thomas Hylland Eriksen iden-tifies the "tyranny of the moment" as the most conspicuous feature of contemporary society and arguably its most semi-nal novelty: "The consequences of extreme hurriedness are overwhelming: both the past and the future as mental catego-ries are threatened by the tyranny of the moment . . . Even the 'here and now' is threatened since the next moment comes so quickly that it becomes difficult to live in the present."[7]

This is a paradox indeed, and an inexhaustible source of ten-sion: the more voluminous and capacious becomes the mo-ment, the smaller (briefer) it is; as its potential contents swell, its dimensions shrink. "There are strong indications that we are about to create a kind of society where it becomes nearly impossible to think a thought that is more than a couple of inches long."[8] But contrary to the popular hopes beefed up by the consumer-market promises, changing one's identity, were it at all plausible, would require much more than that.

While undergoing the "punctuation" treatment, the moment is thereby cut off on both sides. Its interfaces with both the past and the future turn into gaps—hopefully unbridgeable. Ironically, in the age of instant and effortless connection and the promise of being constantly "in touch," communication between the experience of the moment and whatever may precede or follow it needs to be permanently, and hopefully irreparably, broken. The gap behind should see to it that the past is never allowed to catch up with the running self. The gap ahead is a condition of living the moment to the fullest, of abandoning oneself totally and unreservedly to its (admittedly fleeting) charm and seductive powers—something that wouldn't be feasible were the currently lived-through moment contaminated with worry about mortgaging the future. Ideally, each moment would be shaped after the pattern of credit card use, a radically depersonalized act: in the absence of face-to-face intercourse it is easier to forget, or rather never to think in the first place, of the unpleasantness of repayment. No wonder the banks, eager to get cash moving and so earning yet more money than it would while lying idle, prefer to have their clients fingering credit cards instead of visiting branch managers.

Following Bertman's terminology, Elżbieta Tarkowska, a most prominent chronosociologist in her own right, develops the concept of "synchronic humans" who "live solely in the present," who "pay no attention to past experience or future consequences of their actions"—a strategy that "translates into absence of bonds with the others." The "presentist culture" "puts a premium on speed and effectiveness, while favoring neither patience nor perseverance."[9]

We may add that it is such frailty and the apparently easy

disposability of individual identities and interhuman bonds that are represented in contemporary culture as the substance of individual freedom. One choice that such freedom would neither recognize, grant, nor allow is the resolve (or indeed the ability) to persevere in holding to the identity, once constructed—that is, in the kind of activity that presumes, and necessarily entails, the preservation and security of the social network on which that identity rests, while actively reproducing it.

To serve all these new needs, urges, compulsions, and addictions, as well as to service new mechanisms motivating, guiding, and monitoring human conduct, the consumerist economy must rely on *excess* and *waste*.

The speed with which the cavalcade of novelties dashes along in order to overshoot any target made to the measure of the already recorded demand must be so mind-boggling as to cast the prospect of taming and assimilating innovations well beyond the ordinary human's capacity. In the consumerist economy, products as a rule appear first and only then seek their applications; many of them travel to the dumping site without finding any. But even the lucky few products that manage to find or conjure up a need, a desire, or a wish for which they might demonstrate themselves to be (or eventually to become) relevant soon tend to succumb to the pressure of "new and improved" products (that is, products that promise to do all they can do, only quicker and better—with an extra bonus of doing a few things that no consumer has as yet thought of needing and intended to buy) well before their working capacity reaches the point of its preordained exhaustion. As Eriksen points out, most of the life aspects and the life-servicing gadgets grow at an *exponential rate*—whereas in each case of exponential growth, a point must be reached when the offer exceeds the capacity of the genuine or contrived demand; more often than not that point arrives before another, more dramatic point, the point of the natural limit to supply, has been reached.

Such pathological (and eminently wasteful) tendencies of any and all exponentially growing output of goods and services could conceivably be spotted in time and be recognized for what they are, and could perhaps even manage to inspire remedial or preventive measures—if not for one more, and in many ways special, exponential process, which results in the *excess of information*. As Ignazio Ramonet points out, during the past thirty years, more information has been produced in the world than during the previous 5,000 years, while "a single copy of the Sunday edition of the *New York Times* contains more information than a cultivated person in the eighteenth century would consume during a lifetime."[10] Just how difficult, nay impossible, to absorb and assimilate—and how endemically wasteful—such a volume of information is, one can glean, for instance, from Eriksen's observation that "more than a half of all published journal articles in the social sciences are never quoted," and that many articles are never read by anyone except the "anonymous peer reviewers" and copy editors.[11] It is anybody's guess how small a fraction of their content manages to find its way into the social-sciences discourse.

"There is far too much information around," Eriksen concludes. "A crucial skill in information society consists in protecting oneself against the 99.99 per cent of the information offered that one does not want."[12] We may say that the line separating a meaningful message, the ostensible object of communication, from background noise, its acknowledged adversary and obstacle, has all but disappeared. In the cut-throat competition for that scarcest of scarce resources, the attention of would-be consumers, the suppliers of would-be consumer goods desperately search for the scraps of consumers' time still lying fallow, for the tiniest gaps between moments of consumption that could still be stuffed with more information—in the (vain) hope that some section of the Internauts at the receiving end of the communication channel will, in the course of their desperate search for the bits of information they need, come by chance across the bits that *they* don't need but the *suppliers* wish them to absorb, and that they will be sufficiently impressed to pause or slow down enough to absorb those bits instead of the bits they had originally sought.

Picking up fragments of the noise and molding them, kneading and converting them into meaningful messages, is by and large a random process. "Hypes," those products of the PR industry meant to separate "desirable objects of attention" from the nonproductive (read: unprofitable) noise (like the full-page advertisements announcing a premiere of a new film, the launching of a new book, the broadcasting of a TV show heavily subscribed by the advertisers, or an opening of a new exhibition), serve to divert for a moment and channel in a direction chosen by promoters the continuous and desperate, yet rambling and scattered, search for "filters," and focus attention, for a few minutes or a few days, on a selected object of consuming desire.

Moments are few, however, in comparison with the number of contenders, who in all probability also multiply at an exponential rate. Hence the phenomenon of "vertical stacking"—a notion coined by Bill Martin to account for the amazing piling up of musical styles—as gaps and fallow plots have been or are about to be all filled to overflowing by the ever-rising tide of supplies, while promoters struggle feverishly to stretch them beyond capacity.[13] The images of "linear time" and "progress" were among the most prominent victims of the information flood. In the case of popular music, all imaginable retro styles, together with all conceivable forms of recycling and plagiarism that count on the short span of public memory to masquerade as the latest novelties, find themselves crowded into one limited span of music fans' attention. The case of popular music is just one manifestation of a virtually universal tendency that affects in equal measure all areas of life serviced by the consumer industry. To quote Eriksen once more: "Instead of ordering knowledge in tidy rows, information society offers cascades of decontextualized signs more or less randomly connected to each other . . . Put differently: when growing amounts of information are distributed at growing speed, it becomes increasingly difficult to create narratives, orders, developmental sequences. The fragments threaten to become hegemonic. This has consequences for the ways we relate to knowledge, work and lifestyle in a wide sense."[14]

The tendency to take a "blasé attitude" toward "knowledge, work, and lifestyle" (indeed, toward life as such and everything it contains) had been noted by Georg Simmel, with astonishing foresight, at the start of the last century, as surfacing first among the residents of the "metropolis"—the big and crowded modern city: "The essence of the blasé attitude consists in the blunting of discrimination. This does not mean that the objects are not perceived, as is the case with the half-wit, but rather that the meaning and differing values of things, and thereby the things themselves, are experienced as insubstantial. They appear to the blasé person in an evenly flat and grey tone; no one object deserves preference over any other . . . All things float with equal specific gravity in the constantly moving stream of money."[15]

Something like a fully fledged version of the tendency Simmel spotted and described, so to speak, *avant la lettre*— an ever more salient phenomenon strikingly similar to that discovered and dissected by Simmel and that he called "blasé attitude"—is currently discussed under a different name, that of melancholy. Writers who use this term tend to bypass Simmel's augury and foreboding and go even further back, to the point where the ancients, like Aristotle, left it and the Renaissance thinkers, like Ficino and Milton, rediscovered and reexamined it. In Rolland Munro's rendering, the concept of melancholy in its current use "represents not so much a state of indecision, a wavering between the choice of going one way or another, so much as it represents a backing off from the very divisions"; it stands for a "disentanglement" from "being attached to anything specific." To be melancholic is "to sense the infinity of connection, but be hooked up to nothing." In short, melancholy refers to "a form without content, a refusal from knowing just *this* or just *that*."[16] I would suggest that the idea of "melancholy" stands in the last account for the generic affliction of the consumer, *Homo eligens* (man choosing), by behest of the consumer society, resulting from the fatal coincidence of the compulsion/addiction of choosing with the inability to choose. To repeat after Simmel, it stands for the inbuilt transitoriness and contrived insubstantiality of things that surf with the same specific gravity over the tide of stimulations; insubstantiality that rebounds in consumer behavior as indiscriminate, omnivorous gluttony—that most radical, ultimate form of hedging bets and a last-resort life strategy, considering the "pointillization" of time and the unavailability of the criteria that would allow consumers to separate the relevant from the irrelevant and the message from the noise.

That humans at all times prefer happiness to unhappiness is a banal observation, or, more correctly, a pleonasm, since the concept of "happiness" in its most common uses refers to the states or events that humans desire, while "unhappiness" stands for the states or events humans desire to avoid; both "happiness" and "unhappiness" refer to a distance between reality as it is and reality as it is wished to be. For that reason, all attempts to compare degrees of happiness experienced by people living in spatially or temporally separate forms of life are idle efforts.

Indeed, if people A spent their lives in a different sociocultural setting from that in which people B lived, it is vain to pronounce which one of them was "happier" than the other; as the sentiment of happiness or its absence depends on hopes and expectations, as well as on the learned habits admittedly different in different settings, what is meat for people A may well be poison for people B; if transported to conditions known to make people A happy, people B may feel excruciatingly miserable, and vice versa. And as we know from Freud: the end to toothache makes one happy, but nonpainful teeth hardly do. The best we can expect from comparisons that ignore the factor of unshared experience is information about the time- or place-bound proclivity to complain or tolerance of suffering.

For those reasons, the question of whether the liquid-modern consumerist revolution has made people happier or less happy than, say, people who spent their lives in the solid-modern society of producers or even in the premodern era is as moot as a question can be; in all probability it will remain moot forever. Whatever assessment is made, it makes sense and sounds convincing solely in the context of preferences specific to the assessors, since the registers of blessings and banes must be composed according to the notions of bliss and misery dominant at the time when the inventory is conducted.

Relations between two compared populations are doubly and hopelessly asymmetrical. The assessors never lived nor *would live* (as distinct from paying a brief visit, while retaining the special status of visitors/tourists for the duration of the trip) under conditions normal to the assessed, while the assessed would never have a chance to respond to the assessors' assessment; and even if they had such a (posthumous) chance, they would not be able to present an opinion of the relative virtues of a totally unfamiliar setting of which they did not have first-hand experience. And so, since the judgments pronounced on the (frequent) relative advantages or (infrequent) disadvantages of the society of consumers' happiness-generating capacity are devoid of cognitive value (except for the insight they offer into the outspoken or implicit values of their authors), one is well advised to focus on the data that may shed light on that society's ability to live up to *its own* promise; in other words, to evaluate its performance by the values it itself promotes while promising to facilitate the effort of their acquisition.

The value most characteristic of the society of consumers, indeed the metavalue, the supreme value in relation to which all other values are called to justify their worth, is *happy life*. Our society of consumers is perhaps the only society in human history that promises happiness in *earthly life*, and happiness *here and now*, in every successive "now"—an undelayed and continuous happiness—and the only society that refrains from justifying any variety of *un*happiness, refuses to tolerate it, and presents it as an abomination that calls for punishment of the culprits and compensation for the victims. The question, "Are you happy?" addressed to members of the liquid-modern society of consumers has therefore a status hardly similar to the same question addressed to members of societies that did not make such promises and commitments. More than any other society, the society of consumers stands and falls by the happiness of its members. The answers they give to the question, "Are you happy?" may be viewed as the ultimate test of the consumer society's success and failure.

By now, the answers are fully predictable—and the verdict they insinuate is not at all flattering. And this is true on two counts.

The first: as the evidence collected by Richard Layard in his book on happiness suggests, it is up to only a certain threshold (coinciding with the point of providing for the "essential" or "natural" needs, "survival needs"—the very motives for consumption that the society of consumers denigrated as the source of demand and on which it declared war, aiming to substitute desires and impulsive wishes for needs) that the sentiment of being happy grows with the increments of income (and so also with the intensifications of consumerist bustle). Above that fairly modest threshold, the correlation between wealth (and so presumably the level of consumption) and happiness vanishes. More income does not add happiness. What such findings suggest is that, contrary to its official and most often restated *plaidoyer,* "consumption for consumption's sake," consumption as an autotelic activity and a source of happiness in its own right ("the hedonic treadmill," in Layard's terminology), fails to increase the sum total of satisfaction among its practitioners. The happiness-enhancing capacity of consumption is fairly limited; it can't easily be stretched beyond the level of the satisfaction of "basic needs," as famously defined by Abraham Maslow.

The second: there is no evidence whatsoever that with the overall growth of the volume of consumption, the number of people reporting that they "feel happy" grows. Andrew Oswald of the *Financial Times* suggests that the opposite tendency is more likely to be recorded.[17] His conclusion is that the highly developed, well-off countries with consumption-driven economies have not become happier as they've grown richer and as consumerist preoccupations and activities have grown more voluminous. It may be also noted, at the same time, that negative phenomena, causes of discomfort and unhappiness such as stress or depression, long and unsocial working hours, deteriorating relationships, lack of confidence, and nerve-racking uncertainty about "being in the right" and secure, tend to increase in both their frequency and their overall volume.

The case for rising consumption, in its plea to be recognized as the royal road to the greatest happiness of the greatest numbers, has not been proved, let alone closed: it stays wide open. Indeed, as deliberations of the facts of the matter proceed, the evidence in favor of the plaintiff grows thinner and more dubious. In the course of the trial, more serious doubts have been raised: is it not, rather, the case that, in opposition to the plaintiff's argument, a consumption-oriented economy actively promotes disaffection, saps confidence, and deepens the sentiment of insecurity—the major factors behind the insecurity and ambient fear saturating liquid-modern life and the principal causes of the liquid-modern variety of unhappiness?

While consumer society rests its case on the promise to gratify human desires like no other society in the past could do or dream of doing, the promise of satisfaction remains seductive only so long as the desire stays *ungratified*. More important, it tempts only so long as the client is not "completely satisfied"— so long as the desires that motivate the consumers to further consumerist experiments are not believed to have been truly and fully gratified. Just as the easily satisfied "traditional worker" (a worker who wished to work no more than absolutely necessary to allow his habitual way of life to continue) was the nightmare of the budding society of producers, so the traditional consumer, guided by yesterday's familiar needs and immune to seduction, would (were she or he allowed to survive) sound the death knell of a mature society of consumers, consumer industry, and consumer markets. Setting targets low, ensuring easy access to the goods that meet the targets, and a belief in objective limits to "genuine" and "realistic" desires are the major adversaries of consumer-oriented economy earmarked for extinction. It is the *non*satisfaction of desires, and a firm and perpetual belief that each act of their satisfaction *leaves much to be desired and can be bettered,* that are the genuine flywheels of the consumer-targeted economy.

Consumer society thrives so long as it manages to render dissatisfaction (and so, in its own terms, unhappiness) permanent. One way of achieving this effect is to denigrate and devalue consumer products shortly after they have been hyped into the universe of consumers' desires. But another way, yet more effective, tends by and large to be kept out of the limelight: the satisfying of every need/desire/want in such a fashion that cannot help giving birth to new needs/desires/wants. What starts as a need must end up as a compulsion or an addiction. And it does, as the urge to seek in shops, and in shops only, solutions to problems and relief from pain and anxiety turns into a behavior that is not just allowed but eagerly encouraged as a habit.

The realm of hypocrisy stretching between popular beliefs and the realities of consumers' lives is therefore a necessary condition of the properly functioning society of consumers. If the search for fulfillment is to go on and if the new promises are to be alluring and catching, promises already made must be routinely broken and the hopes of fulfillment regularly frustrated. Each single promise *must* be deceitful or at least exaggerated, lest the search lose its intensity or even grind to a halt. Without the repetitive frustration of desires, consumer demand could quickly run dry and the consumer-targeted economy would run out of steam. It is the *excess* of the sum total of promises that neutralizes the frustration caused by the excessiveness of each one of them, and stops the accumulation of frustrating experiences short of sapping consumers' confidence in the ultimate effectiveness of the search.

In addition to being an economics of excess and waste, consumerism is for this reason also an economics of deception. Just like the excess and waste, deception does not signal its malfunctioning. On the contrary—it is a symptom of its good health and a signal that it is on the right track; a distinctive mark of the sole regime under which the society of consumers may be assured of its survival.

The discarding of successive consumer offers expected (promised) to satisfy desires is paralleled by the rising mountains of dashed expectations. Among the expectations the mortality rate is high, and in a properly functioning consumer society it must be steadily rising. The life expectancy for hopes is minuscule, and only an extravagantly high fertility rate may save them from thinning out to the point of extinction. For expectations to be kept alive and for new hopes to promptly fill the voids left by the hopes already discredited and discarded, the road from the shop to the garbage bin needs to be short and the passage swift.

There is even more, though, that sets the society of consumers apart from all other known arrangements, including the most ingenious among them, for skillful and effective "pattern maintenance" and "tension management" (to recall Talcott Parsons's prerequisites of the "self-equilibrating system"). The society of consumers has developed to an unprecedented degree the capacity to absorb any and all dissent it inevitably, and in common with other types of society, breeds—and then to recycle it as a major resource for its own wellbeing and expansion. The society of consumers derives its animus and momentum from the *disaffection* it itself expertly produces. It provides the prime example of a process that Thomas Mathiesen has recently described as the "silent silencing" of potential system-born dissent and protest through the stratagem of "absorption": "The attitudes and actions which in origin are transcendent [that is, threatening the system with explosion or implosion—Z. B.] are integrated in the prevailing order in such a way that dominant interests continue to be served. This way, they are made unthreatening to the prevailing order."[18]

It was Stephen Bertman who coined the terms "nowist culture" and "hurried culture" to denote the way we live in our kind of society.[19] Apt terms they are indeed—and such as come in particularly handy whenever we try to grasp the nature of the liquid-modern human condition. I would suggest that, more than for anything else, this condition stands out for its (thus far unique) *renegotiation of the meaning of time.*

Time in the liquid-modern society-of-consumers era is neither cyclical nor linear, as it used to be in other known societies of modern or premodern history. I would suggest that it is *pointillist* instead—broken up into a multitude of separate morsels, each morsel reduced to a point ever more closely approximating its geometrical idealization of nondimensionality. As we surely remember from school lessons in geometry, points have no length, width, or depth: they exist, one is tempted to say, *before* space and time; both space and time are yet to begin. But like that unique point that, as state-of-the-art cosmogony postulates, preceded the big bang that started the universe, each point is presumed to contain an infinite potential to expand and an infinity of possibilities waiting to explode if properly ignited. And remember, there was nothing in the "before" that preceded the eruption of the universe that could offer the slightest inkling that the moment of the big bang was approaching. The cosmogonists tell us a lot about what happened in the first fractions of a second *after* the big bang; but they keep odiously silent about the seconds, minutes, hours, days, years, or millennia before.

Each time-point (but there is no way to know in advance which) might—just might—be pregnant with the chance of another big bang, though this time on a much more modest, "individual universe" scale, and successive points continue to be believed to be so pregnant, regardless of what might have happened with the previous ones and despite the accumulating experience showing that most chances tend to be wrongly predicted, overlooked, or missed, that most points prove to be barren and most stirrings stillborn. A map of pointillist life, if one were charted, would look like a graveyard of imaginary or unfulfilled possibilities. Or, depending on the point of view, like a cemetery of wasted chances: in a pointillist universe, hope's rates of infant mortality and miscarriage are very high.

Precisely for that reason, a "nowist" life tends to be a "hurried" life. The chance that each point might contain will follow it to its grave; for *that* particular, unique chance, there will be no "second chance." Each point might be lived through as a new beginning, but more often than not the finish will arrive right after the start, with pretty little happening in between. Only an unstoppably expanding multitude of new beginnings may—just may—compensate for the profusion of false starts. Only the vast expanses of new beginnings believed to be waiting ahead, only a hoped-for multitude of points whose big-bang potential has not yet been tried, and so remains thus far undiscredited, may salvage the hope from the debris of premature endings and stillborn beginnings.

As I said earlier, in the "nowist" life of the avid consumer of new *Erlebnisse* (lived-through experiences), the reason to hurry is not to *acquire* and *collect* as much as possible, but to *discard* and *replace* as much as one can. There is a latent message behind every commercial promising a new unexplored opportunity for bliss: no point crying over spilt milk. Either the big bang happens right now, at this very moment and on the first try, or loitering at that particular point makes sense no longer; it is time to move on to another point.

In the society of producers that is now receding into the past (at least in our part of the globe), the advice in such a case would have been "try harder"; but not in the society of consumers. Here, the failed tools are to be abandoned rather than sharpened and tried again with greater skill, more dedication, and better effect. And the appliances that stopped short of delivering the promised "full satisfaction," as well as the human relationships that delivered a "bang" not exactly as "big" as expected, should be chucked as well. The hurry ought to be at its most intense when one is running from one point (failed, failing, or about to start failing) to another (yet untried). One should be wary of the bitter lesson of Christopher Marlowe's Faust: of being cast into hell when wishing the moment—just because it was a pleasing one—would last forever.

Given the infinity of promised and assumed opportunities, what makes a most attractive novelty of time into pulverised "points," a novelty one could be sure would be avidly embraced and explored with zeal, is the double expectation or hope of pre-empting the future and of disempowering the past. Such a double accomplishment is, after all, the ideal of liberty.

Indeed, the promise of emancipating actors from the choice-limiting remnants and echoes of the past, particularly resented for their nasty habit of growing in volume and weight as the "past" expands and devours ever greater chunks of life, together with the promise of denying the future its similarly discomforting propensity to devalue successes currently enjoyed and dash the presently entertained hopes, augur between them a complete, unrestrained, well-nigh absolute freedom. Liquid-modern society offers such liberty to a degree unheard of, and downright inconceivable, in any other society on record.

Let us consider first the uncanny feat of disabling the past. It boils down to just one change in the human condition, but a truly miraculous one: the facility of being "born again." From now on, it's not just cats that can live nine lives. Into one abominably short lifespan on earth, bewailed not that long ago for its loathsome brevity and not radically lengthened since, humans—like the proverbial cats—are now offered the ability to squeeze many lives, an endless series of "new beginnings." Being born again means that the previous birth(s), together with their consequences, have been annulled; it feels like the arrival of the always dreamt of, though never before experienced, divine-style omnipotence.[20] The power of causal determination can be disarmed, and the power of the past to cut down the options of the present can be radically limited, perhaps even abolished altogether. What one was yesterday would no longer bar the possibility of becoming someone totally different today.

Since each point in time is, let's recall, full of potential, and each potential is different and unique, the number of ways in which one can be different is genuinely uncountable: indeed, it dwarfs even the astonishing multitude of permutations and the mind-boggling variety of forms and likenesses that the haphazard meetings of genes have managed thus far and are likely in the future to produce in the human species. It comes close to the awe-inspiring capacity of *eternity,* in which, given its infinite duration, everything may/must sooner or later happen, and everything can/will sooner or later be done. Now that wondrous potency of eternity seems to have been packed into the not-at-all-eternal span of a *single* human life.

Consequently, the feat of defusing and neutralizing the power of the past to reduce subsequent choices, and thus to severely limit the chances for "new births," robs eternity of its most seductive attraction. In the pointillist time of the liquid-modern society, *eternity no longer is a value and an object of desire*—or rather, what was its value and what made it an object of desire has been excised and *grafted onto the moment.* Accordingly, the late-modern "tyranny of the moment," with its precept of carpe diem, gradually yet steadily and perhaps unstoppably replaces the premodern tyranny of eternity, with its motto of memento mori.

That transformation stands behind the new centrality accorded in the present society to the preoccupation with "identity." Though remaining an important issue and an absorbing task since the early-modern passage from the "ascription" to the "achievement" society, identity has now shared the fate of other life pursuits and undergone the "pointillization" process. Once a whole-life project, a project coterminous with the duration of *life,* it has now turned into an attribute of the *moment.* It is no longer designed once and built to last forever but is intermittently, and ever anew, assembled and disassembled— each of those two apparently contradictory operations carrying equal importance and being equally absorbing. Instead of demanding advance payment and a lifelong subscription with no cancellation clause, identity (or, more correctly, identification) is now an activity akin to watching pay-per-view movies on your television set (or using a pay-as-you-go phone card). While still a constant preoccupation, identification is now split into a multitude of exceedingly short (and, with the progress in marketing techniques, ever shorter) efforts fully within the capacity of even a most fleeting attention span; a series of sudden and frenetic spurts of no predesigned, predetermined, or even predictable succession—but instead with effects following the beginnings comfortably closely and quickly, and so freeing the joys of wanting from the dark prison of waiting.

The skills required to meet the challenge of the liquid-modern manipulation of identity are akin to those of the famous Claude Lévi-Strauss's *bricoleur,* a juggler, or—even more to the point—to the artfulness and dexterity of a prestidigitator. The practice of such skills has been brought within reach of the ordinary, run-of-the-mill consumer by the expedient of *simulacrum*—a phenomenon, in Jean Baudrillard's memorable description, similar to psychosomatic ailments, known to cancel the distinction between "things as they are" and "things as they pretend to be," or reality and illusion, the true state of affairs and its simulation. What once was viewed and suffered as an interminable drudgery calling for the mobilization and onerous straining of any and all of one's "inner" resources can now be accomplished with the help of ready-to-use contraptions and gadgets, purchasable for a modicum of money and time. To be sure, the attractiveness of identities patched together from bought trappings rises in proportion to the amount of money spent; most recently it has also risen with the length of waiting, as the most prestigious and exclusive designer shops introduce waiting lists—clearly for no other purpose except to enhance the distinction with which the waited-for tokens of identity endow their buyer. As Georg Simmel pointed out a long time ago, values are measured by the volume and painfulness of the sacrifice of other values required to obtain them (and delay is arguably the most excruciating of sacrifices that members of the society of consumers may be required to accept).

Annulling the past, "being born again," acquiring a different self, reincarnating as "someone completely different"—these temptations are difficult to resist. Why work on self-improvement, with all the strenuous effort and painful self-sacrifice such toil notoriously requires? Why send good money after bad? Is it not cheaper, and quicker, and more thorough, and more convenient, and easier to cut the losses and start again, to shed the old skin—spots, warts, and all—and buy a new one? There is nothing new in seeking escape when things get really hot; people have tried that in all times. What is new is the prospect of a leopard's actually changing its spots, the dream of *escaping from one's own self,* complemented by the conviction that making such a dream a reality is within reach; this is not just one of many options but the easiest option, the one most likely to work in case of trouble—a shortcut less cumbersome, less time- and energy-consuming, and so, all in all, a cheaper option.

Joseph Brodsky, the Russian-American philosopher-poet, vividly described the kind of life guided by trust invested in this kind of escape. For acknowledged losers, like the "flawed consumers" (the poor, eliminated from the consumerist game), the liquid-modern variety of social outcasts, the sole form of escape from oneself (from being tired of oneself, or as Brodsky prefers, from being *bored*) is alcohol or drug addiction: "In general, a man shooting heroin into his vein does so largely for the same reason you buy a video," Brodsky told the students of Dartmouth College in July 1989; this is as far as flawed consumers, the social rejects barred from entry to the more refined and ostensibly more effective (but also more expensive) escape routes, can go. As to the potential haves, which the Dartmouth College students aspired to become, they need not stop at buying a new video. They may try to live out their dream. "You'll be bored with your work, your spouses, your lovers, the view from your window, the furniture or wallpaper in your room, your thoughts, yourselves," Brodsky warned. "Accordingly, you'll try to devise ways of escape. Apart from the self-gratifying gadgets mentioned before, you may take up changing jobs, residence, company, country, climate, you may take up promiscuity, alcohol, travel, cooking lessons, drugs, psychoanalysis."[21]

The haves may indeed pick and choose their ways of escape from uncountable numbers of options on offer. And they are likely to be tempted to try as many as they can afford, one by one or all together, since what is much less likely is that any of the chosen ways will indeed deliver that freedom from "boredom with oneself" that all of them promise to bring: "In fact, you may lump all these together, and for a while that may work. Until the day, of course, when you wake up in your bedroom amid a new family and a different wallpaper, in a different state and climate, with a heap of bills from your travel agent and your shrink, yet with the same stale feeling toward the light of day pouring through your window."[22]

Andrzej Stasiuk, an outstanding Polish novelist and insightful analyst of the contemporary human condition, suggests that "the possibility of becoming someone else" is the present-day substitute for the now largely discarded and uncared-for salvation or redemption. "It is highly probable that the quantity of digital, celluloid, and analogue beings met in the course of a bodily life comes close to the volume that eternal life and resurrection in flesh could offer," Stasiuk suggests. "Applying various techniques, we may change our bodies and re-shape them according to different patterns . . . When browsing through glossy magazines, one gets the impression that they tell mostly one story—about the ways in which one can remake one's personality, starting from diets, surroundings, homes, and up to rebuilding of psychical structure, often code-named as a proposition to 'be yourself.'"[23]

Sławomir Mrożek, a Polish writer of worldwide fame and a man with firsthand experience of many lands and cultures, compares the world we inhabit to a "market-stall filled with fancy dresses and surrounded by crowds seeking their 'selves' . . . One can change dresses without end, so that a wondrous liberty the seekers enjoy can go on forever . . . Let's go on searching for our real selves, it's smashing fun—on condition that the real self will never be found. Because if it were, the fun would end."[24]

If happiness is permanently within reach, and if reaching it takes but the few minutes needed to browse through the yellow pages and to pull the credit card out of the wallet, then obviously a self that stops short of reaching happiness can't be "real"—not really the one that spurred the self-seeker to embark on the voyage of self-discovery. Such a fraudulent self needs to be discarded on the grounds of its "inauthenticity," while the search for the real one should go on. And there is little reason to stop searching if one can be sure that the next moment another moment will duly arrive, carrying new promises and bursting with new potential.

Blaise Pascal suggested that "the sole cause of man's unhappiness is that he does not know how to stay quietly in his room."[25] Pascal wrote these words almost four centuries ago, but even if he were to have written them a mere fifty years ago, little would he have known that, first, a time would arrive when men *and* women would be unhappy for much the same reason, and second, that however keenly they tried to remain in their own respective rooms at this time, they would hardly manage to stay quiet, since their rooms, set on castors rather than solid and durable foundations, would be exquisitely mobile; and they, the men and women of *our* times, would have no inkling, let alone any reliable knowledge, of when their rooms would be moved, where to, and with what speed. Don't blame Pascal, though. He was born, and he died, long before the advent of our liquid-modern world.

It is inside this liquid-modern world that we've been called to consider the fate, the value, and the prospects of memory. And no wonder that nowadays we believe these questions to be worthy of our particularly acute attention. As Martin Heidegger pointed out, we human beings start pondering the essence of something only when that "something" goes bust on us: when we can't find it in the place in which it "always was," or if it begins to behave in a way that for all we know and are used to expecting can be described only as odd, surprising, baffling, and puzzling. As Hegel remarked a century earlier, the owl of Minerva, that goddess of wisdom, spread its wings only at dusk—at the end of the day.

Memory has recently fallen into just that category of "something" of which you become suddenly aware—things that have gone bust, or things that the eye of wisdom has not spotted since they started dissolving in the darkness of night and so stopped hiding in the dazzling light of the day. If these days we return, compulsively and obsessively, to the issue of memory, it is because we have been transported from a civilization of duration, and for that reason of *learning and memorizing*, into the civilization of transience, and thus of *forgetting*. Of that seminal departure, memory is the prime victim, disguised as its collateral casualty.

It took more than two millennia after the ancient Greek sages invented the notion of *paidea* for the idea of "lifelong education" to be transformed from an oxymoron (a contradiction in terms) into a pleonasm (akin to a "buttery butter" or "metallic iron"). But that remarkable transformation has occurred quite recently—in the past few decades—under the impact of the radically accelerated pace of change taking place in the social setting in which both principal actors in education, the teachers and the learners alike, have found themselves obliged to act.

The moment they start moving, the direction of ballistic missiles and the distance they will travel have been already decided by the shape and the position of the barrel from which they are fired and the amount of gunpowder in the shell; one can calculate with little or no error the spot on which the missile will land, and one can choose that spot by shifting the barrel or changing the amount of gunpowder used. These qualities of ballistic missiles make them ideal weapons to use in positional warfare—when the targets stay dug into their trenches or bunkers and the missiles are the sole bodies on the move.

The same qualities, however, make the guns useless or almost useless once the targets, invisible to the gunner, start to move—particularly if they move faster than the missiles can fly, and even more so if they move erratically, in an unpredictable fashion that plays havoc with all preliminary calculations required for setting the missile's trajectory. A smart, "intelligent missile" is needed then—a missile that can change its direction in full flight, depending on changing circumstances, one that can spot immediately the target's movements, learn from them whatever can be learned about the target's current direction and speed—and extrapolate from the gathered information the spot in which their trajectories may cross. Such smart missiles cannot suspend, let alone finish the gathering and processing of, information as it travels—as its target may never stop moving and changing its direction and speed, and the place of encounter needs to be constantly updated and corrected.

We may say that smart missiles follow the strategy of "instrumental rationality," although in its, so to speak, liquidized, fluid version; that is, in the version that drops the assumption that the end is given, steady and immovable for the duration, and that only the means are variable and can and must be calculated and manipulated. Even smarter missiles won't be confined to a preselected target at all but will choose the targets as they go. They will be guided solely by two considerations: what are the greatest effects they can achieve, given their technical capacity, and which potential targets are they best equipped to hit? This provides, we may say, the case for instrumental rationality in reverse: targets are selected as the missile travels, and it is the available means that decide which "end" will be selected. In such cases the "smartness" of the flying missile and its effectiveness would benefit from its equipment's being of a rather "underspecified," "uncommitted" nature, unfocused on any specific category of ends, not overly specialized or adjusted to hitting one particular kind of target.

Smart missiles, unlike their ballistic elder cousins, *learn as they go*. So what they need to be initially supplied with is the *ability* to learn, and learn fast. This is obvious. What is less visible, however, though no less crucial than the skill of quick learning, is the ability to instantly *forget* what has been learned before. Smart missiles wouldn't be smart if they were not able to "change their mind" or revoke their previous "decisions" with no second thoughts and regret. They should not overly cherish the information they acquired a moment earlier and on no account should they develop a habit of behaving in a way that that information suggested. All information they acquire ages rapidly and, instead of providing reliable guidance, may lead astray, if it is not promptly dismissed—erased from memory. What the "brains" of smart missiles must never forget is that the knowledge they acquire is eminently *disposable*, good only until further notice and of only temporary usefulness, and that the warrant of success is not to overlook the moment when that acquired knowledge is of no more use and needs to be thrown away, forgotten, and replaced.

Philosophers of education of the solid-modern era saw teachers as launchers of ballistic missiles and instructed them how to ensure that their products would stay strictly on the predesigned course determined by their initial momentum. And given the "praxeomorphic" nature of human cognition, it's no wonder they did, as ballistic missiles were, at the early stages of the modern era, the topmost achievement of human technical invention.[26] They served flawlessly whoever might have wished to conquer and master the world as it then was; as

Hilaire Belloc confidently declared, referring to African natives, "Whatever happens, we have got / The Maxim Gun, and they have not" (the Maxim gun, let's recall, was a machine to launch great numbers of ballistic bullets in a short time, and was effective only if there were very many such bullets at hand). As a matter of fact, though, that vision of the teacher's task and the pupil's destiny was much older than the idea of the "ballistic missile" and the modern era that invented it—as an ancient Chinese proverb, preceding the advent of modernity by two millennia but still quoted by the Commission of the European Communities in support of its program for "lifelong learning" at the threshold of the twenty-first century, testifies: "When planning for a year, plant corn. When planning for a decade, plant trees. When planning for life, train and educate people." It is only with our entry into liquid-modern times that the ancient wisdom has lost its pragmatic value and people concerned with learning and the promotion of learning known under the name of "education" have had to shift their attention from the ballistic to the smart missiles.

Harvard Business School professor John Kotter advised his readers to avoid being entangled in long-term employment of the "tenure track" sort; indeed, developing institutional loyalty and becoming too deeply engrossed and emotionally engaged in any given job, taking an oath for a long-term, not to mention a lifelong, commitment to anything or anybody in particular, is ill advised, he wrote, when "business concepts, product designs, competitor intelligence, capital equipment and *all kinds of knowledge* have shorter credible life spans."[27]

If the premodern life was a daily rehearsal for the infinite duration of everything except mortal life, the liquid-modern life is a daily rehearsal of universal transience. What the denizens of the liquid-modern world quickly find out is that nothing in that world is bound to last, let alone last forever. Objects recommended today as useful and indispensable tend to "become history" well before settling long enough to turn into a need and a habit. Nothing is believed to stay here forever, nothing seems to be irreplaceable. Everything is born with a brand of imminent death and emerges from the production line with a use-by date printed or presumed. Construction of new buildings does not start unless permission has been issued to demolish them when the time to pull them down comes (as it surely will), and contracts are not signed unless their duration is fixed or their termination on demand is made easy. Few if any commitments last long enough to reach the point of no return, and decisions or rulings, all of which are ad hoc and deemed to bind "for the time being," may stay in force for long only by accident. All things, born or made, human or not, are until-further-notice and dispensable.

A specter hovers over the denizens of the liquid-modern world and all their labors and creations: the specter of superfluity. Liquid modernity is a civilization of excess, redundancy, waste, and waste disposal. In Ricardo Petrella's succinct and pithy formulation, the current global trends direct "economies towards the production of the ephemeral and volatile— through the massive reduction of the life-span of products and services—and of the precarious (temporary, flexible and part-time jobs)."[28] And as the late Italian sociologist Alberto Melucci used to say, "We are plagued by the fragility of the presentness which calls for a firm foundation where none exists."[29] And so, he added, "when contemplating change, we are always torn between desire and fear, between anticipation and uncertainty." Uncertainty means *risk*: undetachable companion of all action and a sinister specter haunting the compulsive decision makers and choosers-by-necessity that we are since, as Melucci put it, "choice became a destiny."

As a matter of fact, to say "became" is not entirely correct, as humans have been choosers as long as they have been humans. But it can be said that at no other time was the necessity to make choices so deeply felt, and that choosing has become poignantly self-conscious since being conducted under conditions of painful yet incurable uncertainty, of a constant threat of "being left behind" and of being excluded from the game and barred from return for failing to rise up to the new demands. What separates the present agony of choice from discomforts that tormented *Homo eligens,* the "man choosing," at all times, is the discovery or suspicion that there are no preordained rules and universally approved objectives that may be followed and that thereby insure the choosers against adverse consequences of their choices. Reference points and guidelines that seem trustworthy today are likely to be discredited tomorrow as misleading or corrupt. Allegedly rock-solid companies are unmasked as figments of their accountants' imagination. Whatever is "good for you" today may be reclassified tomorrow as your poison. Apparently firm commitments and solemnly signed agreements may be overturned overnight. And promises, or at least most of them, seem to be made solely to be betrayed and broken. There seems to be no stable, secure island among the tides. To quote Melucci once more, "We no longer possess a home; we are repeatedly called upon to build and then rebuild one, like the three little pigs of the fairy tale, or we have to carry it along with us on our backs like snails."[30]

In such a world, one is compelled therefore to take life bit by bit, as it comes, expecting each bit to be different from the preceding ones and to call for different knowledge and skills. A friend of mine living in one of the European Union countries, a highly intelligent, superbly educated, uniquely creative person with full command of several languages, a person who would pass most capacity tests and job interviews with flying colors, complained in a private letter of the "labour market being frail like gossamer and brittle like china." For two years she worked as a freelance translator and legal adviser, exposed to a full measure of the usual ups and down of market fortunes. A single mother, she yearned, however, for a more regular income and so opted for steady employment with a salary and a paycheck every month. For one and a half years she worked for a company, briefing its budding entrepreneurs on the intricacies of EU law, but as new adventurous businesses were slow to materialize, the company went promptly bankrupt. For another year and a half she worked for the Ministry of Agriculture, running a section dedicated to developing contacts with the newly independent Baltic countries. Come the next election, the new government coalition chose to "subsidiarize" that problem to private initiative and so disband the department. The next job lasted only half a year, and then the State Board of Ethnic Equality followed the pattern of governmental hand-washing and was declared redundant.

Never before has Robert Louis Stevenson's memorable declaration—"To travel hopefully is a better thing than to arrive"—sounded truer than it does now in our liquidized and fluid modern world. When destinations change places, and those that don't lose their charm faster than legs can walk, cars can drive, or planes can fly—keeping on the move matters more than the destination. Not making a habit of anything practiced at the moment, not being tied up by the legacy of one's own past, wearing one's current identity as one wears shirts that may be promptly replaced when they fall out of fashion, scorning past lessons and disdaining past skills with no inhibition or regret—all are becoming the hallmarks of today's liquid-modern life-politics and the attributes of liquid-modern rationality. Liquid-modern culture no longer feels like a culture of learning and accumulating, as did the cultures recorded in the historians' and ethnographers' reports. It looks and feels instead like a culture of *disengagement, discontinuity, and forgetting.*

In what George Steiner called "casino culture," every cultural product is calculated for maximal impact (that is, for breaking up, forcing out, and disposing of the cultural products of yesterday) and instant obsolescence (wary of outstaying its welcome because of the steadily shortening distance between the fragrance of novelty and the odor of the rubbish bin, it promptly vacates the stage to clear the way for the cultural products of tomorrow). The artists, who once identified the value of their work with their own eternal duration and so struggled for a perfection that would render all further change all but impossible, now put together installations meant to be pulled apart when the exhibition closes, and happenings that will end the moment the actors decide to turn the other way; wrap up bridges until traffic is restarted, or unfinished buildings until the construction work is resumed; and erect or carve "space sculptures" that invite nature to take its toll and to supply further proof (if further proof is needed) of the ludicrous vanity and brevity of all human deeds and the shallowness of their traces. Except dedicated TV-quiz competitors, no one is expected, let alone encouraged, to remember yesterday's talk of the town, though no one is expected, let alone allowed, to opt out of the talk-of-the-town of today. The consumer market is adapted to the liquid-modern casino culture, which in turn is adapted to that market's pressures and seductions. The two chime well with each other and feed on each other. So where does this leave the learners and their teachers?

To be of any use in our liquid-modern setting, education and learning must be continuous and indeed lifelong. No other kind of education or learning is conceivable; the "formation" of selves or personalities is unthinkable in any other fashion but that of an ongoing, perpetually unfinished, open-ended re-formation.

Given the overwhelming trends that shape power relations

and the strategy of domination in our liquid-modern time, the prospects are poor, at best, that the twisted and erratic itinerary of market developments will be straightened out and that "human resources" calculations will become more realistic— and most probably they are nil. In the liquid-modern setting, "manufactured uncertainty" is the paramount instrument of domination, whereas the policy of "precarization," to use Pierre Bourdieu's term, fast becomes the hard core of the domination strategy.[31] The market and "planning for life" are at loggerheads. Once state politics surrenders to the guidance of the "economy," understood as the free play of market forces, the balance of power between the two is switched decisively to the advantage of the first.

This does not augur well for the "empowering of citizens," named by the Commission of the European Communities as the primary objective of lifelong learning. By widespread consent, "empowerment" (a term used in the current debates interchangeably with that of "enablement") is achieved when people acquire the ability to control, or at least to significantly influence, the personal, political, economic, and social forces by which their life's trajectory would be otherwise buffeted; in other words, to be "empowered" means to be *able to make choices and act effectively on the choices made,* and that in turn signifies the *capacity to influence the range of available choices and the social settings in which choices are made and pursued.* To put it bluntly, genuine empowerment requires not only the acquisition of skills that would allow one to play well the game designed by others, but also the acquisition of such *powers* as would allow one to influence the game's objectives, stakes, and rules—in short, not just personal but also *social* skills.

Empowerment requires the building and rebuilding of interhuman bonds, the will and the ability to engage with others in the continuous effort to make human cohabitation into a hospitable and friendly setting for the mutually enriching cooperation of men and women struggling for self-esteem, for the development of their potential and the proper use of their abilities. All in all, one of the decisive stakes of lifelong education aimed at empowerment is the rebuilding of the now increasingly deserted public space, where men and women may engage in a continuous translation between individual and common, private and communal, interests, rights, and duties.

"In light of fragmentation and segmentation processes and increasing individual and social diversity," writes Dominique Simon Rychen, "strengthening social cohesion and developing a sense of social awareness and responsibility have become important societal and political goals."[32] In the workplace, in the immediate neighborhood, and in the street, we mix daily with others who, as Rychen points out, "do not necessarily speak the same language (literally or metaphorically) or share the same memory or history." Under such circumstances, the skills we need more than any others, in order to offer the public sphere a reasonable chance of resuscitation, are the skills of interaction with others—of conducting a dialogue, of negotiating, of gaining mutual understanding, and of managing or resolving the conflicts inevitable in every instance of shared life.

Let me restate what I stated at the beginning: in the liquid-modern setting, education and learning, to be of any use, must be continuous and indeed lifelong. I hope we can see now that one reason, though perhaps the decisive one, for which learning *must* be continuous and lifelong is the nature of the task we confront on the shared road to "empowerment"—a task that is exactly what education should be: continuously confronted, never completed, lifelong.

But the consumer is an enemy of the citizen. All over the "developed" and affluent part of the planet, signs abound of fading interest in the acquisition and exercise of social skills, of people turning their backs on politics, of growing political apathy and loss of interest in the running of the political process. Democratic politics cannot survive for long the citizens' passivity out of political ignorance and indifference. Citizens' freedoms are not properties acquired once and for all; such properties are not secure once locked in private safes. They are planted and rooted in the sociopolitical soil, which needs to be fertilized and watered daily and which will dry up and crumble if it is not attended to day in and day out by the informed actions of a knowledgeable and committed public. Not only do *technical* skills need to be continually refreshed, not only does *job-focused* education need to be lifelong. The same is required, and with a yet greater urgency, for the education in *citizenship*.

Most people would agree today without much prompting that they need to refresh their professional knowledge and digest new technical information if they wish to avoid "being left behind" or being thrown overboard by fast-accelerating "technological progress." And yet, as Henry Giroux meticulously documented in a long series of eye-opening studies, a similar feeling of urgency is conspicuously missing when it comes to catching up with the impetuous stream of political developments and the fast-changing rules of the political game. Survey results testify to the rapid widening of the gap that separates public opinion from the central facts of political life. For instance, soon after the invasion of Iraq, the *New York Times* released a survey indicating that 42 percent of the American public believed that Saddam Hussein was directly responsible for the September 11 attacks on the World Trade Center and the Pentagon. CBS News also released a poll indicating that 55 percent of the public believed that Saddam Hussein directly supported the terrorist organization Al-Qaeda. A Knight Ridder/Princeton Research poll found that 44 percent of respondents said they thought "most" or "some" of the September 11, 2001, hijackers were Iraqi citizens. A majority of Americans also already believed that Saddam Hussein had weapons of mass destruction, that such weapons had been found, that he was about to build a nuclear bomb, and that he would eventually unleash it on an unsuspecting American public. None of these claims had any basis in fact, as no evidence existed to even remotely confirm these assertions. A poll conducted by the *Washington Post* near the second anniversary of the September 11 tragedy indicated that 70 percent of Americans continued to believe that Iraq had played a direct role in the planning of the attacks.

In such a landscape of ignorance, it is easy to feel lost and hapless—and easier yet to be lost and hapless without feeling it. As Pierre Bourdieu memorably remarked, he who has no grip on the present wouldn't dream of controlling the future—and most Americans must have but a misty view of what the present holds. This suspicion is amply confirmed by more incisive and insightful observers. "Many Americans," wrote Brian Knowlton in the *International Herald Tribune,* "said the hot-cold-hot nature of recent alerts had left them unsure just how urgently, and fearfully, they should react."[33]

Ignorance leads to the paralysis of will. One does not know what is in store, one has no way to count the risks. For the authorities, impatient with the constraints imposed on power holders by a buoyant and resilient democracy, the ignorance-incurred impotence of the electorate and the widespread disbelief in the efficacy of dissent and unwillingness to get politically involved are much-needed and welcome sources of political capital: domination through deliberately cultivated ignorance and uncertainty is more reliable and comes cheaper than rule grounded in a thorough debate of the facts and a protracted effort to agree on the truth of the matter and on the least risky ways to proceed. Political ignorance is self-perpetuating, and the rope plaited of ignorance and inaction comes in handy whenever democracy's voice is to be stifled or its hands tied.

We need lifelong education to give us choice. But we need it even more to salvage the conditions that make choice available and within our power.

CHAPTER FIVE

Out of the Frying Pan and into the Fire,

or the Arts between Administration

and the Markets

◆

THE IDEA OF "CULTURE" was coined and named, in the third quarter of the eighteenth century, as a shorthand term for the management of human thought and behavior.

The concept of culture was born as a declaration of *intent.* Its present use as a descriptive term, a generic name for the already achieved, observed, and recorded regularities of population-wide conduct, arrived about a century later—when the culture managers looked back on what they had already come to view as their product and, as if following the example set by God in His six days of creation, declared it to be "good." Since then, the term "culture" has come to mean, in its most common use, the way in which one specimen of "normatively regulated" human conduct differs from another specimen under different management.

Let me repeat, however: the term "culture" entered the vocabulary as a name of a *purposeful* activity. At the threshold of the modern era men and women—viewed theretofore as tough "brute facts," the nonnegotiable and not-to-be-meddled-with links in the chain of Divine creation, indispensable even when mean, paltry, and leaving much to be desired—came to be seen as pliable: amenable to, and in need of, repair and improvement.

The term "culture" was conceived within the semantic family of concepts that included terms like "cultivation," "husbandry," "breeding," "grooming"—all denoting improvement, prevention of impairment, arresting deterioration. What the farmer did with the seed, all the way from a planting to seedling to crop, through constant attentive care—could and ought to be done with incipient human beings, through education and training (obviously, by educators and trainers). "Being human" was no longer viewed as a matter of fact, a gift of God or Nature, but as an explicitly human task—and a task that needed to be supervised and monitored in order to be fulfilled. Humans were not *born* but *made*. Newborns had yet to *become* human, and in the course of becoming human they had to be guided by the already accomplished humans: humans who had been duly educated and trained in the art of educating and training other humans.

"Culture" appeared in the vocabulary less than a hundred years *after* another crucial modern concept—that of "managing," which, according to the *Oxford English Dictionary,* meant "to cause (persons, animals, etc.) to submit to one's control," "to operate upon," "to succeed in accomplishing"—and more than one hundred years *earlier* than another, synthesizing sense of "management": "to contrive to get along or pull through." To manage, in a nutshell, meant to get things done in a way in which they would not move on their own; to *redirect* events according to one's design and will. To put it in a yet another way: to manage (to get control over the flow of events) came to mean to *manipulate probabilities*—to make certain conduct (openings or responses) of "persons, animals, etc.," more likely to take place than it would otherwise be, while making some other kinds of conduct less likely or utterly unlikely to happen. In the last account, to manage means to *limit the freedom of the managed.*

Just as the idea of "agriculture" posited the field as seen from the perspective of the farmer, as an object of farming activity, the idea of "culture," when metaphorically applied to humans, was a vision of the *social* world as viewed through the eyes of the managers, the "farmers of humans": an object of management. The postulate or tacit (but axiomatic) presumption of management was not a later addition: it had been from the beginning and throughout its history *endemic* to the concept of "culture." Deep in the heart of that concept lies the premonition and/or acceptance of an unequal, *asymmetrical social relation:* of a neat division between acting and bearing the impact of action, between the managers and the managed, the powerful and the submissive, the knowing and the ignorant, the refined and the crude.

Theodor Wiesegrund Adorno points out that the "inclusion of the objective spirit of an age in the single word 'culture' betrays from the onset the administrative view, the task of which, looking down from on high, is to assemble, distribute, evaluate and organize."[1] And he goes on to unpack the defining traits of that spirit: "The demand made by administration upon culture is essentially heteronomous: culture—no matter what form it takes—is to be measured by norms not inherent to it and which have nothing to do with the quality of the object, but rather with some type of abstract standards imposed from without."[2]

But as one could only expect in the case of an asymmetrical social relation, quite a different sight greets the eyes when the relationship is scanned from the opposite, receiving end (in other words, through the eyes of the "managed"), and quite a different verdict is then voiced (or rather would be voiced, if people assigned to that end acquired a voice): it is the sight of unwarranted and uncalled-for repression, and the verdict is one of illegitimacy and injustice. In that other version of the relationship's story, culture appears to be "opposed to administration," since, as Oscar Wilde put it (provocatively, in Adorno's opinion), culture is useless—or so it at least appears to be, so long as the managers hold the monopoly on drawing the line separating use from waste. In that rendition, "culture" represents the claims of the *particular* against the homogenizing pressure of the *general,* and it "involves an irrevocably critical impulse towards the status quo and all institutions thereof."[3]

The clash, one of simmering antagonism and occasionally open conflict, between the two perspectives and narratives is inevitable. It can be neither prevented from coming into the open nor pacified once it does. The managers-and-managed relationship is intrinsically agonistic; the two sides pursue two opposite purposes and are able to cohabit solely in a conflict-ridden, suspicion-infected, and battle-ready mode.

The conflict is particularly pronounced, most ferociously acted out, and pregnant with particularly morbid consequences in the case of the arts. After all, the arts are the advance units of culture—engaged in reconnaissance battles whose purpose is to explore, pave, and chart the roads that human culture may (or may not) follow. ("Art is not a better, but an alternative existence," said Joseph Brodsky. "It is not an attempt to escape reality but the opposite, an attempt to animate it."[4]) The artists are either adversaries or competitors in the job that the managers wish to monopolize.

The more they distance themselves from the realities of the day and so resist being accommodated by them, the less fit the arts and the artists are to be deployed in the service of the status quo; and that means that, from the managerial point of view, they may well be seen as useless if not downright harmful. Managers and artists are at cross-purposes: the managerial spirit is at war with contingency, which is the natural habitat of the arts. Besides, busy as they are in designing imagined alternatives to the status quo, the arts are, willy-nilly, in competition with the managers, whose control over human conduct and the manipulation of probabilities is in the last account a bid to control the future. There is more than one reason that no love is lost between management and the arts.

Speaking of culture but having mainly the arts in mind, Adorno recognizes the inevitability of the culture-management conflict. But he also points out that the antagonists *need each other;* more important, the arts need management, as their mission can't be fulfilled without it. However inconvenient and unpleasant the state of an overt or clandestine enmity may be, the greatest misfortune that might befall culture (more precisely, the arts) is a complete and finite victory over its antagonist: "Culture suffers damage when it is planned and administrated; if it is left to itself, however, everything cultural threatens not only to lose possibility of effect, but its very existence as well."[5] In these words, Adorno restates the sad conclusion at which he arrived when working (with Max Horkheimer) on *Dialectics of Enlightenment:* that "the history of the old religions and schools like that of the modern parties and revolutions" teaches us that the price of survival is "the transformation of ideas into domination."[6] This lesson of history ought to be studied particularly diligently, absorbed, and put into practice by the artists, the professional "culture creators" who carry the main burden of the transgressive propensity of culture, making of it their consciously embraced vocation and practicing critique and transgression as their own mode of being: "The appeal to the creators of culture to withdraw from the process of administration and keep distant from it has a hollow ring. Not only would this deprive them of the possibility of earning a living, but also of every effect, every contact between work of art and society, something which the work of greatest integrity cannot do without, if it is not to perish."[7]

A paradox, indeed. Or a vicious circle. On the one hand, culture cannot live in peace with management, particularly with an obtrusive and insidious management, and most particularly with a management aimed at twisting the culture's exploring and experimenting urge so that it fits into the frame of rationality the managers have drawn—the selfsame rationality that the artistic exploration of the "not yet" and the "merely possible" needs to transgress and cannot but transgress; whereas the managers, being bent (as they are, professionally, bound to be) on defending the cause of that rationality tooth and nail, must view the arts as adversaries—and the more so the better the arts perform their own mission. Management's plot against the endemic freedom of the arts is for the artists a perpetual casus belli. On the other hand, however, culture creators need managers if they wish (as most of them, bent on "improving the world," must) to be seen, heard, listened to—and so to stand a chance of seeing their mission/task/project through to its completion. Otherwise they risk marginality, impotence, and oblivion.

Culture creators have no choice but to live with that paradox. However loudly they protest against managers' pretensions and interference, the alternative to seeking a modus covivendi with administration is to sink into irrelevance. They may choose between alternative managements pursuing different purposes and thus using different means and deploying different strategies to trim liberty from cultural creation—but certainly not between *acceptance* and *rejection* of management as such. Not realistically, at any rate.

This is the case because the paradox in question stems from the fact that, despite all the conflicts of interests and mutual mudslinging, culture creators and managers are bound to share the same household and partake of the same endeavor. Theirs is a *sibling rivalry*. They are after the same target, sharing the same goal: to make the world different from what it would be likely to be or would turn into if left alone. Both of them are critical toward the ability of the status quo to sustain, direct, and assert itself. They quarrel not about whether the world should be an object of constant intervention or left to its own inner tendencies—but about the direction that the intervention should take. Ultimately, at stake in their strife is the right to be in charge and the capacity to make that "being in charge" effective. Each of the antagonists claims the right to decide the direction for intervention and to select the tools with which its pursuit is monitored, as well as the measures by which progress toward the goal is assessed.

Hannah Arendt flawlessly spotted and spelled out the gist of the conflict:

> An object is cultural depending on the duration of its permanence: its durable character is opposed to its functional aspect, that aspect which would make it disappear from the phenomenal world through use and wear and tear . . .
>
> Culture finds itself under threat when all objects of the world, produced currently or in the past, are treated solely as functions of the vital social processes—as if they had no other reason but satisfaction of some need—and it does not matter whether the needs in question are elevated or base.[8]

Culture aims above the head of the realities of the day. It is not concerned with whatever has been put on the daily agenda and defined as the imperative of the moment—or at least it strives to transcend the limiting impact of "topicality," however and by whomever defined, and struggles to free itself of its demands.

Being used or consumed on the spot, let alone dissolving in the process of instantaneous consumption, is neither the cultural products' destination nor the criterion for their value. Arendt would say that culture is after *beauty*—and I suggest that she chose that name for culture's concerns because the idea of "beauty" is the very epitome of an elusive target that stubbornly and steadfastly defies rational or causal explanation, which has no purpose or obvious use, serves nothing, and cannot legitimate itself by reference to any need already felt, defined, and scheduled for gratification; whatever needs it may in the end gratify are yet to be enticed into being by the act of artistic creation. An object is "cultural" insofar as it outlives any use that might have attended to its creation.

Such an image of culture differs sharply from the common opinion, which was until recently also prevalent in academic literature; an opinion that, in contrast, cast culture among the homeostatic appliances meant to preserve the monotonous reproduction of social reality, its *mêmeté,* and thereby to help ensure the continuation of its sameness over time. The notion of culture common to the writings classified under the rubric of social science (and by and large unquestioned until recently) has been one of a stabilizing, routine- and repetition-begetting and servicing mechanism, an instrument of inertia—and not at all an instrument of the ferment that prevents social reality from standing still and forces it into perpetual self-transcendence, as Adorno and Arendt would insist it must.

The classic notion of culture, whose domination coincided with the solid phase of modernity guided by managerial reason, was as an element of self-renewing order, rather than of its eternal disruption and overhaul. In the orthodox anthropological descriptions (one society = one culture), culture appears as an efficient tool for "pattern maintenance," a handmaiden of social structure—of a permanent distribution of behavioral probabilities that retains its shape over time and successfully fights back all occasional breaches of the norm, disruptions, and deviations that threaten to throw the system out of its equilibrium. This conception of culture was, to be sure, simultaneously an extrapolation and the utopian horizon of a properly managed (or, to recall Talcott Parsons's once widely used phrase, "principally coordinated") social totality, marked by a stable distribution of probabilities and tightly controlled by a number of homeostatic contraptions, among which culture was assigned the pride of place; a kind of totality inside which wrong manners or deviant actions of individual human units are promptly spotted, isolated before irreparable harm can be done, and swiftly defused or eliminated. Inside that vision of the society as a self-equilibrating system (that is, one remaining obstinately the same despite all the pressures of countervailing forces) *"culture" stands for the managers' dream come true: an effective resistance to change*—but above all, resistance to, and preferably the preempting of, unplanned, undesigned change, haphazard change, change caused by anything other than the will of the manager and the manager's definition of what is useful, sensible, and proper.

That dream, if fulfilled, would usher into the world what Joseph Brodsky described under the name of "tyranny," referring to an arrangement of human togetherness that "structures your world for you. It does this as meticulously as possible, certainly much better than democracy does . . . The dream is to make every man its own bureaucrat."[9] As Milan Kundera insists, while calling that tyranny by the name of "totalitarianism," in such a "world of repetitions" that "excludes relativity, doubt and questioning," there is no room for the arts.[10] "The history of novel writing (painting, music) was born of human freedom, of human personal achievement, of human choice"— and was developed through improvisation and the creation of its own rules as it went.[11]

It was, however, in the spirit of managerialism that the role of culture used to be most commonly perceived even two to three decades ago, at a time when culture was annexed, or intended to be annexed, by the managerial project that mastered (or struggled to master) the perception of the human world.

Much has happened in the last two to three decades, though. To start with, we have experienced the "managerial revolution, mark II," conducted surreptitiously under the banner of "neoliberalism." The cultural managers switched from "normative regulation" to "seduction," from day-to-day surveillance and policing to PR, and from the stolid, overregulated, routine-based, panoptical, all-surveilling and all-monitoring model of power to domination through casting the dominated into a state of diffuse uncertainty, *précarité,* and a continuous though haphazard disruption of routine. And then, the state-serviced frame in which the paramount parts of individual life-politics used to be held was gradually dismantled as well, and life-politics shifted/drifted into the domain operated by consumer markets. In stark opposition to state bureaucracy, consumer markets are known to thrive on the *frailty* of routines and their rapid *supercession*—rapid enough to prevent their hardening into habits or norms.

In this new setting, there is little demand for bridling and taming the transgressive urge and compulsive experimentation dubbed culture in order to deploy it in the service of self-equilibration and continuity. Or at least the traditional and the most stalwart carriers of that demand at one time, the would-be managers of the nation-building states, have lost their interest in such deployment, whereas the new scriptwriters and directors of cultural drama, who joined or replaced them, would wish from humans, now transformed into consumers first and last, anything but tamed, regular, routine-bound, inflexible conduct.

With the principal characters of the solid-modernity drama leaving the stage or being downgraded to the half-mute role of supernumeraries, and with their replacements failing—and possibly also not particularly eager—to emerge from the wings, our contemporaries found themselves acting in what can be properly called, following Hannah Arendt, who in turn took her inspiration from Bertolt Brecht, "dark times." This is how Arendt unpacked the nature and the origins of that darkness:

> If it is the function of the public realm to throw light on the affairs of men by providing a space of appearances in which they can show in deed and word, for better and worse, who they are and what they can do, then darkness has come when this light is extinguished by "credibility gap" and "invisible government," by speech that does not disclose what is but sweeps it under the carpet, by exhortations, moral or otherwise, that, under the pretext of upholding old truths, degrade all truth to meaningless triviality.[12]

And this is how Arendt described its consequences:

> The public realm has lost the power of illumination which was originally part of its nature. More and more people in the countries of the Western world, which since the decline of the ancient world has regarded freedom from politics as one of the basic freedoms, make use of this freedom and have retreated from the world and their obligations

within it . . . But with each such retreat an almost demon-
strable loss to the world takes place: what is lost is the specific and usually irreplaceable in-between which should
have formed between the individual and his fellow men.[13]

Withdrawal from politics and the public realm will turn,
therefore, wrote Hannah Arendt prophetically, into the "basic
attitude of the modern individual, who in his alienation from
the world can truly reveal himself only in privacy and in the in-
timacy of face-to-face encounters."[14]

It is that newly gained and enforced privacy and the "inti-
macy of face-to-face encounters"—the inseparable companion,
simultaneously outcome and cause, of "dark times"—that are
serviced by the consumer markets, which in turn promote
the universal contingency of the consumer's life while cap-
italizing on the fluidity of social placements and the growing
frailty of human bonds; on the contentious, unstable, and unpredictable status of individual rights, obligations, and commitments; and on a present that eludes the grasp of its denizens and a future obstinately uncontrollable and uncertain.
Acting under pressure and out of impotence, yet with little
resistance, if not willingly, the state managers abandon the ambitions of normative regulation of which they once stood
accused by Adorno and other critics who feared the all-too-
real prospect of a "fully administered mass society." The state
managers put themselves instead in the "agentic state" and assume the role of "honest brokers" of the market's needs (read:
the demands of commodity promoters). In other words, they
subsidiarize or contract out the risks, chores, and responsibilities of "running the show" to the market forces, turning them
over to the play of demand and offering up the once jealously
guarded right to call the tune, together with the duty to pay the
pipers. These agent-managers now declare their own neutral-

ity in the hotly contested issue of cultural, including artistic, choices. With culture no longer needed as a tool for the design, building, and maintenance of order, and for the mass mobilizations those steps all require, things cultural have been decommissioned and put on sale to individual shoppers, in updated versions of the army and navy surplus stores.

Culture creators may nevertheless still be up in arms against the obtrusive intervention of the managers, who all—political and commercial alike—tend to insist on measuring cultural performance by *extrinsic* criteria alien to the irrationality, spontaneity, and inherent freedom of creativity, and who use their power and the resources they command to secure obedience to the rules and standards they have set, thus clipping the wings of artistic imagination and jarring with the principles that guide the artists' creativity. It needs to be repeated, however, that the arts' principal objection to managerial interference is not, as it has been argued, a novel departure—it is but another chapter in a long story of "sibling rivalry" that has no end in sight. For better or worse, for better *and* worse, cultural creators at all times need managers—lest they should die far from the madding crowd, in the same ivory tower in which they were conceived.

What *are* truly novel are the criteria that the present-day managers, in their new role as agents of market forces rather than of nation-building state powers, deploy to assess, audit, monitor, judge, censure, reward, and punish their wards. Naturally, these are *consumer-market* criteria, which reflect a set preference for *instant* consumption, *instant* gratification, and *instant* profit. A consumer market catering to long-term needs, not to mention eternity, would be a contradiction in terms. The consumer market promotes rapid circulation, shorter distances from use to waste and from consignment to waste to waste disposal, all for the sake of the immediate replacement of no-longer-profitable goods. And all that stands in jarring opposition to the nature of artistic creation and the message of the arts, which, in Kundera's words, "is silenced in the hubbub of easy and speedy answers that preempt and annihilate the questions."[15] And so the novelty, one may conclude, is the parting of ways followed by the siblings still being engaged in rivalry.

At stake in the new chapter of their age-old tug-of-war is not just the answer to be proffered to the question "Who is in charge?" but the very meaning of "being in charge"—its purpose and its consequences. I might go a step (a small step, as it were) further, and say that what is at stake now is the survival of the arts as we have known them since the Altamira cave paintings were made. Can culture survive the devaluation of duration, the demise of infinity—that first "collateral casualty" of the consumer market's victory? The answer to that question is that we don't really know—though one could be excused for favoring a "no" answer, and though one might, following Hans Jonas's advice to the denizens of the "era of uncertainty," put more trust in the dark premonitions of the "prophets of doom" than in the reassurances of the brave-new-consuming-life's promoters.

To subordinate cultural creativity to the standards and criteria of consumer markets means to demand that cultural creations accept the prerequisite of all would-be consumer products: that they legitimize themselves in terms of market value (the *current* market value, to be sure)—or perish.

The first query addressed to artistic products bidding for recognition of their (market) value is that of market demand (is it already sufficient or likely to be speedily and expediently boosted?), followed by whether demand is supported by an adequate capacity to pay. Let us note that, consumer demand being notoriously capricious, freak, and volatile, the records of the consumer market's rule over artistic products are full of mistaken prognoses, wide-of-the-mark evaluations, and grossly incorrect decisions. In practice, that rule boils down to compensating for the absent *quality* analysis with the *quantitative* overshooting of potential targets and a lot of bets-hedging, both resulting in a wasteful excess and excessive waste (G. B. Shaw, a dedicated and skillful practitioner of photography in addition to his consummate playwriting, advised fellow photographers to follow the example of the codfish, which must spawn a thousand eggs in order to hatch one mature offspring; it seems that the whole consumer industry, and the marketing managers who keep it alive, follow Shaw's advice). Such a strategy may sometimes insure against the exorbitant losses caused by mistaken cost-and-effect analysis; it does little or nothing, however, to assure artists that their creations stand a chance of revealing their true quality if no market demand for them is in sight (this being an eminently *short* sight, given the endemic "short-termism" of market calculations).

It is now the prospective clients, their numbers and the volume of cash in their bank accounts, that decide (though unknowingly) the fate of artistic creations. The line dividing the "successful" products (which therefore command public attention) from the failed ones (that is, those unable to break through into the notoriety achievable solely in and through art galleries) is drawn by sales, ratings, and box-office returns. According to Daniel J. Boorstin's witty definitions, a "celebrity is a person who is known for his well-knownness," while "a best seller" is a book that somehow sold well "simply because it was selling well." The same can be said about best-selling objets d'art. And not much more than the one-directional correlation suggested by Boorstin's tongue-in-cheek definitions has been established thus far by the theorists and critics of contemporary art between the intrinsic artistic virtues of creations and the celebrity status of their authors. If the effective cause of the artist's celebrity is sought, it is most likely to be found in the celebrity status of the brand (the gallery, the periodical) that, through its promotion of his or her work, has lifted the incipient artist from obscurity into the limelight.

The contemporary equivalent of good fortune or a stroke of luck, which has always been an indispensable factor in the artist's worldly success, is a Charles Saatchi stopping his car in front of an obscure side-street shop selling bric-a-brac patched together by an obscure side-street person who craved in vain to convince the accidental and rare visitors of its artistic valor. That bric-a-brac promptly turns into works of art once it is transferred to a gallery whose walls and gates separate good art from bad (and, for the cognoscenti, art from nonart). The glory of the gallery name rubs off on the names of the artists on exhibition. In the vexingly confusing liquid-modern world of flexible norms and floating values, this is—not unexpectedly—a universal trend, rather than a specifically artistic oddity. As Naomi Klein succinctly put it, "Many of today's best-known manufacturers no longer produce products and advertise them, but rather buy products and 'brand' them."[16] The brand and the logo attached (it is the shopping bag with the name of the gallery that gives meaning to the purchases carried inside) do not add value—they *are* value, the *market* value, and thus value *as such*.

It is not just companies that lend value to artistic products through branding (or devalue products by withdrawing their logo); the act of branding is as a rule supplemented by an *event*—short-lived but all-stops-pulled-out, multimedia "hype." Events seem to be the most potent sources of value: the promotional events, "hyped" events, are massively attended, of course, thanks to being known to be massively attended, and they sell masses of tickets because tickets are known to command long queues.

Such events steer clear of the risks involved in the mere display of art products in even the most celebrated galleries. Unlike the galleries, they don't need to reckon on the dubious loyalty of the faithful in a world attuned to the notoriously short span of public memory and the cut-throat competition among countless attractions vying for the consumer's attention. Events, like all bona fide consumer products, bear a "use-by" date; their designers and managers can leave long-term concerns out of their calculations (with the double benefit of huge savings and the confidence inspired by being in tune with the spirit of the age). Events producers plan and cater, to recall George Steiner's apt phrase, for "maximal impact and instant obsolescence."

The spectacular, mind-boggling rise of fixed-time events (that is, of the events with a time span not exceeding the life expectancy of public interest) as the most prolific sources of market value chimes well with the universal tendency of the liquid-modern setting. Culture products—whether inanimate objects or educated humans—tend these days to be enlisted in the service of "projects," admittedly one-off and short-lived undertakings. And, as the research team quoted by Naomi Klein found out, "You can indeed brand not only sand, but also wheat, beef, brick, metals, concrete, chemicals, corn grits and an endless variety of commodities, traditionally considered immune to the process"—that is, such objects as are believed (wrongly, as it transpires) to be able to stand on their own feet and prove their point just by unfolding and demonstrating their own valor and excellence.[17]

For centuries, culture lived in an uneasy symbiosis or love-hate relationship with management, tussling uncomfortably, sometimes suffocating in the managers' embrace, but also running to the managers for shelter and emerging reinvigorated and strengthened from the encounter. Would culture survive the change of management? Would it be allowed anything but a butterfly-like, ephemeral existence? Won't the new management, true to the new managerial style, limit its wardenship to asset-stripping? Won't the cemetery of deceased or aborted "cultural events" replace the rising slope as a fitful metaphor for culture?

Willem de Kooning suggests that in this world of ours, "content is a glimpse," a fugitive vision, a look in passing.[18] Meanwhile, a most incisive analyst of the twists and turns of post-postmodern culture, Yves Michaud, suggests that aesthetics, art's forever-elusive and stubbornly pursued target, is these days consumed and celebrated in a world emptied, devoid, of the works of art.[19]

Aside from happiness, beauty was one of the most exciting modern promises and guiding ideals of the restless modern spirit. The convoluted history and semantic adventures of the dream of happiness, I have briefly described elsewhere.[20] Now is the turn of beauty; its history may be seen as paradigmatic for the birth and development of the liquid-modern culture of waste.

The idea of beauty, I suggest, used to be—at least since the Renaissance—made to the measure of managerial ambitions. The concepts most often cropping up in the early stages of the modern debate about the meaning of "beauty" were harmony, proportion, symmetry, order, and such like (John Keats, in "Endymion," would add health and quiet breathing)—all converging on an ideal perhaps most pithily formulated by Leon Battista Alberti: the ideal of a state in which any change can be only a change for the worse; a state to which Alberti gave the name of *perfection*. Beauty meant perfection, and it was the perfect that had the right to be called beautiful. Many a great modern artist struggled to conjure up such a state of perfection, and indeed to make the search for perfection, in Alberti's sense, the subject matter of his work. Think, for instance, of Mondrian, Matisse, Arp, or Rothko. Cut the colorful rectangles out of Mondrian's paintings and attempt to rearrange them in an order different from the one that Mondrian selected, and the odds are that you will find your arrangements, indeed *all and any* alternative arrangements, inferior—less pleasing, "ugly" by comparison. Or cut out the figures in Matisse's *Dance* and try to position them so they relate to one another in a different way; you will most certainly experience a similar frustration.

But what, in the last account, is the meaning of "perfection?" Once the object has acquired the "perfect" form, all further change is undesirable and unadvisable. Perfection means change should come to an end. No more changes. Short of being transported to another universe, everything from now on will be the same—eternally. What is perfect will never lose its value, never become redundant, never be rejected and disposed of and so will never turn into waste; it is, on the contrary, all further searching and experimenting that will from now on be redundant. And so, when pining after perfection, we need to stretch our imagination to the utmost, to deploy all our creative powers—but only in order to render imagination a wasteful pastime and creativity not just unnecessary but undesirable. If beauty means perfection, then once beauty has been reached, nothing is going to happen anymore. There is nothing *after* beauty.

We humans are, and cannot help being, "transgressive," "transcending" sorts of animals, and the artists (or at least the "true" artists, whatever that may mean) more so than other humans. They live ahead of the present. Their representations may be cut loose from the senses and run ahead of them. The world they inhabit is always a step, or a mile, or a stellar year ahead of the world we are experiencing. That part of the world that sticks out ahead of the lived experience we call "ideals"; ideals are to guide us into the territory as yet unexplored and unmapped.

"Beauty" was one such ideal that guided artists beyond the world that already was. Its value was fully entailed in its guiding power. Had the artists ever reached the point that the ideal of beauty marks, it would have lost that power—their journey would have come to an end. There would be nothing left to transgress and transcend, and so also no room for exploration and experiment.

We call many things beautiful, but of none of them would we be able to honestly say that it could not be improved. Perfection *is forever "not-yet."* Only people who have a lot to improve may dream of a state of affairs in which no further improvement would be desirable. The vision of perfection may be a eulogy of stillness, but the job of that vision is to pull and push us away from what is, to bar us from standing still. *Stillness* is what the graveyards are about—and yet, paradoxically, it is the *dream of stillness* that keeps us alive. So long as the dream remains unfulfilled, we count the days and the days count—there is a purpose and there is an unfinished job to do.

Not that such work, which stubbornly, infuriatingly refuses to be finished, is an unmixed blessing and brings unpolluted happiness. The condition of "unfinished business" has many charms, but like all other conditions, it falls short of perfection. For Picasso, artistic creation was divine when rejecting the pursuit of beauty, because God was not a perfectionist. According to the testimony of Françoise Gilot and Carlton Lake, Picasso considered God as "really only another artist. He invented the giraffe, the elephant, and the cat. He has no real style. He just goes on trying other things." Musing on the state and prospects of contemporary art, Tom Wolfe wondered: "We've got rid of representational objects, third dimension, dye stuff, technique, frame and canvas . . . but what about the wall itself? The image of the work of art as a thing on the wall—is it not premodern?"[21]

Jacques Villeglé, a practicing artist, keen photographer, and painter of huge canvases that hang on the walls of all the most prestigious Parisian salons of art (or at least I found them hanging there four years ago . . .), thinks of a different kind of wall: a thoroughly postmodern contraption, a wall facing the street where the action unfolds, a window rather than a part of the cage/shelter that, under the modernist rule, used to define the difference between the "inside" and the "outside" in the arts. The walls that gape from Villeglé's canvases pasted on the *gallery* walls are the walls in the city, those living, constantly unfinished and constantly updated records of the eminently modern art—the art of modern living. Such walls are the very places where the evidence of living can be found—revealed and recorded in order to be later transferred inside to the museum walls, to be reincarnated as objets d'art. Villeglé's objects are the walls and customized billboards that carry public notices and announcements, posters and advertisements; or just the stretches of wall that separate and hide private residences and public places. Those plots of blank brickwork and spans of bland concrete are a constant challenge and temptation for the printers, distributors, and hangers of bills, a temptation impossible to resist in a liquid-modern city filled to the brim with sights and sounds vying for attention.

Once fixed on Villeglé's canvases, the billboards and the walls invaded and annexed by advancing troops from the empire of information hardly betray their different pasts. They all look shockingly alike. Whether they have been pasted and then pasted over again on the Boulevard de la Chapelle, or on Haussmann, Malesherbes, or rue Littré; or on Boulevard Marne, or rue des Écoles; or on Saint-Lazare, on Faubourg Saint-Martin, or at the crossing of Sèvres and Montparnasse. Each is a haphazard medley of graveyards and building sites; a meeting point for things about to die and things about to be born in order to die a bit later. The fragrance of fresh glue fights with the odor of putrefying corpses. *Affiches lacérées,* Villeglé calls his canvases. Scraps of paper already torn fly over would-be scraps yet to be torn. Half smiles on salvaged halves of faces; single eyes or solitary ears with no twins, knees and elbows with nothing to connect them and hold them together. Cries that fall silent before reaching comprehension, messages that dissolve and vanish in a fraction of a sentence, arrested and garroted well short of the birthplace of meaning; unfinished calls, or sentences with nowhere to start.

These scrap heaps are full of life, though. Nothing rests still here; everything that is, is on a temporary leave from elsewhere, or on a trip to somewhere else. All homes are but highway inns. These boards and walls, overcrowded with layer after layer of have-been, would-have-been, or would-be meanings, are snapshots of a history in the making, history that proceeds by shredding its traces: history as a *factory of rejects, of waste.* Neither creation nor destruction, neither learning nor genuine forgetting; just livid evidence of the futility—nay, utter silliness—of such distinctions. Nothing is born here to live long and nothing dies definitely. Duration? Sorry, what do you mean? Things made to last? What a strange idea . . .

Manolo Valdés's canvases are also huge and also remarkably like each other. Whatever message they convey, they repeat, with unctuous yet passionate persistence, over and over again, canvas by canvas. Valdés paints/collates/composes/sticks together *faces.* Or, rather, a single face—a single woman's face.

Each canvas is material evidence of another beginning, another go, another attempt to finish the portrait—not of bringing it to an end, whatever that word "end" might mean. Or is it, rather, a testimony to a job completed a while ago but, soon after, decried as obsolete and condemned? The canvas has been frozen, for sure, the moment it was pinned to the gallery wall—but on the way up or down? *Aller* or *retour*? You tell me. For my money, you won't be able to tell the "forward" from the "backward." Just like the opposition between creation and destruction, this distinction has lost its sense—or perhaps it never had any—though that void, now laid bare, where meaning was assumed to reside used to be a secret, closely guarded by all those who insisted that "forward" is the right name for where they, the forward-looking people, look and who averred that "creation" is the proper name for the destruction they, the creative people, accomplish. At least this is the message that Valdés's canvases, in unison, intone; perhaps their only message.

Valdés's collages have been laboriously patched together, layer by layer, with bits and pieces of hessian, or burlap—some of them dyed, some unashamed of the erstwhile blandness of jute or hemp; some primed to be painted over, some already shedding crumbs of the dried-up paint with which they were overlaid before. Or have they been torn apart from a canvas already complete, seamless, whole and wholesome? Patches are poorly glued—loose ends hang in the air—but again it is anything but clear whether they are about to be pressed to the other cuttings beneath or are in the course of getting unstuck and coming off. Are these collages snapshots caught in the process of creation, or in a state of advanced decomposition? Are these bits and pieces of hessian not yet fixed or already unfixed? Fresh and immature, or used up and putrescent? The message is: It does not matter, and you would not know what it is even if it did.

Villeglé and Valdés are representative artists of the liquid-modern era—of an era that has lost self-confidence, resigned itself to the whirlwind of consumerist existence, and forfeited the boldness of sketching (let alone pursuing) models of perfection, a condition that would put an end to the whirlwind. Unlike the preceding era of solid modernity that lived toward "eternity" (shorthand for a state of perpetual, monotonous, and irrevocable sameness), liquid modernity sets itself no objective and draws no finishing line; more precisely, it assigns the quality of permanence solely to the state of transience. Time *flows;* time no longer "marches on." There is change, always change, ever new and different change—but no destination, no finishing point, no anticipation of a mission accomplished. Each lived-through moment is pregnant, *simultaneously,* with a new beginning *and* the end—once sworn antagonists, now Siamese twins.

The artists discussed here replicate in their works the defining features of liquid-modern experience. Canceling the oppositions between creative and destructive acts, learning and forgetting, forward and backward steps—as well as cutting the pointer off the time arrow—these are all marks of lived reality that Villeglé and Valdés recycle onto canvases fit to be hung on the gallery walls. Nor are they alone; digesting those novel qualities of the *Lebenswelt* and articulating the experience are perhaps the major preoccupations of the arts, now cast into a world with no "sitters"—a world no longer trusted to sit still long enough to allow the artist to complete its portrait. That preoccupation expresses itself over and over again in the tendency to reduce the life span of art products to a performance, a happening, the brief time span between the opening and the dismantling of an exhibition; in the preference for frail and friable, eminently degradable, and perishable materials among the stuff of which art objects are made; in the earthworks unlikely either to be visited by many or to survive for long the caprices of inclement weather; all in all, in incorporating the imminence of decay and disappearance into the material presence of the object.

Imperceptibly, the meaning of "beauty" undergoes a fateful change. In the current uses of the word, philosophers would hardly recognize the concepts they so earnestly and laboriously constructed over past centuries. More than anything else, they would miss the link between beauty and eternity, between aesthetic value and durability. However furiously they quarreled, all philosophers used to agree, in the now-by-gone times, that beauty rises above fickle and fragile private whims, and that even if there could be such a thing as "beauty at first sight," only the (endless?) flow of time would put it to the trustworthy, ultimate, and clinching test ("A thing of beauty is a joy forever," as Keats insisted). Today's philosophers would also miss the "claim to universal validity" that used to be viewed as an indispensable attribute of any properly aesthetic judgment. It is these two points that fell by the board with the advent of the liquid-modern "casino culture," and they are conspicuously absent from the current popular uses of the word "beauty."

In order not to waste their clients' time or to prejudice their future, yet unpredictable joys, consumer markets offer products meant for immediate consumption, preferably for one-time use, and then rapid disposal and replacement, so that the living space won't stay cluttered once the objects admired and coveted today fall out of fashion. The clients, confused by the whirlwind of products, mind-boggling variety of offers, and vertiginous pace of change, can no longer rely on their own ability to learn and memorize—and so they must (and do, gratefully) accept the market's reassurances that the product currently on offer is "*the* thing," the "*hot* thing," the "*must-*

have," and the "must-be-seen (-in or -with) thing." It is Lewis Carroll's hundred-year-old fantasy turned now into reality: "It takes all the running *you* can do, to keep in the same place. If you want to get somewhere else, you must run at least twice as fast as that!"

The everlasting or "objective" aesthetic value of the product is the last thing to worry about. And beauty is not "in the eye of the beholder": it is instead located in today's fashion, and so the beautiful is bound to turn ugly the moment the current fads are replaced by others, as they surely will be soon. If not for the market's wondrous capacity to impose a regular, even if short-lived, pattern on the ostensibly individual and so potentially random and diffuse customer choices, customers would feel totally disoriented and lost. Taste is no longer a safe guide, learning and relying on one's already acquired knowledge is a trap rather than a help, yesterday's *comme il faut* may well turn, without warning, into *comme il ne faut pas*.

"Beauty rules"—observes Yves Michaud in his trenchant report on the state of the arts in the liquid-modern world. "In all respects it has become an imperative: be beautiful, or at least spare us your ugliness."[22] To be ugly means to be condemned to the rubbish heap. Conversely, having been condemned to the rubbish heap is all the proof one needs of ugliness. This was, wasn't it, what the modern artists, and the learned philosophers of aesthetics who reflected on their labors, dreamed of all along. So what do we witness—the final triumph of the beautiful? The fulfillment of at least one of the most ambitious "modern projects"?

Not so, Michaud would say. In fact, aesthetics *has* triumphed—but over its own object. Aesthetics won through the *trivialization* of beauty—by sapping the status of the so-called works of art ("precious and rare," "invested with [an] aura and magic qualities," "unique, refined and sublime"). "The 'aesthetic' is cultivated, diffused and consumed in a world emptied of the works of art," Michaud writes. Art has evaporated into a sort of "aesthetic ether," which, like the ether of the pioneers of modern chemistry, permeates all things and condenses in none. "Beautiful" are sweaters bearing the currently celebrated designer's label; or bodies reshaped after the latest fashion, with gym workouts and plastic surgeries and makeup; or packaged products on supermarket shelves. Says Michaud, "Even the corpses are beautiful—neatly wrapped in plastic covers and aligned in front of the ambulances."[23] Everything has, or at least may have and should try to have, its fifteen minutes, perhaps even fifteen days, of beauty on the road to the dump.

What the graveyards are to living humans, museums are to the works of art: sites in which to keep or dispose of the objects that are no longer vital and animate. Some human corpses are laid in graves and overlaid with gravestones to be visited by those who feel orphaned or bereaved by their disappearance; some others vanish forever in unmarked mass burial places or disintegrate without a trace in scorched villages, burning ovens, and the depths of Rio de la Plata. Some works of art are placed in museums, where their once-acclaimed beauty is sanitized, sterilized, and embalmed, to be preserved alongside archaeological findings for the fans of history or the passengers of tourist coaches. Graveyards and museums alike are set away from the hurly-burly of daily life, separated from life's business in their own enclosed spaces and with their own visiting hours. In museums, as at the cemeteries, one does not talk loudly, one does not eat, drink, run, or touch the objects of the visit.

The scene of daily life is different. That scene is the site of aesthetics, not objets d'art. It is the stage for ephemeral performances and happenings, for installations scrambled together out of manifestly and self-consciously perishable materials or sewn together with the yarn of immaterial thoughts—for all those things and events that would swear not to overstay their welcome and would keep their solemn promise. Nothing put and seen on that stage is meant to last or to intrude and vex once its time is over—frailty and transience are the names of the game. Whatever happens there can carry only as much meaning as its own tiny carrying capacity can embrace and hold. That meaning will be, after all, sought and gleaned by people drilled in the art of "zapping"—and "zappers" enter "after [the name of the] editor and before 'the end' appears on the screen."[24] Michaud writes of the "new regime of attention which privileges scanning over reading and deciphering of meanings. The image is fluid and mobile, less a spectacle or a datum than an element of a chain of action."[25] Having cut itself loose from the referential sequence of which it was a part, the image is free to be harnessed at will to any cortège or sequence of phantasms.

The relocation of images from the focus of attention to the attention's own refuse pile—irrelevance and invisibility—is random. The difference between "the object" and its indifferent surroundings has been all but obliterated, much as has the time separating being in the focus from being cast out of sight. Objects and waste change places easily. I remember admiring in a Copenhagen art gallery an installation put together out of a series of TV screens, each with huge captions reading, "the promised land." I found the installation thoughtful and thought provoking—not least because of the broom and bucket standing in the corner at the end of the series. Before I had time, though, to think that meaning through to its end, a cleaner returned to collect her work tools, which she had left in the corner for the duration of her coffee break.

Only numbers may offer the perplexed viewers, lost on their search for beauty, a hope of rescue from the chaos conjured up by a culture of free-floating aesthetics with no fixed objects. Salvation is in numbers. As the writers of commercial copy untiringly repeat—all those people who proudly sport the latest fashion can't all be wrong. Magically, the massiveness of a choice ennobles its object. That object *must* be beautiful, everyone thinks; otherwise it would not have been chosen by so many choosers. Beauty is in high sales figures, box-office records, platinum discs, sky-high television ratings. (Andy Warhol once mused: imagine a bunch of banknotes hanging on a string—one hundred sixty thousand dollars . . . What a beautiful picture!) Perhaps beauty is also somewhere else, as some philosophers stubbornly insist—but how would you know? And who would approve of your findings, if you searched for them in bizarre places *à qui on ne parle plus?* Even the Old Masters, whose reputation is sure, one would think, thanks to their venerable age and the number of tests they have triumphantly passed over the centuries, cannot ignore the new rules of the beauty game. It is Vermeer today, Matisse the other day, and Picasso the day after, that you *must see* and *be seen* to be seeing—depending on the latest hype of a successive "everybody who is anybody is talking about" exhibition. As in all other cases, beauty is not a quality of their canvases but a (*quantitatively* evaluated, by the carefully counted and promptly publicized number of visitors) quality of the *event*.

In our liquid-modern society, beauty met the fate suffered by all the other ideals that used to motivate human restlessness and rebellion. The search for ultimate harmony and eternal duration has been recast as, purely and simply, an ill-advised concern. Values are values insofar as they are fit for instantaneous, on-the-spot consumption. Values are attributes of *momentary experiences*. And so is beauty. And life? Life is a succession of momentary experiences.

"Beauty has no obvious use; nor is there any clear cultural

necessity for it. Yet civilization could not do without it," Freud mused. "This useless thing which we expect civilization to value is beauty. We require civilized man to reverence beauty whenever he sees it in nature and to create it in the objects of his handiwork so far as he is able." Beauty and, with it, cleanliness and order "obviously occupy a special position among the requirements of civilization."[26]

Let us note that all three objectives named by Freud as "the requirements of civilization" are *imaginary horizons* of the civilizing process. It would be perhaps better, less misleading and controversial, to speak of *beautification, purification,* and *ordering,* rather than of beauty, purity, and order. We see now, more clearly than our ancestors could possibly have noted seventy years ago, that the "civilizing process" is not a time-limited, transitory period leading to civilization—but the very substance of "civilization." The idea of a civilization that has completed the effort to civilize (brought to an end the cleaning job, the ordering bustle, and the search for beauty) is as incongruous as that of a wind that does not blow and a river that does not flow. It is out of the *hunger* for beauty that civilizations (that is, the efforts to "civilize," the "civilizing processes") have been born. But far from placating that hunger, they seem to have made it insatiable.

The gradual yet resolute dismantling of the administrative wardenship over the arts was greeted by the denizens of the art worlds with mixed feelings. Some were pushed to the edge of despair—just as Voltaire had been two hundred years before, when the Louis XIV court, which had supplied everything needed to set the creative effort on a firm track (that is, the purpose of creation and the relative values of creations), had fallen apart and the creators moved to the Parisian salons with their endless *querelles,* interminable games of musical chairs, and proclivity to melt all and any solid convictions. Some others were elated: Now, finally, we are free, they thought. If freedom can't be gained without uncertainty—so be it. At least now "creating" would be tantamount to self-creation, and this was a gain that justified all losses.

A word of warning is, however, in order—and for that purpose I'll quote one more time Joseph Brodsky's reflections on exile from the land of administrative tyranny or tyrannical administration—that, one would (rightly!) say, extreme and most radical case of liberation conceivable. Brodsky warns: "A freed man is not a free man . . . [L]iberation is just the means of attaining freedom and is not synonymous with it." And he concludes: "A free man, when he fails, blames nobody."[27]

CHAPTER SIX

Making the Planet Hospitable to Europe

•

THE TITLE OF this chapter implies that our planet is not at the moment hospitable to Europe. It also suggests, obliquely, that we, the Europeans, experience the lack of such hospitality as a problem—that is, as a deviation from what could be legitimately expected, an abnormality that needs to be put right again. And I say "again" since, presumably, we used to be made to feel at home on the planet. Wherever and whenever we went, we would have expected hospitality to be extended to us and our daring pursuits as our birthright; and we would have assumed that the homey feeling would continue as part of the natural order of things. This "hospitality" came to us so naturally that it hardly ever occurred to us to view it as a "problem" calling for special attention. As Martin Heidegger would have put it, it remained in the gray and misty area of *zuhanden*—and so long as things worked as they were expected to, there was no occasion to move it into the sphere of *vorhanden*—into the focus of attention, into the universe of "troubles" and "tasks."[1]

In 1784, Immanuel Kant shared with his contemporaries a few thoughts conceived in his tranquil, off-the-beaten-track seclusion in Königsberg. They were, in his own rendering, ideas of "universal history," considered from the point of view of "worldwide citizenship." Kant noted that the planet we inhabit is a *sphere*—and he thought through the consequences of that admittedly trivial observation: that we all stay and move about on the surface of that sphere, have nowhere else to go, and hence are bound to live forever in each other's neighborhood and company. Moving on a spherical surface, we cannot but shorten our distance on one side as we try to stretch it on the other. All efforts to lengthen a distance can only be ultimately self-defeating. And so, Kant mused, citizenship-style unification of the human species is the destination that Nature itself has chosen for us—the ultimate horizon of our universal history. Prompted and guided by reason and our interest in self-preservation, we are bound to pursue that horizon and (in the fullness of time) to reach it. Sooner or later, Kant warned, there will be no empty space left into which those of us who have found the already populated places too cramped—or too inconvenient, awkward, and uncomfortable—can venture. And so Nature commands us to view *hospitality* as the supreme precept, which we all in equal measure will have to embrace sooner or later—as we must seek an end and a resolution to the long chain of trials and errors, the catastrophes our errors have caused, and the ruin left in the wake of those catastrophes.

But unlike other books by the same author, this little book on the peaceful coexistence of humankind, on the imminent age of "citizenship of the world" and worldwide hospitality, gathered dust for two centuries in academic libraries. It was read only (if at all) by a few dedicated archivists of ideas, and read by them mostly as a historical curiosity, a freak product of an uncharacteristically lighthearted moment in the great philosopher's life of exemplary self-discipline and scholarly pedantry. Only quite recently, after two centuries of exile in the footnotes and bibliographies of scholarly monographs, did it suddenly burst into the very center of contemporary historiography. These days, it would be a tall order to find a learned study of the challenges of the current stage of planetary history that does *not* quote Kant's little book as a supreme authority and source of inspiration. As Jacques Derrida, for instance, observed, Kant's time-honored insights would easily expose present buzzwords like "culture of hospitality" or "ethics of hospitality" as mere pleonasms: "L'hospitalité, c'est la culture même et ce n'est pas une éthique parmi d'autres . . . *L'éthique est hospitalité.*"[2]

Indeed, if ethics is a work of reason, as Kant wished it to be, then hospitality is—must be, or must sooner or later become—the first rule of human conduct. Strange turn of fortune for a little book? Heidegger, with his depiction of the tortuous journey from the universe of *zuhanden* to that of *vorhanden*, would have no difficulty in explaining the puzzling *fatum* of this particular *libellae*. Hospitality has been noted as a universal commandment since the moment it stopped going unnoticed because it was "always there" and became instead conspicuous through its sudden (discomforting and painful) absence.

Ryszard Kapuściński, arguably the most acute and insightful reporter and recorder of the turn-of-century state of our world, noted a most fateful, if surreptitious and subterranean, change in the mood of the planet.[3] In the course of the past five centuries, Europe's military and economic dominance tended to be topped with the belief that its unchallenged position made it both the reference point for evaluation, praise, or condemnation of all other forms of human life, past and present, and the supreme court where such assessments were authoritatively pronounced and made binding. It was enough just to be a European, says Kapuściński, to feel everywhere else like a boss and a ruler. Even a mediocre person of humble standing and low opinion in his native (but European!) country rose to the highest social position once landing in a Malaysia or a Zambia. This is no longer the case, though, as Kapuściński notes. The present time is marked by the ever more self-assured and outspoken self-awareness of peoples who, half a century ago, still genuflected to Europe and placed it on the altar of cargo cults, but who now exhibit a fastgrowing sense of their own value and an evident ambition to gain and retain an independent and weighty place in the new, increasingly polycentric and multicultural world. Once upon a time, remembers Kapuściński, everyone he met in distant lands asked him about life in Europe, but no one does it anymore: today the "natives" have their own tasks and problems awaiting their attention, and theirs alone. No one seems to wait impatiently for news from Europe. What indeed could happen in Europe that would make a difference to their lives? Things that truly matter may happen in any place; Europe is no longer the site of preference. "The European presence" is ever less visible, physically as much as spiritually.

And another profound change has taken place on the planet to make us Europeans feel uncomfortable, uneasy, and apprehensive. The wide world "out there," at the other end of a long-distance flight from London, Paris, or Amsterdam, seldom if ever appears now to be a playground, a site for adventure—challenging and exciting but safe, with a happy ending certain and assured. Unless the flight in question is part of an all-inclusive holiday trip to a fashionable tourist resort, the places at the other end look more like a wilderness than a playground, teeming with unspoken and unspeakable dangers—the kind of "no-go," "keep out and away" areas that the ancient Romans used to mark out on their world maps with *hic sunt leones*. This is quite a change, a shocking change, traumatic enough to put paid to European self-confidence, courage, and ardor.

Indeed, until quite recently (the older among us still remember those times) Europe was the *center* that made the rest of the planet a *periphery*. As Denis de Rougemont crisply put it, Europe discovered all the lands of Earth, but no one ever discovered Europe.[4] Europe dominated all continents in succession but was never dominated by any, and it invented a civilization that the rest of the world tried to imitate, but the reverse process has never (thus far, at any rate) happened. I might add: European wars, and only those wars, have been *world* wars.

Until quite recently, one could still define Europe as de Rougemont suggested not that long ago, by its "globalizing function." Europe was for most of the past few centuries a uniquely adventurous continent, unlike any other. Having been the first continent to enter the mode of life that it subsequently dubbed modern, Europe created locally, in Europe, problems that no one on earth had heard of before and no one had the slightest inkling how to resolve. Then Europe invented their resolution—but in a form unfit to be universalized and deployed by all those for whom the problems, originally exclusively European, would arrive later. Europe resolved the problems it produced internally (and so locally) by transforming other parts of the planet into sources of cheap energy or cheap minerals, inexpensive and docile labor, and, above all, into so many dumping grounds for its excessive and redundant products and excessive and redundant people—the products it could not use and people it could not employ. To put it in a nutshell, Europe invented a *global* solution to its *locally* produced problems—and, by doing so, forced all other humans to seek, desperately and in vain, *local* solutions to the *globally* produced problems.

All this is over now—and thus the shock and the trauma we feel, the anxiety and the wilting and fading of our confidence. It is over because global solutions to locally produced problems can be available only to a few inhabitants of the planet, and only so long as they enjoy superiority over all the rest, as the benefit of a power differential large enough to remain unchallenged (or at least not challenged effectively) and widely believed to be unchallengeable, and for that reason, one that offers an apparently credible, reliable, and reassuring prospect of a long and secure future. But Europe no longer enjoys such privilege and cannot seriously hope to recover what it lost.

Hence the abrupt loss of European self-confidence, and the sudden explosion of acute interest in a "new European identity" and in "redefining the role" of Europe in the planetary game in which the rules and the stakes have drastically changed and continue to change—and to change outside Europe's control and with minimal, if any, European influence. Hence, also, the tide of neotribal sentiment swelling from Copenhagen to Rome and from Paris to Sofia, magnified and beefed up by deepening fears about "enemies at the gate" and "fifth columns," and the resulting besieged-fortress spirit manifested in the fast-rising popularity of securely locked borders and firmly shut doors.

It has become common to blame all such worrying developments on Europe's loss of economic and military domination as a result of the spectacular rise of the United States to the position of sole planetary superpower and the metropolis of the worldwide empire—and on the parallel dismantling of all Europe-centered empires and the loss of Europe's past imperial standing as a whole.

All roads now lead to Washington, so it is widely believed and even more widely said. All loose threads are tied up there. Amid the planetary chaos, it is the White House, Capitol Hill, and the Pentagon that, among themselves, define the meaning of the new planetary order, design its shape, and manage, monitor, equip, and police its implementation. The West, as Jürgen Habermas proclaimed, is divided, with Europe assigned thus far the role of a sometimes sympathetic, some other times resentful, but most of the time lukewarm, uninvolved, and/or ignored bystander.[5] More often than not, when the chances that a new worldwide order will emerge out of the present planetary chaos are pondered, thoughts focus on the intentions and actions of the United States of America, while the planet itself figures as the site of the American Empire in-the-making or, at best, as a most-favored province granted a "special relationship" with the metropole.

When the role of Europe in the emergent empire is contemplated, most efforts go into constructing and comparing various scenarios that the close though occasionally stormy European-American relations may follow: roles veering from those of an obedient courtier or witty, perspicacious, and clever court jester all the way to those of the dauphin's sage mentor or a wise, experienced, and respected member of a brain trust or advisory board; nowhere, however, along the spectrum of scenarios is the location of the court, or the incumbency of the highest office, treated as a moot or contentious point.

But is indeed the United States the "World Empire" in the sense with which Europe endowed the concept of empire through its own past practices, and which Europe bequeathed to the planet's residents through its own collective memory? There are many reasons to doubt that it is, and the reasons currently seem to multiply at an almost exponential rate. Quoting a recent summary by Immanuel Wallerstein, Morris Berman suggests that "Europe and Asia see [the U.S.] as much less important on the international scene, the dollar is weaker, nuclear proliferation is probably unstoppable, the U.S. military is stretched to the limit, and our [American] national and trade deficit is enormous. Our days of hegemony, and probably even leadership, would thus seem to be over."[6] In conclusion, Berman ventures so far as to insist that, rather than of the past empires in their heyday, the present plight of the "American World Empire" is reminiscent of "late-empire Rome and the subsequent slide into the Dark Ages" (as the third century A.D. was marked by almost continuous warfare, the collapse of the currency, and the spectacular rise of the military to political power, followed by the fourth century's repressive reactions, leading to chaos and anxiety and the fifth-century collapse).

There is little if any doubt that in terms of sheer expenditure on high-tech military equipment and the stockpiles of all kinds of weapons of mass destruction, the United States has no equal, and that no single state or combination of states can realistically contemplate matching the U.S. military power in the foreseeable future. (The United States spends annually on armaments a sum equal to the joint military expenditures of the twenty-five states next in rank.) It is also true, however, that the "U.S. military is stretched to its limits," without coming anywhere nearer to preventing new emergencies and resolving the problems lingering after unsuccessful efforts to respond adequately to the past ones. Perhaps even more important is the ever more obvious inadequacy of the American military machine for the kinds of tasks posed by the new shape of conflict, violence, and warfare.

Before sending U.S. troops to Iraq in 2003, Secretary of Defense Donald Rumsfeld declared that the "war will be won when Americans feel secure again."[7] But sending troops to Iraq pushed the mood of insecurity, in America and elsewhere, to new heights. Far from shrinking, the spaces of lawlessness, the highly effective training grounds for global terrorism, stretched to unheard-of dimensions. Five years have passed since Rumsfeld's decision, and terrorism has been gathering force—extensively and intensively—year by year. Terrorist outrages have been recorded in Tunisia, Bali, Mombasa, Riyadh, Istanbul, Casablanca, Jakarta, Madrid, Sharm el-Sheikh, and London; altogether, according to the U.S. State Department, there were 651 "significant terrorist attacks" in 2004 alone—198 of those, nine times more than a year before (not counting daily attacks on U.S. troops), in Iraq, to which the troops had been sent with the explicit order to put an end to the terrorist threat. In May 2005 there were 90 suicide bombings just in Baghdad; since then, massive atrocities, in Baghdad and elsewhere in Iraq, have gathered in frequency and force and become the daily routine. Iraq, as some observers aver, has become a grotesque advertisement for the power and efficacy of terror—and for the impotence and inefficiency of the alleged World Empire's "war on terror."

This is not a matter of tactical blunders committed by inept generals. Given the nature of contemporary terrorism, and above all the "negatively globalized" setting in which it operates, the very notion of the war on terrorism is all but a *contradictio in adiecto.*

Modern weapons, conceived and developed in the era of territorial invasions and conquests, are singularly unfit to locate, strike, and destroy the extraterritorial, endemically elusive, and eminently mobile targets, tiny squads or just single men or women traveling lightly, armed with weapons that are easy to hide. While difficult to pick out when on their way to commit another atrocity, such would-be "targets" perish on the site of the outrage or disappear from it as rapidly and inconspicuously as they arrived, leaving behind few if any traces.

To deploy Paul Virilio's apt terms, we have now passed (an event only belatedly noted and grudgingly admitted by the military) from the times of "siege warfare" to those of "wars of movement."[8] Given the nature of the modern weapons at the disposal of the military, its responses to terrorist acts must appear awkward, clumsy, and fuzzy, spilling over a much wider area than the one affected by the terrorist outrage, and causing yet more numerous "collateral casualties," greater volumes of "collateral damage," and so also more terror, disruption, and destabilization than the terrorists could possibly produce on their own—as well as provoking a further leap in the volume of accumulated grievance, hatred, and pent-up fury and stretching yet further the ranks of potential recruits to the terrorist cause. We may surmise that this circumstance is an integral part of the terrorists' design and the principal source of their strength, which exceeds many times the power of their numbers and arms.

Unlike their declared enemies, the terrorists need not feel constrained by the limits of the forces they themselves muster and directly command. When working out their strategic designs and tactical plans, they may include among their assets the probable reactions of the "enemy," as these are certain to magnify considerably the intended impact of their own atrocities. If the declared (immediate) purpose of the terrorists is to spread terror among the enemy population, then the target population's army and police forces, with the whole-hearted cooperation of the mass media, will certainly see to it that this purpose is achieved far beyond the degree to which the terrorists themselves would be capable of carrying out. And if the terrorists' long-term intention is to destroy human freedoms in liberal democracies and to "close" open societies, they may count again on the immense capacities commanded by the governments of the "enemy countries." As journalist Ted Koppel pointed out in his trenchant analysis of the impact in the United States of global terrorism, the present American administration uses the images of the terrorist iniquity to justify a new worldview, within which even associating with someone who belongs to an organization on the United States' terrorist list justifies persecution here at home. This practice falls into the category of what Deputy Attorney General Paul J. McNulty calls "preventive prosecution" . . . Faced with the possible convergence between terrorism and a weapon of mass destruction, the argument goes, the technicality of waiting for a crime to be committed before it can be punished must give way to preemption.[9]

As a result, Americans "are advised to adjust to the notion of warrantless wiretaps at home, unaccountable C.I.A. prisons overseas and the rendition of suspects to nations that feature prominently on the State Department list of human rights abuses." Koppel warns that "even liberties voluntarily forfeited are not easily retrieved. All the more so for those that are removed surreptitiously." Indeed, a few packets of explosives and a few desperadoes eager to sacrifice their lives "for the cause" can go a long way—much, much further than the terrorists themselves could dream of going with the resources they themselves can procure, command, and administer.

Terrorist forces hardly budge under the answering military blows. On the contrary, it is precisely from the clumsiness and the extravagant and wasteful prodigality of their adversary's efforts that they draw, replenish, and magnify their own strength. A dozen or so ready-to-kill Islamic plotters proved to be enough to create the atmosphere of a besieged fortress in large, affluent, and resourceful countries and to raise waves of "generalized insecurity."

Insecure people tend to seek feverishly to unload their gathering anxiety on a fit target, and to restore their lost self-confidence by easing the frightening and humiliating helplessness they feel. The besieged fortresses that multiethnic and multicultural cities are now becoming are shared by the terrorists and their victims. Each side adds to the fear, passion, fervor and obduracy of the other. Each side confirms the worst fears of the other and adds substance to its prejudices and hatreds. Between themselves, locked in a sort of the liquid-modern rendition of the *danse macabre,* the two sides won't allow the phantom of siege ever to rest.

In all parts of the planet, the soil for the seeds of terrorism is well prepared, and the traveling "masterminds" of terrorist outrages can reasonably hope to find some fertile plots wherever they stop. They don't even need to design, build, and maintain a tight structure of command. There are no terrorist armies, only terrorist *swarms,* synchronized rather than coordinated, with little or no supervision and only ad hoc platoon commanders or corporals. More often than not, for a "task group" to be born apparently *ab nihilo,* it will suffice to set a properly spectacular example, which will then be obligingly and promptly disseminated and hammered into millions of homes by the constantly spectacle-hungry TV networks and through all the information highways on which messages can be sent moving. In the bizarre "war against terrorism" there are no front lines—only separate, widely dispersed, and eminently mobile battlefields; no regular troops, only civilians turned soldier for a day and soldiers on indefinite civilian leave. Terrorist "armies" are all *home* armies, needing no barracks, no rallies, and no parade grounds.

If there is a World Empire, it is confronted with a kind of adversary that can't be caught in the nets it has or is able to weave or acquire. That empire may be armed to the teeth, but its teeth are much better fit for gnawing than for biting. By *military* means (and most certainly by military means alone) the war on terrorism *can't be won.* Its continuation may only further expose the "soft underbelly" of the seemingly invincible superpower, with disastrous consequences for planetary cohabitation, not to mention the prospect of planetary peace of the kind dreamt of, more than two centuries ago, by Immanuel Kant.

The fact that the *military* might of the United States is stretched "to its limits" is also a principal reason, arguably *the* principal reason, that the *economic* resources of the metropolis are being stretched to the limit—those very resources that could conceivably be deployed in assuring genuine victory over global terrorism. It is the economic resources that could be used to cut terrorism off at its roots, through arresting and possibly reversing the current polarization of standards of living and life prospects, that most effective fertilizer in the terrorist-growing plantations.

Nowadays, America is perhaps deeper in debt than any other country in history. Paul Krugman, who points out that "last year America spent 57 percent more than it earned on world markets," asks: "How did Americans manage to live so far beyond their means?" and answers: "By running up debts to Japan, China and Middle Eastern oil producers."[10] America is addicted to (and dependent on) imported money, as it is addicted to and dependent on imported oil. A budget deficit of 300 billion dollars was recently hailed by the White House because it was a few billion less than the previous year's deficit. Imported money that sooner or later will need to be repaid is spent not on financing potentially profitable investments but on sustaining the consumer boom, and so the "feel-good factor" in the electorate, and on financing growing federal deficits— which are in turn regularly exacerbated (despite cuts in social provisions) by continuing tax cuts for the rich. Krugman calculates that "the dollar will eventually have to fall by 30 percent or more" and "both American consumers and the U.S. government will have to start living within their means"—and awakening from their current superpower or World Empire version of the American dream.

All that does not augur well for the prospects that the aspiring World Empire will acquit itself in the task of settlement-and-peace enforcement, which the empires of the past could neglect or fail in only at the cost of their decline and demise. It seems that the United States entered the stage of undivided world domination while already dangerously close to the exhaustion of its expansive potential. *Pax Americana* may stretch territorially well beyond the boundaries of *Pax Romana,* yet its life expectancy is hardly measured in centuries. Like everything else in our "negatively globalized," liquid-modern world, the disassembling and self-destructive mechanisms built into every empire on record work faster now and need much less time to run their full cycle.

Starting the calculation of Europe's tasks and missions from the axiom of America's monopoly on world power and world policing is therefore patently and conspicuously wrong: the present challenge to Europe *does not* derive from the fact that "since we play at best a second fiddle, we can't, and won't be allowed, to do much to make a difference to the state of the planet." It would be equally wrong, and very dangerous, to exculpate ourselves for not trying to make such a difference by invoking that false axiom, and thereby to placate our collective conscience so that the state of not-trying might continue until it is too late to try. The *real* challenge to Europe derives from the fast-accumulating evidence that the sole superpower of the planet fails abominably to lead the planet toward peaceful coexistence and away from imminent disaster. Indeed, there are ample reasons to suppose that this superpower may become a prime cause of disaster's not being averted.

At all levels of human cohabitation, power holders tend to deploy power for rendering the habitat more congenial and supportive for the kind of power they hold; in other words, to create an environment in which the particular resource that is the main source of the power holders' strength is assured the decisive, clinching role in crisis management and conflict resolution. The American superpower is no exception. Its strongest asset being military might, it naturally tends to redefine all planetary problems—whether economic in nature, social, or political—as problems of military threat and military confrontation, as problems amenable solely to military solutions and calling for no solutions other than military solutions. Reversing the memorable formula of Clausewitz, the United States views and treats politics as continuation of war by other means. As George Soros recently remarked, "the Cheney clique of American supremacists believe that international relations are relations of power, not law. In their view, international law merely ratifies what power has wrought, and they define power in terms of military might." And then: "A fearful giant striking about wildly is a good definition of a bully."[11]

As a result, poverty, inequality, deprivation, and all other urgent social problems yearning for global attention and remedy fall as collateral victims of endless and prospectless military expeditions. As successive armed interventions exacerbate the misery of a growing number of the world's deprived populations, and as they further intensify the peoples' already deep and bitter resentment of the callousness and arrogance with which their needs and ambitions are treated by the high and mighty of the planet, conflicts and antagonisms multiply, the chances for peaceful cohabitation become ever more remote, and *the one-sided perception of the world as the site of armed confrontations between incompatible interests becomes a self-fulfilling vision.*

Si vis pacem, para bellum is a contagious attitude particularly prone to globalization; it prompts the worldwide armament chase and threatens to turn every unsatisfied need for vindication and every case of suffering into a *casus belli*. To secure its domination while counting and relying on its sole undisputed advantage—military superiority—America needs to remake the rest of the world in its own image and so render it, so to speak, "hospitable" to its own preferred policies: to make the planet a place where economic, social, and political problems are tackled (and hoped to be resolved) with military means and military actions, while all other means and types of action are devalued and disabled. It is from here that the true challenge to Europe has arisen.

Europe can't seriously contemplate matching the American military might, and so resisting the push toward militarization of the planet by playing the American game; neither can it hope to recover its past industrial domination, irretrievably lost in our increasingly polycentric world, now subjected *in its entirety* to the processes of economic modernization. It can, however, try—and should try—to make the planet hospitable to other values and other modes of existence than those represented and promoted by the American military superpower, to the values and modes that Europe, more than any other part of the world, is predisposed to offer the world, which more than anything else needs to design, to enter, and to follow the road leading to Kant's *allgemeine Vereinigung der Menschheit* and perpetual peace.

Having admitted that "it is nonsense to suppose that Europe will rival the economy, military and technological might" of the United States and the emergent powerhouses (particularly those in Asia), George Steiner insists that Europe's assignment "is one of the spirit and the intellect." Writes Steiner: "The genius of Europe is what William Blake would have called 'the holiness of the minute particular.' It is that of linguistic, cultural, social diversity, of a prodigal mosaic which often makes a trivial distance, twenty kilometres apart, a division between worlds . . . Europe will indeed perish if it does not fight for its languages, local traditions and social autonomies. If it forgets that 'God lies in the detail.'"[12]

Similar thoughts can be found in the literary legacy of Hans-Georg Gadamer.[13] It is its variety, its richness bordering on profligacy, that Gadamer places at the top of the list of Europe's unique merits; he sees the profusion of differences as the foremost among the treasures that Europe has preserved and can offer to the world. "To live with the Other, live as the Other's Other, is the fundamental human task—on the most lowly and the most elevated levels alike . . . Hence perhaps the particular advantage of Europe, which could and had to learn the art of living with others." In Europe, as nowhere else, the Other has been and is always close, in sight, and at a hand's stretch; metaphorically or even literally, the Other is a next-door neighbor—and Europeans can but negotiate the terms of that neighborliness, despite the alterity and the differences that set them apart. The European setting, marked by "the multilingualism, the close neighborhood of the Other, and equal value accorded to the Other in a space tightly constrained," could be seen as a school from which the rest of the world may well carry away crucial knowledge and skills that make the difference between survival and demise. To acquire and share the art of learning from one another is, in Gadamer's view, "the task of Europe." I would add: it is Europe's mission, or more precisely, Europe's *fate* waiting to be recast into *destiny*.

The importance of this task—and the importance of Europe's determination to undertake it—is impossible to exaggerate, as "the decisive condition [for] solving vital problems of [the] modern world," writes Gadamer, a truly sine qua non condition, is the friendship and "buoyant solidarity" that alone can secure "an orderly structure" of human cohabitation. In confronting the task, we need to look back for inspiration to our shared European heritage: for the ancient Greeks, the concept of "friend," Gadamer reminds us, "articulated the totality of social life."[14] Friends tend to be mutually tolerant and sympathetic. Friends are able to be friendly with each other however they differ, and to be helpful to each other despite or rather because of their differences—and to be friendly and helpful without renouncing their uniqueness, while never allowing that uniqueness to set them apart from and against each other.

More recently, Lionel Jospin invested his hopes for a new importance for Europe in the world in its "nuanced approach to current realities."[15] Europe has learned, he said, the hard way, and at an enormous price paid in the currency of human suffering, "how to get past historical antagonisms and peacefully resolve conflicts" and how to bring together "a vast array of cultures" and to live with the prospect of permanent cultural diversity, no longer seen as only a temporary irritant. Let's note that these are precisely the sorts of lessons that the rest of the world most badly needs.

When seen against the background of the conflict-ridden planet, Europe looks like a laboratory where the tools necessary for Kant's universal unification of humanity keep being designed, and a workshop in which they keep being "tested in action," though for the time being in the performance of less ambitious, smaller-scale jobs. The tools that are currently being put to the test in Europe serve above all the delicate operation (for some less sanguine observers, *too* delicate to have anything more than a sporting chance of success) of separating the bases of political legitimacy, of democratic procedure and the willingness to engage in a community-style sharing of assets, from the principle of national and territorial sovereignty with which they have been for most of modern history inextricably linked.

The budding European federation is now facing the task of repeating, on a grander (and therefore potentially planetary) scale, the feat accomplished by the nation-states of early modernity: the rejoining of power and politics, once closely interlinked, but which have since navigated (or drifted) in opposite directions. The road to implementing that task is as rocky now as it was then, at the start of the modern era and its nation- and state-building stage. As then, it is strewn with snares and encumbered with incalculable risks. Worst of all, this road is unmapped, and each successive step seems like a leap into the unknown.

Many observers doubt the wisdom of the endeavor and rate low the chances of its success. The skeptics don't believe in the viability of a "postnational" democracy, or any democratic political entity above the level of the nation, insisting that allegiance to civic and political norms would not replace ethnocultural ties and that citizenship is unworkable on a purely "civilizational" (legal-political) basis without the assistance of "Eros" (the emotional dimension).[16] They assume that the ethnocultural ties and Eros are uniquely and inextricably linked to the kind of the past- and destiny-sharing sentiment that went down in history under the name of "nationalism," and believe that communal solidarity can set down roots and grow only inside this connection and cannot be rebuilt or established anew in any other way. The possibility that the nationalistic legitimation of state power was but a historically confined episode and but one of many alternative forms of the politics-power reunion, or that the modern blend of statehood and nationhood bore more symptoms of a marriage of convenience than of the verdict of providence or historical inevitability—or that the marriage itself was not a foregone conclusion and when arranged proved to be as stormy as most divorce proceedings tend to be—are thereby dismissed by the simple expedient of begging the question.

Jürgen Habermas, arguably the most consistent and authoritative spokesman for the opposition to that kind of skepticism, points out, however, that "a democratic order does not inherently need to be mentally rooted in 'the nation' as a pre-political community of shared destiny. The strength of the democratic constitutional state lies precisely in its ability to close the holes of social integration through the political participation of its citizens."[17]

This is evidently convincing—but the argument may be pushed yet further. The *nation,* as any promoter of any "national idea" would eagerly admit, is as vulnerable and frail without a sovereign state to protect it (indeed, to assure its continuing identity) as the *state* would be without a nation to legitimize its demands for obedience and discipline. Modern *nations* and modern *states* are twin products of *the same historical constellation.* One might "precede" the other only in the short run, and will try to make that short run as short as possible—filling it with efforts to replace priority with simultaneity, and inserting the equals sign between the ostensibly autonomous partners. The French state was "preceded" by Savoyards and Bretons, not Frenchmen; the German state by Bavarians and Prussians, not Germans. Savoyards and Bretons would have hardly turned into Frenchmen, or Bavarians and Prussians into Germans, had not their reincarnation been "power assisted" by, respectively, the French and the German *states.*

For all practical intents and purposes, modern nations and modern states alike emerged in the course of two simultaneous and closely intertwined processes of nation- and state-building—anything but cloudless processes, and anything but processes guaranteed, a priori, to succeed. To say that a political framework cannot be established without a viable ethno-cultural organism already in place is neither more nor less con-vincing than to say that no ethnocultural organism is likely to become and remain viable without a working and workable political framework. A chicken-and-egg dilemma if there ever was one.

Habermas's comprehensive and grinding analysis points in a very similar direction: "Precisely the artificial conditions in which national consciousness arose argue against the defeatist assumption that a form of civic solidarity among strangers can only be generated within the confines of the nation. If this form of collective identity was due to a highly abstractive leap from the local and dynastic to national and then to democratic consciousness, why shouldn't this learning process be able to continue?"[18]

Shared nationhood is *not* a *necessary* condition of the state legitimacy, if the state is a genuinely democratic body: "The citizens of a democratic legal state understand themselves as the authors of the law, which compels them to obedience as its addressees."[19]

We may say that nationalism fills the legitimation void left (or not filled in the first place) by the democratic participation of the citizens. It is in the *absence* of such participation that the invocation to the nationalist sentiments and the efforts to beef them up are the state's sole recourse. The state must invoke the shared national destiny, building its authority on the will-ingness of its subjects to die for their country, *if and only if* the rulers of the country need its residents solely for their readi-ness to sacrifice their lives, while not needing, or even shun-ning, their contributions to the daily running of the country.

At the moment, however, Europe seems to be looking for an-swers to the new and unfamiliar problems in inward-facing policies rather outward-looking ones—centripetal rather than

centrifugal, implosive rather than expansive—like retrenchment, falling back upon itself, building fences topped with
X-ray machines and closed-circuit television cameras, putting
more officials inside the immigration booths and more border
guards outside, tightening the nets of immigration and natural-
ization law, keeping refugees in closely guarded and isolated
camps or turning them back before they have a chance to claim
refugee or asylum-seeker status—in short, sealing its own doors
while doing little, if anything, to repair the situation that
prompted their closure. (Let's recall that the funds that the European Union transferred most willingly and with no haggling
to the Eastern and Central European countries applying for
accession were those earmarked for the fortification of their
eastern borders.)

Casting the victims of the rampant globalization of the
financial and commodity markets as, first and foremost, a security threat, rather than as people needing aid and entitled to
compensation for their damaged lives, has its uses. First, it
puts paid to the ethical compunctions: no failing of moral duty
eats at the soul when one is dealing with enemies who "hate
our values" and cannot stand the sight of men and women living in freedom and democracy. Second, it allows us to divert
funds that could be used "unprofitably" on the narrowing of
disparities and defusing of animosities to the profitable task of
beefing up the weapons industry, arms sales, and stockholders'
gains, and thus improving the statistics on home employment
and raising the home feel-good gradient. Last but not least, it
builds up the flagging consumerist economy by retargeting diffuse security fears on the urge to buy the little private fortresses on wheels (like the notoriously unsafe, gas-guzzling,
and pricey Hummers and sport-utility vehicles), and by impos-
ing lucrative "brand rights" or "intellectual rights" on the excuse that the government must prevent profits from illegal
trade and pirating from being diverted to terrorist cells.

It also allows the governments to shake off the more irritating constraints of popular, democratic control by recasting political and economic *choices* as military *necessities*. America, as always, takes the lead—but it is closely watched and eagerly followed by a large number of European governments. As William J. Bennett recently stated in a book aptly titled *Why We Fight: Moral Clarity and the War on Terrorism*, "The threats we face today are both external and internal: external in that there are groups and states that want to attack the United States: internal in that there are those who are attempting to use this opportunity to promulgate the agenda of 'blame America first.' Both threats stem from either a hatred for the American ideals of freedom and equality or a misunderstanding of those ideals and their practice."[20] Bennett's credo is an ideological gloss on a practice already in full swing—like the USA Patriot Act, which is aimed explicitly at people engaged in the kinds of political action protected by the American Constitution, legalizing clandestine surveillance, searches without warrants, and other invasions of privacy, as well as incarceration without charge and trials before military courts.

Admittedly, there are reasons for Europe to be increasingly inward-looking. The world no longer looks inviting. It appears to be a hostile world, a treacherous, vengeance-breathing world, a world that needs to be made safe for us, the tourists. This is a world of the imminent "war of civilizations"; a world in which any and all steps taken are fraught with risks, just as much as not taking them promptly would be. The tourists who dare to take such risks must look out and stay constantly on the alert; most crucially, they should stick to the safe havens, the marked and protected paths cut out from the wilderness for their exclusive use. Whoever forgets those precepts does so at her or his own peril—and must be ready to bear the consequences.

In an insecure world, security is the name of the game. Security is the main purpose of the game and its paramount stake.

It is a value that in practice, if not in theory, dwarfs and elbows out all other values—including the values dearest to "us" while hated most by "them," and for that reason declared the prime cause of "their" wish to harm "us." In a world as insecure as ours, personal freedom of word and action, right to privacy, access to truth—all those things we used to associate with democracy and in whose name we still go to war—need to be trimmed or suspended. Or this at least is what the official version, confirmed by official practice, maintains.

The truth is, nevertheless, that *we cannot effectively defend our freedoms here at home while fencing ourselves off from the rest of the world and attending solely to our affairs here at home.*

There are valid reasons to suppose that on a globalized planet, where the plight of everyone everywhere determines the plight of all the others, while also being determined by them, one can no longer live in freedom and democracy "separately"—in isolation, in one country, or in a few selected countries only. The fate of freedom and democracy in each land is decided and settled on the global stage; and only on that stage can it be defended with a realistic chance of lasting success. It is no longer in the power of any state acting alone, however resourceful, heavily armed, resolute, and uncompromising, to defend chosen values at home while turning its back on the dreams and yearnings of those outside its borders. But turning our backs is precisely what we, the Europeans, seem to be doing, when we keep our riches and multiply them at the expense of the poor outside.

A few examples will suffice. While forty years ago the income of the richest 5 percent of the world population was 30 times higher than the income of the poorest 5 percent, fifteen years ago it was 60 times higher, and by 2002 it had reached the factor of 114.

As pointed out by Jacques Attali in *La voie humaine*,[21] half of the world's trade and more than half of global investments benefit just twenty-two countries that accommodate a mere 14 percent of the world population, whereas the forty-nine poorest countries, inhabited by 11 percent of the world population, receive among them but one-half of 1 percent of the global product—an amount just about equal to the combined income of the three wealthiest men on the planet. Ninety percent of the total wealth of the planet remains in the hands of just 1 percent of the planet's inhabitants.

Tanzania earns 2.2 billion dollars a year, which it divides among 25 million inhabitants. The Goldman Sachs Bank earns 2.6 billion dollars a year, which is then divided among 161 stockholders.

Europe and the United States spend 17 billion dollars each year on animal food while, according to experts, there is a 19-billion-dollar shortfall in the funding needed to save the world population from hunger. Joseph Stiglitz wrote in the *Guardian*, as trade ministers prepared for their 2003 meeting in Mexico, that the average European subsidy per cow "matches the 2 dollars per day poverty level on which billions of people barely subsist"—whereas America's 4 billion dollars in cotton subsidies paid to 25,000 well-off farmers "bring misery to 10 million African farmers and more than offset the U.S.'s miserly aid to some of the affected countries."[22] One occasionally hears Europe and America accusing each other publicly of "unfair agricultural practices." But, Stiglitz observes, "neither side seems to be willing to make major concessions"—whereas nothing short of a major concession would convince others to stop looking at the unashamed display of "brute economic power by the U.S. and Europe" as anything but an effort to defend the privileges of the privileged, to protect the wealth of the wealthy and to serve their interests—which, in their opinion, boil down to more wealth and yet more wealth.

*   *   *

If they are to be lifted and refocused at a level higher than the nation-state, the essential features of human solidarity (like the sentiments of mutual belonging and of shared responsibility for the common future, or the willingness to care for one another's well-being and to find amicable and durable solutions to sporadically inflamed conflicts), need support from an *institutional* framework of opinion building and will formation. The European Union aims (and moves, however slowly and haltingly) toward a rudimentary or embryonic form of such an institutional framework, although the most obtrusive obstacles it encounters on its way are the existing nation-states, which are reluctant to part with whatever is left of their once fully-fledged sovereignty. The current direction is difficult to plot clearly, and predicting its future turns is even more difficult, in addition to being unwarranted, irresponsible, and unwise.

The EU's present momentum seems to be shaped by two different (perhaps complementary, perhaps incompatible) logics—and it is impossible to decide in advance which will ultimately prevail. One is the *logic of local retrenchment;* the other is the *logic of global responsibility and global aspiration.*

The first logic is that of the quantitative expansion of the territory-and-resource basis for the *Standortskonkurrenz* strategy—competition between localities, or locally grounded competition; more precisely, competition between territorial states. Even if no attempts had ever been made by the founders of the European Common Market and their successors to emancipate the economy from its relatively incapacitating confinement in the *Nationalökonomie* frames, the "war of liberation" currently conducted by global capital, finance, and trade against "local constraints," a war triggered and intensified not by local interests but by the global diffusion of opportunities, would have been waged anyway and gone on unabated. The role of European institutions *does not* consist in eroding the member states' sovereignty and in exempting economic activity from their controlling (and constraining) interference; in short, it *does not* consist in facilitating, let alone initiating, the divorce procedure between power and politics. For such a purpose the services of European institutions are hardly required. The real function of European institutions consists, on the contrary, in *stemming the tide:* stopping the capital assets that have escaped the nation-state cages inside the continental stockade and keeping them there to prevent them from evaporating or leaking beyond the confines of the Union. If, in view of the rising might of global capital, the effective enclosure inside a single nation-state of capital, financial, commodity, and labor markets, along with the balancing of the books, becomes ever more daunting, then perhaps severally, or all together, the combined powers of the nation-states will be able to match and confront the task on more equal terms. In other words: the logic of local retrenchment is that of reconstructing, at the Union level, the legal-institutional web that no longer holds the "national economy" within the boundaries of the nation-state's territorial sovereignty. But, as Habermas put it, "the creation of larger political unities in itself changes nothing about the mode of *Standortskonkurrenz* as such."[23] Viewed from the planetary perspective, the joint strategy of a continental union of states is hardly distinguishable from the single nation-states' codes of conduct that it came to replace. It is still guided by the logic of division, separation, enclosure, and retrenchment; of seeking territorial exemptions from the general rules and trends—or, to put it bluntly, *local solutions for globally generated problems.*

At the same time, the logic of global responsibility (and once that responsibility is acknowledged and acted upon, also the logic of global aspiration) is aimed, at least in principle, at confronting the globally generated problems point-blank—at their own level. It stems from the assumption that a lasting and truly effective solution to planetwide problems can be found and can work only through the *renegotiation and reform of the web of global interdependencies and interactions.* Instead of aiming for the least local damage and most local benefits to be derived from the capricious and haphazard drifts of global economic forces, it would rather pursue a new kind of global setting, in which the itineraries of economic initiatives anywhere on the planet would not be whimsical any longer or guided haphazardly by momentary gains alone, with no attention paid to the side effects and collateral casualties and no importance attached to the social dimensions of the cost-and-effect balances. In short, that logic is aimed, to quote Habermas again, at the development of "politics that can catch up with global markets."[24]

Unlike the logic of local retrenchment, which replays the perseverant tunes of *raison d'état,* tunes familiar since universally (or almost) dominant in the nation-state era, the logic of global responsibility and global aspiration ushers us into unknown territory and opens an era of political experimentation. It rejects, as swerving dangerously into a blind alley, the strategy of a purely local defense against planetary trends; it also abstains (by necessity, if not for reasons of conscience) from falling back to another orthodox European strategy, that of treating the planetary space as a "hinterland" (or, indeed, the *Lebensraum*) onto which the problems that are home-produced but unresolvable at home can be unloaded. It accepts that it would be utterly pointless to follow the first strategy with a realistic hope of even a modicum of success, whereas having lost its global dominance, and living instead in the shadow of an empire that aspires to become planetary, an empire that it can at best try to contain and mitigate, but hardly to control, Europe is not in a position to follow the second strategy either, however successful that course might have been in the past and however tempting it may still be.

And so, willy-nilly, new unexplored strategies and tactics must be sought and tried without first reliably calculating, let alone ensuring, their ultimate success. "At the global level," Habermas warns, "coordination problems that are already difficult at the European level grow still sharper." This is because "civic solidarity is rooted in particular collective identities," whereas "cosmopolitan solidarity has to support itself on the moral universalism of human rights alone." The "political culture of a world society lacks the common ethical-political dimension that would be necessary for a corresponding global community."[25]

A genuine catch-22: the community that could conceivably underlie a common ethical sensibility and make political coordination feasible (thus providing the necessary condition that must be met if the supranational and supracontinental solidarity is to sprout and take root) is difficult to attain precisely because the "ethical-political dimension" is thus far missing, and it is likely to remain missing—or to fall short of what is needed—so long as the ethical-political dimension is incomplete. What Europe faces now is the prospect of developing, gradually and *simultaneously,* and possibly through a long process of trial and error, the objectives *and* the tools fit to tackle and resolve it. To make the task even more daunting, the ultimate destination of all that labor, an effective planetary policy based on a continuous polilogue rather than on the soliloquy of a single planetary government, is equally unprecedented. Only historical practice may prove (though never disprove) its feasibility—or, more correctly, *render* it feasible.

We feel, guess, suspect what needs to be done. But we cannot know in which shape and form it eventually will be done. We can be pretty sure, though, that the ultimate shape will not be familiar. It will be—it must be—different from all we've gotten used to in the past, in the era of nation building and nation-states' self-assertion. It can hardly be otherwise, as all political institutions currently at our disposal were made to the measure of the *territorial sovereignty* of the nation-state; they resist stretching to the planetary, supranational scale, and the political institutions serving the self-constitution of the planetwide human community won't be, can't be "the same, only bigger." If invited to a parliamentary session in London, Paris, or Washington, Aristotle could perhaps approve of its procedural rules and recognize the benefits it offers to the people whom its decisions affect, but he would be baffled when told that what he has been shown is "democracy in action." It is not how he, who coined the term, visualized a "democratic polis."

We may well sense that the passage from international agencies and tools of action to universal—humanitywide—institutions must be and will be a *qualitative* change, not merely a *quantitative* one. So we may ponder, worryingly, whether the currently available frames for "global politics" can accommodate the practices of the emergent global polity or indeed serve as their incubator; what about the UN, for instance—briefed at its birth to guard and defend the undivided and unassailable sovereignty of the state over its territory? The *binding force* of global law—can it depend on the (admittedly revocable!) agreements of sovereign members of the "international community" to obey them?

To grasp the logic of the fateful departures in seventeenth-century European thought, Reinhardt Kosseleck, the great German historian of ideas, deployed the trope of the "mountain pass." I suggest that this is an apt and felicitous metaphor for us as much as it was for our ancestors of four centuries ago, as we struggle to anticipate the twists and turns that the twenty-first century will inevitably follow, and to give shape to the seminal departures by which it is likely to be retrospectively described and "made sense of" in the accounts penned by future historians.

Like our seventeenth-century ancestors, we are moving up a rising slope toward a mountain pass that we have never crossed before—and so we have no inkling what sort of view will open once we have reached it; we are not sure where the winding and twisted gorge will eventually lead us. One thing we can be sure of is that where we are now, at some point on a steeply rising slope, we cannot rest for long, let alone settle. And so we go on moving; we move not so much "in order to" as "because of"—we move because we can neither stop nor stand still. Only when (if) we reach the pass and survey the landscape on its other side will the time come to move "in order to"; then we will be pulled ahead by the sight of a visible destination, by the goal within our reach, rather than pushed to move by current discomforts.

For the time being, little can be said of the shape of that vexingly distant *allgemeine Vereinigung der Menschengattung,* except that it will (we hope) gradually acquire more visible and manageable contours; that is, it will if there are still climbers left to find out that it has and to say so. I suggested as much to Kosseleck, pointing to the current rarity of prophetic talents and the notorious deficiencies of scientific prediction. In his reply, however, Kosseleck added an argument yet more decisive: we don't even have the concepts with which we could articulate and express our anticipations. Concepts fit to grasp realities that are *not yet* are formed in the practice of climbing, and not a moment before. And it is not just the concepts that keep emerging as we keep moving, but also—as Claus Offe would add—the rules of forming and accepting them; the rules of decision making cannot but be made as we go, in a sort of "reflexive loop." On the shape of things yet to emerge on the other side of the mountain pass, prudent climbers ought to keep silent.

The climbers' ignorance about their final destination does not mean that they should stop moving. And in the case of Europeans, known for their fondness for adventure and knack for experimentation, it is unlikely that they will stop. We will need to make many stark choices, all under the condition of severely limited knowledge (this is exactly what sets adventure apart from routine and acting on command), and the adversarial odds against us seem truly daunting—but there is also hope, rooted firmly in our acquired skills of living with difference and engagement in meaningful and mutually beneficial dialogue, skills that stay mostly hidden yet come to the surface in moments of crisis. In a conversation held in May 2003, Jürgen Habermas and Jacques Derrida called 15 February 2003 "another Fourth of July" but this time on an all-European scale: the day on which "a genuine shared European conscience" was born.[26] On that day, millions of Europeans went into the streets of Rome, Madrid, Paris, Berlin, London, and other capitals of Europe to manifest their unanimous condemnation of the invasion of Iraq that was about to be launched—and obliquely their shared historical memory of past sufferings and shared revulsion against such violence and atrocities committed in the name of national rivalry.

The choice we confront is between allowing our cities to turn into places of terror, "where the stranger is to be feared and distrusted," and sustaining the legacy of mutual civility among citizens and the "solidarity of strangers," a solidarity strengthened by the ever harder tests to which it is subjected and which it survives—now and in the future.

The logic of global responsibility and global aspiration, if adopted and given preference over the logic of local retrenchment, may help to prepare the Europeans, those eminently adventurous people notorious for their fondness for experimentation, for their next adventure, greater perhaps than all previous ones. Despite the formidable volume of adverse odds, it could once more cast Europe in the role of a global pattern-setter; it may enable Europe to deploy the values it has learned to cherish and managed to preserve, and the political-ethical experience it has acquired of democratic self-government, in the awesome task of replacing the collection of territorially entrenched entities engaged in a zero-sum game of survival with a fully inclusive, planetary human community. Only when (and if) such a community is achieved, may Europe consider its mission accomplished. Only within such a community can the values enlightening Europe's ambitions and pursuits, values that *are Europe,* be truly safe.

What lies ahead has been prophetically put into writing by Franz Kafka—as a premonition, a warning, and encouragement: "If you find nothing in the corridors open the doors, if you find nothing behind these doors there are more floors, and if you find nothing up there, don't worry, just leap up another flight of stairs. As long as you don't stop climbing, the stairs won't end, under your climbing feet they will go on growing upwards."[27]

Notes

•

Introduction

1. Richard Jones, "Why Insects Get Such a Buzz Out of Socializing," *Guardian*, 25 January 2007.

2. *Doxa:* a set of assumptions about the ways and means of the world that are seldom if ever questioned—assumptions one thinks *with*, but not of or about; paradigm: a preconceived idea of what is relevant and what is not, and what should be therefore recorded as exemplifying the norm and what should be dismissed and left out of the account as abnormal or accidental.

3. François de Singly, *Les uns avec les autres: Quand l'individualisme crée du lien* (Paris: Colin, 2003), pp. 108–109.

4. See Claude Dubar, *La socialisation: Construction des identités sociales et professionelles* (Paris: Colin, 1991), p. 113.

5. Singly, *Les uns avec les autres*, p. 108.

6. See Jean-Claude Kaufmann, *L'invention de soi: Une théorie d'identité* (Paris: Hachette, 2004), p. 214.

7. Ibid., pp. 212–213.

8. Theodor W. Adorno, *Critical Models: Interventions and Catchwords*, trans. Henry W. Pickford (New York: Columbia University Press, 1998), p. 14.

9. Jürgen Habermas, *The Postnational Constellation: Political Essays*, trans. Max Pensky (Cambridge: Polity, 2001), p. 109.

1. What Chance of Ethics in the World of Consumers?

1. Sigmund Freud, "Civilization and Its Discontents," in *The Standard Edition of the Complete Psychological Works of Sigmund Freud*, trans. James Strachey (London: Hogarth Press, 1961).

2. Quotations in this paragraph are from Sigmund Freud, *Civilization, So-*

ciety and Religion, trans. James Strachey, Penguin Freud Library, vol. 12 (London: Penguin, 1991), pp. 300, 303.

3. See Michel Agier, *Aux bords du monde, les réfugiés* (Paris: Flammarion, 2002), pp. 55–56.

4. Emmanuel Levinas, *The Theory of Intuition in Husserl's Phenomenology,* trans. André Orianne (Evanston, IL: Northwestern University Press, 1995), pp. 36, liv.

5. Harvie Ferguson, *Phenomenological Sociology: Experience and Insight in Modern Society* (Thousand Oaks, CA: Sage, 2006), p. 73.

6. See Georg Simmel, *The Sociology of Georg Simmel,* trans. and ed. Kurt H. Wolff (New York: Free Press, 1964), pp. 134ff.

7. See Zygmunt Bauman, *Postmodernity and Its Discontents* (Cambridge: Polity Press, 1997), chap. 4.

8. Compare Emmanuel Levinas, "L'Autre, utopie et justice," *Autrement* 102 (November 1988): 52–60.

9. See François Poirié, *Emmanuel Lévinas: Qui êtes-vous?* (Lyon: Editions la Manufacture, 1987); translation is mine.

10. Simmel, *Sociology of Georg Simmel,* p. 137.

11. Joseph Brodsky, "The Condition We Call Exile," in *On Grief and Reason* (New York: Farrar, Straus and Giroux, 1998), p. 34.

12. Emmanuel Levinas, *Ethics and Infinity: Conversations with Phillipe Nemo,* trans. Richard A. Cohen (Pittsburgh, PA: Duquesne University Press, 1985), pp. 98–99.

13. Ibid., p. 80.

14. See Alain Ehrenberg, *La fatigue d'être soi* (Paris: Odile Jacob, 1998).

15. "Adiaphoric," a term borrowed from language of the church, meant originally a neutral or indifferent belief in the matters of faith and its doctrine. In the metaphorical use here, "adiaphoric" means amoral: subject to no moral judgment, having no moral significance.

16. Colette Dowling, *Cinderella Complex* (New York: Pocket Books, 1991).

17. See Arlie Russell Hochschild, *The Commercialization of Intimate Life* (Berkeley: University of California Press, 2003), pp. 21ff.

18. See Frank Mort, "Competing Domains: Democratic Subjects and Consuming Subjects in Britain and the United States since 1945," in *The Making of the Consumer: Knowledge, Power and Identity in the Modern World,* ed. Frank Trentmann (Oxford: Berg, 2006), pp. 225ff. Mort quotes the Henley Centre's reports *Planning for Social Change* (1986), *Consumer and Leisure Futures* (1997), and *Planning for Consumer Change* (1999). The Henley Centre is a marketing organization that provides consumer industries with information about the changing patterns of leisure time use among their prospective British customers.

19. Knud Ejler Løgstrup, *The Ethical Demand,* trans. Hans Fink and Alisdair MacIntyre (Notre Dame, IN: University of Notre Dame Press, 1977), p. 8.

20. Leon Shestov, "All Things Are Perishable," in *A Shestov Anthology,* ed. Bernard Martin (Athens: Ohio University Press, 1970), p. 70.

21. See J. Livingstone, "Modern Subjectivity and Consumer Culture," here quoted from Russell W. Belk, "The Human Consequences of Consumer Culture," in *Elusive Consumption,* ed. Karin M. Ekström and Helen Brembeck (Oxford: Berg, 2004), p. 71.

22. Colin Campbell, "I Shop Therefore I Know That I Am," in *Elusive Consumption,* ed. Karin M. Ekström and Helen Brembeck (Oxford: Berg, 2004), pp. 41–42.

23. See Hochschild, *Commercialization of Intimate Life,* pp. 208ff.

24. Ibid.

25. See Arlie Russell Hochschild, *The Time Bind: When Work Becomes Home and Home Becomes Work* (New York: Henry Holt, 1997), pp. xviii–xix.

26. Knud Løgstrup, *After the Ethical Demand,* trans. Susan Dew and van Kooten Niekerk (Aarhus, Denmark: Aarhus University Press, 2002), p. 26.

27. Ibid.

28. See Levinas, *Ethics and Infinity,* pp. 10–11.

29. Nan Ellin, "Fear and City Building," *Hedgehog Review* 5, no. 3 (Fall 2003): 43–61.

30. B. Diken and C. Laustsen, "Zones of Indistinction: Security, Terror, and Bare Life," in *Space and Culture* 5 (2002): 290–307.

31. G. Gumpert and S. Drucker, "The Mediated Home in the Global Village," in *Communication Research* 25, no. 4 (1998): 422–438.

32. M. Schwarzer, "The Ghost Wards: The Flight of Capital from History," *Thresholds* 16 (1998).

33. Richard Sennett, *The Uses of Disorder: Personal Identity and City Life* (London: Faber and Faber, 1996), pp. 39, 42.

34. Ibid., p. 194.

35. Italo Calvino, *Invisible Cities,* trans. William Weaver (New York: Vintage, 1997), p. 165.

2. Categorial Murder

1. See Giorgio Agamben, *Homo Sacer: Il potere sovrano e la nuda vita* (1995), here quoted in translation from *Homo Sacer: Sovereign Power and Bare Life,* trans. Daniel Heller-Roazen (Stanford, CA: Stanford University Press, 1998), pp. 11, 18.

2. Helen Fein, *Genocide: A Sociological Perspective* (London: Sage, 1993), p. 6.

3. Frank Chalk and Kurt Jonassohn, *The History and Sociology of Genocides* (New Haven, CT: Yale University Press, 1990), p. 23.

4. Agamben, *Homo Sacer: Sovereign Power and Bare Life*, pp. 8, 82.

5. Quoted in Kristina Boréus, "Discursive Discrimination: A Typology," in *European Journal of Social Theory* 3 (2006): 405–424.

6. John P. Sabini and Mary Silver, "Destroying the Innocent with a Clear Conscience: A Sociopsychology of the Holocaust," in *Survivors, Victims, Perpetrators: Essays on the Nazi Holocaust*, ed. Joel E. Dimsdale (Washington, DC: Hemisphere, 1980), pp. 329–330.

7. See Tzvetan Todorov, "Ni banalisation ni sacralisation: Du bon and du mauvais usage de la mémoire," *Le Monde diplomatique*, April 2001, pp. 10–11.

8. Ibid., translation is mine.

9. See Jim Hoagland, "Viewing Vietnam and Algeria with the Luxury of Hindsight," *New York Herald Tribune*, 5–6 May 2001, p. 6.

10. Tzvetan Todorov, "Les illusions d'une justice universelle," in *Le Monde de débats*, May 2001, p. 27; translation is mine.

11. For quotation, see "Secret U.S. Endorsement of Severe Interrogations," *New York Times*, 10 October 2007.

12. See "Choephori, or The Libation Bearers," in Aeschylus, *The Oresteian Trilogy*, trans. Philip Vellacott (London: Penguin, 1959), pp. 108–109, 114–115, 118, 143; and "The Eumenides," ibid., p. 174.

13. Ryszard Kapuściński, "Un siècle de barbarie: De la nature des génocides," *Le Monde diplomatique*, March 2001, p. 3.

14. See particularly René Girard, *Violence and the Sacred*, trans. Patrick Gregory (Baltimore: Johns Hopkins University Press, 1977; originally published in French, 1972), and *The Scapegoat*, trans. Yvonne Freccero (Baltimore: Johns Hopkins University Press, 1986; originally published in French, 1982).

15. Kapuściński, "Un siècle de barbarie"; translation is mine.

3. Freedom in the Liquid-Modern Era

1. Anders quoted here after the French translation, *L'obsolescence de l'homme* (Paris: Editions Ivrea, 2001); English translation is mine.

2. Richard Rorty, "The Intellectuals at the End of Socialism," *Yale Review* 80, nos. 1 and 2 (April 1992).

3. John Locke, "A Letter Concerning Toleration" in *Political Writings*, ed. David Wootton (Indianapolis: Hackett, 2003), p. 407.

4. Albert Camus, *L'homme révolté* (1951), here quoted from Anthony

Bower's translation, *The Rebel* (Harmondsworth, UK: Penguin, 1971), p. 32.

5. See her conversation (in Polish) with Joanna Sokolińska in "Wysokie Obcasy," *Gazeta Wyborcza,* 6 November 2006; translation is mine.

6. See "On the Genealogy of Ethics: An Overview of Work in Progress," in *The Foucault Reader,* ed. Paul Rabinow (New York: Random House, 1984), p. 350.

7. See Ernst Kris and Otto Kunz, *Legend, Myth and Magic in the Image of the Artist,* trans. Alistair Lang and Lottie M. Newman (New Haven, CT: Yale University Press, 1979), p. 113.

8. See Jon Lanchaster, "A Bigger Bang," *Guardian Weekend,* 4 November 2006.

9. See Arlie Russell Hochschild, *The Commercialization of Intimate Life* (Berkeley: University of California Press, 2003), pp. 213ff.

10. See Robert Taylor, *Sweden's New Social Democratic Model* (London: Compass, 2005), p. 32; *http://www.compassonline.org.uk/publications/.*

4. Hurried Life

1. A correction is, however, needed: speaking of the approval or rejection of the "style pack," one can speak only (to use Jacques Derrida's terms) *sous rature*—harking back to the no longer operating mechanisms of normative regulation, social pressure, and group control. It would be more proper to talk of the difference between success and failure as being determined by conformity or nonconformity with the patterns set and publicized by the style pack.

2. All following quotations of Freud come from "The Future of an Illusion" and "Civilization and Its Discontents," trans. James Strachey, in *The Penguin Freud Library,* vol. 12: *Civilization, Society and Religion* (Harmondsworth, UK: Penguin, 1991), pp. 179–341.

3. The point, though, is that even if before the advent of the modern era the room for coercion was no less ample than it was bound to be in the course of building the modern order (and it was), there was hardly room there for the self-assurance and matter-of-factness with which Jeremy Bentham could and did draw an equation between obedience to law, on the one hand, and, on the other, a "work-or-die" situation into which he cast the law's intended subjects, locking the exits from their compulsory confinement and putting the wardens in the observation tower to make sure that no other choices seeped in.

4. Lucy Siegle, "Is Recycling a Waste of Time?" *Observer Magazine,* 15 January 2006.

5. See Helen Haste, "Joined Up Texting: The Role of Mobile Phones in

264 Notes to Pages 159–179

Young Peoples' Lives," Nestlé Social Research Programme Report 3 (2005), p. 29.

6. See Zygmunt Bauman, *Wasted Lives: Modernity and Its Outcasts* (Cambridge: Polity Press, 2004).

7. Thomas Hylland Eriksen, *Tyranny of the Moment: Fast and Slow Time in the Information Age* (London: Pluto Press, 2001), pp. 2–3.

8. Ibid., p. vii.

9. Elżbieta Tarkowska, "Zygmunt Bauman o czasie i procesach temporalizacji," *Kultura i Społeczeństwo* 3 (2005): 45–65; translation is mine.

10. See Ignazio Ramonet, *La tyrannie de la communication* (Paris: Galilée, 1999), p. 184; translation is mine.

11. Eriksen, *Tyranny of the Moment*, p. 92.

12. Ibid., p. 17.

13. See Bill Martin, *Listening to the Future: The Time of Progressive Rock 1968–1978* (Chicago: Open Court, 1997), p. 292.

14. Eriksen, *Tyranny of the Moment*, pp. 109, 113.

15. Georg Simmel, *The Metropolis and Mental Life,* here quoted in Kurt Wolff's 1950 translation, as reprinted in *Classic Essays on the Culture of Cities,* ed. Richard Sennett (New York: Appleton-Century-Crofts, 1969), p. 52.

16. Rolland Munro, "Outside Paradise: Melancholy and the Follies of Modernization," *Culture and Organization* 4 (2005): 275–289.

17. Quoted in George Monbiot, "How the Harmless Wanderer in the Woods Became a Mortal Enemy," *Guardian,* 31 January 2006.

18. Thomas Mathiesen, *Silently Silenced: Essays on the Creation of Acquiescence in Modern Society* (Winchester, UK: Waterside Press, 2004), p. 15.

19. See Stephen Bertman, *Hyperculture: The Human Cost of Speed* (Westport, CT: Praeger, 1998).

20. Leon Shestov, the eminent Russian-French existentialist philosopher, thought that the power to annul the past—to change history, for instance, so that the crime of forcing Socrates to drink hemlock was never committed—was the ultimate sign of God's omnipotence.

21. Joseph Brodsky, "In Praise of Boredom," in *On Grief and Reason* (New York: Farrar, Straus and Giroux, 1995), pp. 107–108.

22. Ibid.

23. Andrzej Stasiuk, *Tekturowy Samolot* (Sekowa, Poland: Czarne Publishers, 2002), p. 59; translations are mine.

24. Sławomir Mrożek, *Małe Listy* (Warsaw: Noir sur Blanc, 2000), p. 122; translation is mine.

25. Blaise Pascal, *Pensées,* trans. A. J. Kreilsheimer (Harmondsworth, UK: Penguin, 1966), p. 67.

26. The "praxeomorphic nature of human cognition" refers to the priority of human praxis over perception of the world—in other words, to the fact that the human vision of the world is shaped at all stages of history by what humans at a particular stage of their history are able to do, are doing, and are inclined to do.

27. John Kotter, *The New Rules* (New York: Dutton, 1995), p. 159; italics added.

28. Ricardo Petrella, "Une machine infernale," *Le Monde diplomatique,* June 1997, p. 17; translation is mine.

29. See Alberto Melucci, *The Playing Self: Person and Meaning in the Planetary Society* (London: Cambridge University Press, 1996), pp. 43ff. This is an extended version of the Italian original published in 1991 under the title *Il gioco dell'io.*

30. Ibid.

31. Precarization: Bourdieu's term refers to the ploys deliberately used by managers to make the situation of subordinates more insecure and vulnerable, and for that reason less predictable and controllable.

32. Dominique Simone Rycher, "Lifelong Learning—But Learning for What?" *LLinE* 1 (2004): 26–33.

33. Brian Knowlton, "Hot-Cold-Hot: Terror Alert Left America Uncertain," *International Herald Tribune,* 5 August 2004.

5. Out of the Frying Pan and into the Fire

1. Theodor W. Adorno, "Culture and Administration," in *The Culture Industry: Selected Essays on Mass Culture,* ed. J. M. Bernstein (London: Routledge, 1991), p. 93. Let me point out that the word "management," rather than "administration," better conveys the gist of the German term *Verwaltung* used in the original.

2. Ibid., p. 98.

3. Ibid., pp. 93, 98, 100.

4. Joseph Brodsky, "The Child of Civilization," in *Less Than One: Selected Essays* (New York: Farrar, Straus and Giroux, 1987), p. 123.

5. Adorno, "Culture and Administration," p. 94.

6. Theodor Adorno and Max Horkheimer, *Dialectics of Enlightenment,* trans. John Cumming (London: Verso, 1979), pp. 216–217.

7. Adorno, "Culture and Administration," p. 103.

8. Hannah Arendt, *La crise de la culture* (Paris: Gallimard, 1968), pp. 266–267; translation is mine.

9. Joseph Brodsky, "On Tyranny," in *Less Than One: Selected Essays* (New York: Farrar, Straus and Giroux, 1987), p. 121.

10. Milan Kundera, *Sztuka powieści* (Warsaw: Czytelnik, 1998), pp. 21–22; translation is mine.

11. Milan Kundera, *Les testaments trahis*, here quoted after the Polish translation by Marek Bieńczyk, *Zdradzone testamenty* (Warsaw: PIW, 1993), pp. 20–23; English translation is mine.

12. Hannah Arendt, *Man in Dark Times* (New York: Harcourt Brace, 1983), p. viii.

13. Ibid., pp. 4–5.

14. Ibid., p. 24.

15. Kundera, *Sztuka powieści*, p. 25.

16. Naomi Klein, *No Logo* (London: Flamingo, 2001), p. 5.

17. Ibid., p. 25.

18. Willem de Kooning, *Écrits et propos* (Paris: Éditions de l'Ensba, 1992), pp. 90ff.

19. Yves Michaud, *L'art à l'état gazeux: Essai sur le triomphe de l'esthétique* (Paris: Stock, 2003), p. 9.

20. See Zygmunt Bauman, *Society under Siege* (Cambridge: Polity Press, 2002), chap. 4.

21. Wolfe quoted in Patrick Barrer, *(Tout) l'art contemporain est-il mal?* (Lausanne: Fauvre, 2000) p. 67; translation is mine.

22. Michaud, *L'art à l'état gazeux*, pp. 7, 9.

23. Ibid., p. 77.

24. S. Daney, *La salaire du zappeur* (Paris: P.O.L., 1993), p. 12; translation is mine.

25. Michaud, *L'art à l'état gazeux*, pp. 120–121.

26. Sigmund Freud, "Civilization and Its Discontents," trans. James Strachey, in *The Penguin Freud Library*, vol. 12: *Civilization, Society and Religion* (Harmondsworth, UK: Penguin, 1991), pp. 271, 281, 282.

27. Joseph Brodsky, "The Condition We Call Exile," in *On Grief and Reason* (New York: Farrar, Straus and Giroux, 1995), p. 34.

6. Making the Planet Hospitable to Europe

1. Heidegger's oppositional terms: in rough translation, *zuhanden* means "given to hand" and thus obvious—unnoticed and handled matter-of-factly; *vorhanden* refers to things "in front of," visible because obstreperous and troublesome.

2. Jacques Derrida, *Cosmopolites de tous les pays, encore un effort!* (Paris: Galilée, 1997), p. 42. "Hospitality *is* culture; it is not an ethic among others . . . Ethics *is* hospitality"; translation is mine.

3. See Ryszard Kapuściński, *Lapidarium V* (Warsaw: Czytelnik, 2002).

4. See Denis de Rougemont, "L'aventure mondiale des Européens" (1962), in *Écrits sur l'Europe* (Paris: Éditions de la Difference, 1994).

5. See Jürgen Habermas, *L'Occidente diviso* (Rome: Editori Laterza, 2005).

6. Immanuel Wallerstein, "Quo Vadis America?" *Commentary* no. 141 (July 15, 2004), Fernand Braudel Center, Binghamton University, State University of New York; *http://fbc.binghamton.edu./commentr.htm.* Morris Berman, *Dark Ages America* (New York: Norton, 2006), pp. 302–303.

7. Quoted after Matthew J. Morgan, "The Garrison State Revisited: Civil-Military Implications of Terrorism and Security," *Contemporary Politics* 10, no. 1 (March 2004): 5–19.

8. Paul Virilio, "Cold Panic," *Cultural Politics* 1 (2005): 27–30.

9. Ted Koppel, "The Long, Cost-Free War," *New York Times*, 6 November 2007.

10. Paul Krugman, "Deep in Debt, and Denying It," *International Herald Tribune*, 14 February 2006.

11. George Soros, *The Age of Fallibility: The Consequences of the War on Terror* (New York: Public Affairs, 2006), pp. 123, 108.

12. See George Steiner, *The Idea of Europe* (Amsterdam: Nexus Institute, 2004), pp. 32–34.

13. See in particular Hans-Georg Gadamer's *Das Erbe Europas* (Frankfurt: Suhrkamp, 1989). Quotations in this paragraph after Philippe Invernel's French translation, *L'héritage de l'Europe* (Paris: Rivages Poche, 2003), pp. 40, 124; English translations are mine.

14. Ibid.

15. See Lionel Jospin, "Solidarity or Playing Solitaire," *Hedgehog Review* (Spring 2003): 32–44.

16. See, for instance, Cris Shore, "Wither European Citizenship?" *European Journal of Social Theory* (February 2004): 27–44.

17. Jürgen Habermas, *The Postnational Constellation: Political Essays*, trans. Max Pensky (Cambridge: Polity Press, 2001), p. 76.

18. Ibid., p. 102.

19. Ibid., p. 101.

20. See Sheldon Rampton and John Stauber, "Trading on Fear," *Guardian Weekend*, 12 July 2003.

21. Jaques Attali, *La voie humaine* (Paris: Fayard, 2004).

22. Joseph Stiglitz, "Trade Imbalances," *Guardian*, 15 August 2003.

23. Habermas, *Postnational Constellation*, p. 104.

24. Ibid., p. 109.

25. Ibid., pp. 104, 108.
26. See Jan-Werner Müller, "Europe: Le pouvoir des sentiments: l'euro-patriotisme en question?" *La vie des idées* (April–May 2004): 19.
27. Franz Kafka, "Advocates," trans. Tania and James Stern, in *The Penguin Complete Short Stories of Franz Kafka*, ed. Nahum N. Glatzer (London: Penguin Books, 1988), p. 451.

Index

◆